Understanding social control

Deviance, crime and social order

CRIME AND JUSTICE
Series editor: Mike Maguire
University College of Wales, College of Cardiff

Crime and Justice is a series of short introductory texts on central topics in criminology. The books in this series are written for students by internationally renowned authors. Each book tackles a key area within criminology, providing a concise and up-to-date overview of the principal concepts, theories, methods and findings relating to the area. Taken as a whole, the *Crime and Justice* series will cover all the core components of an undergraduate criminology course.

Published titles

Understanding youth and crime
Sheila Brown

Understanding crime data
Clive Coleman and
Jenny Moynihan

Understanding white collar crime
Hazel Croall

Understanding justice
(second edition)
Barbara A. Hudson

Understanding crime prevention
Gordon Hughes

Understanding violent crime
Stephen Jones

Understanding risk in criminal justice
Hazel Kemshall

Understanding psychology and crime
James McGuire

Understanding community penalties
Raynor and Vanstone

Understanding criminology
(second edition)
Sandra Walklate

Understanding social control
Martin Innes

Understanding social control

Deviance, crime and social order

Martin Innes

Open University Press

Open University Press
McGraw-Hill Education
McGraw-Hill House
Shoppenhangers Road
Maidenhead
Berkshire
England
SL6 2QL

email: enquiries@openup.co.uk
world wide web: www.openup.co.uk

First published 2003
Copyright © Martin Innes 2003

A catalogue record of this book is available from the British Library

ISBN 0 335 20940 8 (pb)   0 335 20941 6 (hb)

Library of Congress Cataloguing-in-Publication Data
CIP data has been applied for

Typeset by RefineCatch Limited, Bungay, Suffolk
Printed in the UK by Bell & Bain, Glasgow

Contents

For Helen

Series editor's foreword

Martin Innes's book is the tenth in Open University Press's successful *Crime and Justice* series. The series is now established as a key resource in universities teaching criminology or criminal justice, especially in the UK but increasingly also overseas. The aim from the outset has been to give undergraduates and graduates both a solid grounding in the relevant area and a taste to explore it further. Although aimed primarily at students new to the field, and written as far as possible in plain language, the books are not oversimplified. On the contrary, the authors set out to 'stretch' readers and to encourage them to approach criminological knowledge and theory in a critical and questioning frame of mind.

Innes tackles here the tricky but critically important concept of 'social control'. A central focus of theoretical debate in the 1970s and 1980s, the term subsequently became less prominent in criminology in the wake of concerns that it was becoming used in too vague and all-embracing a manner, to cover every aspect of social and institutional life that served to channel individuals towards established norms of behaviour and to challenge or prevent 'deviance'. Confusions also arose with other key terms such as 'socialization' and 'social ordering'. However, Innes argues that social control remains the 'master concept', and that the most fruitful approach is to recognize and articulate the different permutations to be found in how it is enacted across a range of social spaces in contemporary society. His book begins with a very clear summary of the definitional issues and debates, and a succinct history of the development of the idea of social control. He also offers a valuable discussion of its relationship to the concept of social ordering. The remainder of the text is devoted principally to thorough analyses of specific forms of social control in practice, including chapters on policing, punishment, surveillance, regulatory practice, auditing and – unusually among criminologists – control features of the built environment. These chapters all provide a rich combination of theoretical insights and concrete illustrations of how control is exercised in both overt and hidden ways. The value of the policing chapter, in particular, is enhanced by Innes' close knowledge of policing practice, about which he has written widely in other contexts.

Other books previously published in the *Crime and Justice* series – all of whose titles begin with the word 'Understanding' – have covered criminological theory (Sandra Walklate, penal theory (Barbara Hudson), crime data and statistics (Clive Coleman and Jenny Moynihan), youth and crime (Sheila Brown), crime prevention (Gordon Hughes), violent crime (Stephen Jones), community penalties (Peter Raynor and Maurice Vanstone), white collar crime (Hazel Croall) and risk and crime (Hazel Kemshall). Two are already in second editions and other second editions are planned. Other new books in the pipeline include texts on prisons, policing, criminological research methods, sentencing and criminal justice, drugs and crime, race and crime, psychology and crime, and crime and social exclusion. All are major topics in university degree courses on crime and criminal justice, and each book should make an ideal foundation text for a relevant module. As an aid to understanding, clear summaries are provided at regular intervals, and a glossary of key terms and concepts is a feature of every book. In addition, to help students expand their knowledge, recommendations for further reading are given at the end of each chapter.

Mike Maguire
August 2003

Acknowledgements

The subject of social control cuts across a number of disciplinary and thematic boundaries in the social sciences, and I am therefore grateful to a number of friends and colleagues who have helped me make sense of the issues and problems that I have encountered in writing this book. First, I would like to thank Ian Loader for suggesting that I undertake this project. In the process of transforming roughly hewn ideas into slightly less roughly hewn pages, I have discussed issues around the theory and practice of social control with several people including Robin Williams, Nigel Fielding, Bridget Hutter, Louise Westmarland, James Sheptycki and Alan Clarke, and I am indebted to them for their willingness to share their thoughts with me. I would especially like to thank Stan Cohen who generously gave up his time to talk about his work in this area and in the process helped me to identify some of the key themes that I have tried to work through in this study. Likewise I am grateful to Paul Rock, whose advice and comments really pushed me to try and clarify some of the more theoretical components of my analysis. Thanks also to Mike Maguire who, as Series Editor, has been immensely supportive and provided a number of insightful comments on earlier drafts. Justin Vaughan started this project with Open University Press and Mark Barratt concluded it. Both of them have been fantastic to work with, putting up with missed deadlines with good humour and understanding. Finally, thank-you to my family and especially Helen, who has endured numerous drafts, conversations and revisions, and in the process helped me to improve my thinking immeasurably.

chapter one

The argument

A contested concept
Social order and social control
Refining the concept
The late-moderns
Reconfiguring the control apparatus
Summary

We live in a society that is straining for control. Driven by fears about the risks of being a victim of crime, that intermingle with a more diffuse and inchoate sense of insecurity, we clamour for new measures to try and regulate the people, places and behaviours that we believe threaten our sense of security. As a consequence, our public and private lives are increasingly subject to a range of formal and informal controls. For example, public interactions increasingly take place under the gaze of the unblinking electronic eyes of CCTV surveillance systems, whilst many people undergo forms of therapy in an effort to repair what they believe to be their 'flawed' personalities. At the same time, politicians from across the political spectrum respond to our demands, introducing punitive measures to control crime, such as 'three strikes and you're out' laws, or advocate a philosophy of 'zero tolerance', to deal with the seemingly encroaching disorder.

This is not of course a movement in one direction. At the same time as our society is straining for control, it is also straining for freedom. Much has been written about how contemporary late-modern societies are defined by changes in the institutional order and particularly the increasing erosion of the traditional systems of class stratification that were constitutive of modernity. Indeed, perhaps somewhat counter-intuitively and paradoxically, it is in part the increase in freedom that is responsible for the increasing demands for enhanced control. In a world where we believe that the traditions, bonds and social ordering of society are increasingly fragile and fragmented, our cognitive and affective responses are to try to manufacture more of what social scientists term 'social control'.

Social control is one of the key concepts in the lexicon of the modern social and political sciences. It has been found to be present across a range of fields and establishments including: the education system (Willis 1977); the welfare state (Offe 1984; Gough 1979); psychiatry and psychotherapy (Horwitz 1982); workplaces (Zuboff 1988); and more obviously crime control (Garland 2001a). As a concept, its centrality stems from its intimate connection to the issue of social order. One of the central and recurrent concerns for social scientists has been the question of how individuals, groups and societies organize their lives together? How is it that patterns, conventions, routines, traditions, formal organizations and institutions, come into being, are maintained and reproduced? That is, how do social actors, both intentionally and unintentionally, on a personal level and when acting in groups, come to conform with norms and rules so that the social world can be understood as ordered, rather than chaotic? And then relatedly, what happens when they deviate from these orderings?

We can see then that the concept of social control is potentially extremely useful in understanding social life. Indeed, it is because it is so important and so central to the concerns of social scientists that it has become something of a 'fuzzy' concept. It has been used in so many different ways in relation to so many different contexts that its meaning is often difficult to define.

In this book, I will explore what is meant by the concept of social control in order to understand how and why it has been used in different ways by different writers. In so doing, I will also describe and analyse some of the key dimensions of how social control is performed in late modernity, thereby showing how a focus upon the conduct of social control can assist in understanding some important aspects of contemporary society. This approach reflects my belief that ideas about social control, and the ways in which control is carried out in practice, are intimately connected. Ideas shape how social actions are conceived of, in turn though, the conduct of controlling acts and the problems that are experienced in performing them, are often reflected in the ideas that surround practices.

In what remains of this short introductory chapter I will rehearse the argument to be developed throughout the rest of this book. This rehearsal reflects the fact that, as will become apparent, social control is an especially complex area of social life and of social theory, and therefore an overview of the area is useful to the reader in terms of showing how the various ideas and practices to be discussed connect up. I will start by considering how the concept of social control is understood today and then progress to a discussion of how this definition can inform the ways in which we look at and interpret what is going on around us.

A contested concept

Today, the term social control is often used to refer to some form of organized reaction to deviant behaviour. This approach is based upon the seminal work of Stan Cohen, who defined social control as:

> . . . those organized responses to crime, delinquency and allied forms of deviant and/or socially problematic behaviour which are actually conceived of as such, whether in the reactive sense (after the putative act has taken place or the actor been identified) or in the proactive sense (to prevent the act).
>
> (Cohen 1985: 3)

This is very similar to the definition used by Donald Black (1976: 1–2), who posits that:

> . . . social control is the normative aspect of social life, or the definition of deviant behaviour and the response to it, such as prohibitions, accusations, punishment, and compensation.

According to this formulation, social control refers to the purposive mechanisms used to regulate the conduct of people who are seen as deviant, criminal, worrying or troublesome in some way by others. Over time, the ways in which different cultures understand and respond to different forms of problematic behaviour changes and alters. The cause of the problems may be attributed to criminality, deviance, immorality, wickedness, perversity or some combination of these. Similarly, the mechanisms employed to achieve control can variously include forms of punishment, treatment, deterrence, segregation or prevention (Cohen 1985). Whatever the combination of factors that is used to understand and react to trouble, the objective is to enact control over behaviour that is viewed as deviant in some sense.

Cohen developed his 'narrow' definition because, as he saw it, the ways in which social control had previously been defined by some theorists had led to it becoming a 'Mickey Mouse' concept. He was concerned that the more 'open' definitions in circulation lacked sufficient analytic precision to capture a specific quality of social life. The concept had been used in so many different ways and in respect of so many social problems that it had lost all sense of meaning. In his words, it had simply become 'dissolved' into everything (Cohen 1994).

Reviewing the sociological literature in this area, Meier (1982) identifies that social control can be found in three main contexts:

(a) *As a description of basic social process or condition.* This approach is associated with classical sociological theory and as such was the dominant definition in the first half of the twentieth century.

(b) *As a mechanism for ensuring compliance with norms.* This position has its roots in the earlier definition and comes to prominence in the 1950s.

(c) *As a method by which to study (or interpret data about) social order.* This is the most recent formulation, but in many ways represents a return to earlier views.

An example of the loosely defined version of social control that Cohen is so critical of can be found in the work of Joseph Roucek writing in 1947, who understood social control as:

> ...a collective term for those processes, planned or unplanned, by which individuals are taught, or compelled to conform to the useages and life-values of groups.
>
> (Roucek 1970: 3)

And, more recently Horwitz (1990: 5) has suggested that, 'Social control emerges out of and serves to maintain the ways of life and social practices of groups.' Many social scientists would tend to see such descriptions as more akin to processes of 'socialization', than social control. For Cohen, as definitions of social control they are too 'loose' and are so flexible that they could be used to describe too many different types of situation and behaviour.[1] This lack of definition is what Cohen attempted to overcome. Nevertheless, they are important in terms of signalling the extent to which the idea of social control is coherent with and overlaps with some of the central concerns of the social sciences, particularly – processes of inequality, power, coercion, socialization and persuasion.

Although restricting its focus to programmed responses to deviant acts, Cohen's definition remains sufficiently flexible to encompass the direct enactment of social control strategies by the state or by more autonomous professional agents such as employees of private corporations and psychiatrists. This recognition of the part played by non-state agents is afforded an even higher profile in the work of Donald Black (1976; 1984a) and his students. Black, who has been a highly influential figure in the field of social control studies, argues that much work in this area has been overly concerned with the role of the state and legal institutions, ignoring the fact that state action is perhaps only a comparatively minor component in terms of how social actions are controlled in everyday life (Black 1984a). Developing this position, Baumgartner (1984) argues many authors have neglected the potential for 'social control from below'. As Black (1976; 1984a) explains, people tend to use the formal state apparatus of social control, underpinned as it is by the law, relatively infrequently. Most conflicts are resolved without recourse to the law or formal social control. A solution is often negotiated or the deviation tolerated and the imposition of formal social control tends to be a function of increased relational distance. The better people know each other, the less likely they are to use formal social control to resolve their conflicts. Extending the logic of this 'normative' argument, Black (1984b) posits that much of what in Western societies is typically classified as criminal activity, for example violence against the person, can in many cases be understood as a form of self-help, where one person seeks to exert a degree of control over another. Therefore, Black argues, we need to be aware of the extent to which the performance of the majority of social control in society is informally based.

The definition of social control as an organized response to deviant behaviour is not uncontentious. As will be discussed across several chapters in this book, it has been suggested (or at least implied) by a number of contemporary authors that the nature of social control in late-modernity has changed to such an extent that Cohen's definition no longer captures all of the ways in which control is routinely enacted. Stated briefly, they maintain that control-type technologies and processes no longer tend to be restricted to focusing upon those activities that are defined as deviant. Rather, controls have become embedded within our key institutional forms to such an extent that we are all subject to different types and combinations of control as we go about our daily lives, whether our behaviour could be considered deviant or not. Thus it has been suggested that these circumstances necessitate a markedly different conceptualization of social control from that provided by Cohen, and over the course of this book, I will examine the strength of this line of argument. In so doing, I will suggest that this revisionist position is effectively developing an understanding of control as behavioural modification where it is construed as any action intended to change people's behaviour.

Throughout this book I tend to rely upon Cohen's definition to orientate my analyses of different modes of social control, because this is the more established approach. However, in the final chapter I will reflect upon the ways that contemporary developments are stretching Cohen's formulation to such an extent that we need to revisit the definition of the concept. Synthesizing aspects from Cohen's definition and the more revisionist approach, my argument will be that social control can be thought of as a master-concept, comprised of an array of different control modes and technologies. And, as such, if we introduce three additional concepts of 'ambient', 'organic' and 'manufactured' social control, we can reconfigure Cohen's definition in such a way as to retain its analytic purchase for the conditions of late-modernity.

Social order and social control

From my opening remarks it should be apparent that I perceive there to be a close affinity between social control, and social order. Goffman (1971) provides a useful definition of social order where he suggests that:

> When persons engage in regulated dealings with each other, they come to employ social routines or practices, namely, patterned adaptations to the rules – including conformances, by-passings, secret deviations, excusable infractions, flagrant violations, and the like. These variously motivated and variously functioning patterns of actual behaviour, these routines associated with ground rules, together constitute what might be called a 'social order'.
>
> (Goffman 1971: x)

This is a deliberately broadly conceived array of conduct, reflecting Goffman's belief that, 'The study of social order is part of the study of social organization; however, a weakened notion of organization is involved' (Goffman 1971: x).

Drawing upon this definition we can distinguish between the meanings of social order and social control. The enactment of social control is often intended to protect a state of social order, but social order is not solely the product of social controls. Rather, the concept of social order refers to the conditions of existence of a society, in that every society intrinsically has a degree of organization and thus a social order. A social order is not static, but is constantly in process, being produced and reproduced by the combined attitudes, values, practices, institutions and actions of its members. Thus social order is composed of the diverse sets of ideas, actions and interactions, which in some fashion contribute to the ongoing constitution of societal organization. The boundaries between social ordering practices and social controls are neither fixed nor stable, and over time, shift their balance. But as will become apparent, especially in Chapter 4, establishing such a distinction is useful in undoing some of the confusion that has emanated from the ways in which the concept of social control has changed over time. For, if social order refers to the state of a society, and the organized arrangement of its key knowledge, values, actions, institutions and establishments, social control refers to the process by which attempts are made to manage that which deviates from or conflicts with the social order.

Refining the concept

A further layer of complexity, in terms of understanding the idea of social control, stems from the fact that, within the literature, a distinction is routinely made between 'formal' and 'informal' social control. Black (1976) suggests that formal social control relates to any occasion where the imposition of control is based upon, or informed by, the presence of law. Any other controlling activity can be defined as the informal kind.

Whilst Black's solution is attractive, in that it provides a sense of clear unambiguous definition to the territory, its problem is that when applied to many empirical situations it is perhaps too simplistic, failing to capture the complexities involved. For instance, studies of the police and other law enforcement agencies have frequently documented that there is a marked tendency towards the under-enforcement of the law by officials (Hawkins 1984; Reiner 1992). In effect, many conflicts and problems are formally dealt with through informal and negotiated means. Thus we are left wondering whether such incidents should be classified as examples of formal or informal social control? Further ambiguities of this kind are presented if we consider an establishment such as a school. It has been convincingly argued that, through instilling particular norms and knowledge in young people, schooling constitutes one of the most potent and important sources of social control that exist in complex societies (Willis 1977). And yet, whilst many would recognize this function, perhaps few would see it as being the primary intended purpose of the school system to do this. We are therefore left to ponder whether this should be classified as an example of formal or informal social control.

An alternative way of understanding how social control is conducted reflects the fact that social control can be either reactive or proactive. Reactive social controls are those used to respond to something after it has taken place, an example of which would be the conduct of a police investigation into a crime. But some controls are proactive: this involves the calculation of the probability of an act occurring at some point in the future and the manufacture of some form of intervention in anticipation of this. In essence, this is a predictive form of control. As will be discussed in due course, it is the development of forms of proactive social controls and their application in relation to a range of social problems, that has been one of the most important features of the development of the late-modern social control apparatus.

Cohen (1985) usefully differentiates between controls with a 'hard-edge' and those with a 'soft-edge'. Hard-edged controls are those where coercion is present and evident in the controlling action. In contrast, soft controls are more subtle involving psychological and therapeutic forms of diagnosis, persuasion and intervention, that aim to deal with deviancy of different kinds without recourse to the 'harder', more coercive, techniques employed by the formal social control system.

In his study, Black (1976) distinguishes between forms of 'vertical' social control to account for the power differentials that frequently exist between controllers and the controlled. 'Downward' social control is the most common form, involving someone with more power or authority regulating the behaviour of individuals or groups with less. However, social control can also be 'upwards', involving the less powerful shaping the behaviour of normally more powerful individuals or groups.

Black (1976) identifies four key 'pure styles' of social control, each of which has its own way of defining deviant behaviour, its favoured responses, language and logic.[2] In *penal control*, certain conduct is prohibited and enforcement of these prohibitions involves the whole group seeking to determine the guilt or innocence of the alleged offender. In *compensatory control*, the initiative is taken by the victim alleging that someone else has an outstanding obligation to them. Whereas both of these styles of social control are accusatory, *therapeutic* and *conciliatory* styles emphasize a sense of restoration and repair. In the former, a condition is diagnosed for which therapy is taken in order to restore normalcy to an impaired personality. Conciliatory control aims to repair the harm to a relationship caused by some dispute.

It is evident that there are a variety of permutations present in terms of how social control is both understood and practised. The purpose of this discussion has been to review some of the conceptual issues that pertain to understanding the concept of social control. These theoretical concerns will be developed and elaborated upon in the next chapter. For now, in what remains of this chapter I want to sketch out an overview of how these conceptual ideas can be used to diagnose the ways in which social control is conducted in contemporary society.

The late-moderns

Many social scientists are agreed that, to a greater or lesser extent, over the past three decades or so, Western societies have entered a new phase in their ongoing development. A number of different labels have been used to describe this new era, including post-modernity, hyper-modernity, high modernity and late-modernity. For my current purposes, the subtle distinctions and different emphases captured by the different labels are not that important. I will use Giddens's (1990; 1991) analysis of late-modernity to describe the contemporary situation, because of the sense of connection it provides to the earlier period of modernity, thereby suggesting that the current period is probably best understood as marked by an amplification, intensification and acceleration of trends first noticeable in modern societies.

If there is disagreement amongst theorists as to the label that is to be used, there is widespread agreement that we are living through a period where there are fairly profound revisions taking place in respect of some of our key social structures, institutional and organizational arrangements, and modes of understanding both who we are and the world around us. This involves transformations in: the logics of capitalism (Lash and Urry 1997); a shift in the composition and role of the state and its agencies (Rose 1996; Rhodes 1997); the spread of networked forms of social organization (Castells 1996; 2000); a more malleable and fluid sense of identity (Hobsbawm 1994; Bauman 2000; Williams 2000); changes in the use of space (Harvey 1995); and a shift to routinely exchanging, interpreting and storing information through media of interpersonal and mass communication (Thompson 1995; Castells 1997).

Overall then, the late-modern experience is the combined outcome of these social forces, giving the sensation of a world that is constantly undergoing change, moving at pace, and based upon a more fluid form of social order. Traditional systems of stratification have been eroded, if not abolished, and traditional moral orders feel less binding than they did before. People are more mobile and this has implications for the sense of connectedness that they feel with each other. At the same time though, situated in the midst of this flux, in a world that feels as though it is both falling apart and yet still hanging together, many people feel vulnerable and seek a sense of security. For Giddens (1991), the management of this deeply ingrained, existentially based 'ontological insecurity' is a key component of late-modern citizenship. There is a diffuse 'ambient insecurity', and as might reasonably be predicted, its presence has induced important changes in the logics and practices of social control. As Altheide (2002) has suggested, the presence of fear and insecurity has been crucial in articulating demands for more and better controls.

The argument that will be developed in the rest of this book is that recently the ways in which social control is both conceptualized and practised have started to be reconfigured. These changes are part and parcel of wider and deeper shifts in the prevalent conditions of late-modern social order. Stated briefly, the reconfiguration has involved an increasing pluralization, diversification and layering of controls. Social control has also been embedded in the routines of many everyday situations, permeating the fabric of social life and thereby becoming more opaque. As part of these changes, it appears as if previously distinct control institutions and systems are starting to join up, producing a control apparatus composed of interleaved and interlocking practices, mechanisms and objectives. Thus the social control apparatus is expanding, at the same time as parts of it become more intense.

In developing the argument sketched out above, it is important to note that I do not argue that social control in late-modernity *is* a fully-integrated, holistic, all-encompassing system – this is not an accurate description. Rather my argument is that we are experiencing a situation where previously separate systems are *starting* to connect up in new ways. It is not inevitable that such connections will be made or sustained. Furthermore, it is also the case that not all parts of the control apparatus are changing, some continue much as before, whilst others fall out of use. Reflecting on some of these issues, later in this book I will propose that analyses of social control can benefit by separating out the ideas and intentions, programmes, evaluations and explanations that attend to empirical instances of social control. These different dimensions point to some of the tensions that exist in the literature and also in terms of how social control is enacted in late-modernity.

In order to refine this sketched outline, it is necessary to show how and why these ongoing and emerging arrangements have evolved out of those which preceded them. A useful resource in conducting such a diagnosis is Cohen's (1985) metaphor of the 'social control net' and the processes of 'net widening' and 'net deepening'. Describing the 'destructuring' movement of the 1960s, he sought to explain how reforms motivated by well-intentioned, humane interests to limit the spread of state social control and to identify alternative responses to deviance, could have unintended consequences that resulted in the almost paradoxical expansion, rather than contraction, of the social control system (Cohen 1994).

One of the most noticeable aspects of living in late-modernity has been the ways in which new forms of technologically based social control, such as surveillance cameras, listening devices and the analysis of genetic materials, have been introduced in an effort to assist in the control of different forms of deviant behaviour. A metaphor of 'layering' can be used to capture the sense in which the introduction of these new forms of social control has frequently tended to supplement and augment, rather than simply replace those already in use. This is an important dynamic in terms of understanding the nature and logics of social control in the late-modern era. For it is not simply a question of new controls replacing old. Traditional approaches to the control of deviance have continued to be used, but increasingly they are supplemented and/or refined by new laws, technologies and agencies, the overall effect of which is to expand the extent to which different aspects of our lives are regulated and controlled. Increasingly, control has been established as a more explicit function in a variety of social arenas, extending the reach of control, thereby encouraging previously discrete control systems to become joined up.

Reconfiguring the control apparatus

Contemporary definitions of social control tend to combine a sense of it being either conformity inducing or deviance repressing (Hudson 2002). This reflects the sense in which late-modern social life is profoundly shaped by the institutionalization of attempts to exert a degree of control over an array of dangers, hazards and risks that are perceived to impinge on our levels of security (Beck 1992). Garland (2001a) argues though that crucial to understanding the reconfiguring of social control has been the issue of crime. For Garland, it is the problem of crime and the related phenomenon of fear of crime that have emerged as central concerns for late-modern social life. His analysis of the emergence of a 'late-modern crime complex' and its constitutive 'criminologies of everyday life', and 'criminology of the other', suggests that a range of factors have coalesced to produce a situation wherein crime has been established as emblematic of a number of different forms of deviance, over which control is routinely sought and demanded. It is a vehicle where wider concerns about order/disorder and security/insecurity are acted out.

Massive increases in the levels of recorded crime and the spread of 'the criminologies of everyday life' to manage the risks and fears associated with it, have transformed the social problem of crime from an exceptional occurrence to one that appears to be part of everyday living. Crime (or at least the belief of the potential to become a victim of crime) is significant because it is a problem that ordinary people experience fairly regularly, and can thus use as a metaphor and vehicle to articulate the sense of exist-ential insecurity they feel (Girling et al. 2000). By talking about crime and crime threats, they can give a material form, both to their immediate con-cerns about victimization, and to more diffuse and nebulous anxieties that stem from the institutional structures (or felt lack thereof) of late-modern living. It is for this reason that a number of the more profound develop-ments in the late-modern social control apparatus have pivoted around issues of crime and disorder.[3]

Having identified that the logics and practices of social control have changed, what is required is an analytic framework to identify how these have changed in particular ways. A number of theorists including Young (1999), Rose (2000) and Garland (2001a) have argued that there is a detectable trend towards a bifurcation of control. The socially included sections of society, when subject to censure for engaging in deviant acts, tend to be subject to reintegrative forms of control, whereas, individuals drawn from more economically and politically marginalized groups, are dealt with via means that serve to reinforce their exclusion.

As crime has been constructed as a symbolic as well as an actual threat to people's sense of security, so increasingly a diverse array of institutions and establishments have been reconfigured in order that they should play a part in assisting to control crime. So for example, architectural design has increasingly had to incorporate ideas of 'natural surveillance' to help design out crime. Welfare benefit agencies have been given greater enforcement powers to help them detect and censure bogus claimants and their mission is increasingly presented in discourses of control rather than assistance.

One of the defining characteristics of late-modern forms of social control is that, whereas previously different sites and sources of control were fairly distinct and discrete, increasingly the boundaries between them are being blurred. Discourses of welfare have been usurped by those of control, and the implementation and delivery of social control is increasingly based upon and leading to the establishment of overlapping and interspersed strategies, technologies and actors. These connections are 'vertical' in that individuals, communities, and a variety of public agencies have all been enlisted into a plethora of state sponsored programmes designed to tackle crime, fear of crime and antisocial behaviour. They are also 'horizontal' in that public and private agencies have been encouraged to participate in 'multi-agency' partnerships cutting across traditional jurisdictions and boundaries. Thus we have policing, prisons, probation, youth offending teams, private security officers, social workers, drug action teams and doctors, routinely working alongside neighbourhood watch, community renewal projects and crime and disorder partnerships. It should be apparent, that to some extent, we are all both the subjects of control efforts, and at the same time encouraged to participate in the conduct of control, both of ourselves and others.

One field where such trends have been particularly evident is policing, where there has been a succession of new strategies introduced in an attempt to address various dimensions of the problem of fabricating social order from social conflict, as well as preventing and detecting crimes. Community policing programmes have deliberately sought to enhance police–community relations in an effort to encourage community members to participate in order maintenance work and in supplying information to police to assist in solving crimes. Such reforms have focused upon the role of the public police, but increasingly their role has been augmented and supplemented by the provision of private policing services (Johnston and Shearing 2003). Indeed, this is indicative of a broader and more pronounced trend, wherein the performance of formal social control functions has come to rely less on state agencies and to involve a whole host of public and private organizations and individuals.

Equally radical transformations have been taking place in the penal system, in terms of how deviants are punished and the justifications provided in terms of why these punishments are imposed. Of particular consequence to the argument that will be developed over the course of this book, is the implementation of a range of new community based punishments, sometimes utilizing new technological advances, as is the case with electronic tagging schemes.

Technological advances have been especially important in relation to the rapid growth of surveillance. Arguably, it is the growth of a range of different types of surveillance, together with their integration into a variety of social situations, enacted with different purposes, that represents the most important shift in terms of how social control is conducted. But it is not just in the field of surveillance technologies where important changes have occurred. An especially important issue in any discussion of contemporary control strategies is the ways in which the very landscape of late modernity has been transformed to enable more control. Controls have increasingly been designed into the physical environment, in an effort to improve the efficacy and efficiency of social control. Such shifts in practice have been premised upon the idea that reforming deviant people is difficult, it is therefore more practicable to change the nature of the situations in which they act, particularly by reducing their opportunities to engage in deviance (Felson 1998). For a number of commentators and theorists, the reforms associated with situational crime prevention initiatives constitute one of the most important dimensions of late-modern approaches to social control (Hope and Sparks 2000).

Although some of the most profound and noticeable changes in the conduct of social control have pivoted around issues of crime, there have been allied shifts in terms of the reactions provided to other types of deviant behaviour. For example, there has been significant growth in the arenas of economic life that are subject to some form of regulation. In turn, the growth in the number of regulatory agencies and the areas regulated, has been accompanied by an increasing awareness of the importance of acting appropriately in respect of a range of risks. Risk provides a particular way of thinking about potential problems and issues that could be controlled, and also the consequences that might flow from implementing particular strategies to address these problems. In effect, it provides a predictive and anticipatory epistemology, that can be employed to control future uncertainties. Risk has proven to be an important ingredient in relation to some of the transformations I have discussed so far.

Late-modern social control is thus comprised of a range of participants, utilizing a variety of practices and technologies, with the intention of addressing a number of different problems. Taken overall though, there is a feeling that the underpinning logic of social control in late-modernity combines both principles of seeking to reform some deviants and deviance, whilst at the same time identifying exclusion as the only response to other forms of deviants and deviance. In this sense then, there is something of a continuity with past approaches. But significantly, non-deviant members of the population are also increasingly subject to forms of social control and this is accepted as part of an attempt to manufacture a sense of security in insecure times.

Summary

The aim of this chapter has been to anticipate the argument to be developed over the coming chapters. I have sought to give a sense of the complexity involved in trying to understand both what the concept of social control means, and also, how control takes place in a range of situations on a day-to-day basis. The rest of the book will go on to expand, develop and refine the argument I have outlined herein. In the next chapter, I trace the history of the concept of social control in order to identify its beginnings, the conflicting definitions that have been drawn up and its contemporary form. I follow this in Chapter 3 with an equivalent discussion focusing upon the histories of key practices of social control. Chapter 4 considers the operation of social ordering mechanisms in everyday life, in an effort to examine how non-deviant conduct is organized. This serves as a precursor for the subsequent chapters where the focus is explicitly upon different modes of control. Pivoting the discussion around these modes is intended as an analytic device to both identify some of the key themes in studying social control, whilst at the same time appreciating that some developments in terms of how control has come to be practised in late-modernity are coherent, whilst others are apparently contradictory.

The modes have been selected because each of them involves control of individuals, communities, formal organizations and society as a whole. In essence, depending upon the 'analytic lens' adopted, each of these modes of social control can be, and has been, studied at the micro-, meso- and macro-levels of society. In Chapters 5 and 6 I discuss policing and punishment practices respectively, as the principal examples of formal social control. I then move on to examine the role of surveillance and environmental design in facilitating social control. Chapter 9 considers three emergent modes of social control that are increasingly important in late-modernity – risk, regulation and audit. The concluding chapter draws the various themes together and considers the implications that this discussion has for the future of the concept of social control.

chapter two

A history of the idea of social control

The basic idea
Communication and irony: the symbolic interactionist
    perspective
Normative controls: the functionalist tradition
States of control: the legacy of Marx
The dispersal of discipline: post-structuralism
Post-social control
On talking about control?
Summary

The definition of social control as an organized response to deviant acts has become widely established as the dominant conceptualization in the academic literature, having informed a number of studies into the ways in which societies, groups and individuals react to a variety of different forms of deviant behaviour. Indeed, the particular strength of this definition is that although it limits the range of acts that can properly be counted as social control, it remains sufficiently adaptable to be applicable to an array of events and settings. In achieving this balance, the definition draws upon and co-opts a much broader concern with the nature and logics of social order, and its relationship to social control, found throughout a number of different disciplines in the social and behavioural sciences. The concept of social control has been, and continues to be, used and developed in sociology, criminology, political science, social history, anthropology, socio-legal studies, social psychology and geography amongst others.

Whilst a disciplinary framework obviously shapes how the concept of social control is operationalized, cutting across these disciplinary boundaries have been a smaller number of key ideas and values about the theory and practice of social control, associated with some of the fundamental theoretical perspectives in the social sciences. In this chapter, I will trace the development of the concept of social control, to identify how and why these different theoretical perspectives have come to understand the causes and consequences of social control in different ways. In the process of conducting this analysis I will also show how its current accepted meanings have been arrived at.

In performing such an analysis there are a number of general issues to be borne in mind. I identify five key perspectives on social control, which relate to particular traditions in social theory, but in so doing, due to limitations on space, I cannot provide a detailed discussion of the subtleties and complexities that are to be found within each of the perspectives. Rather my aim is to simply identify the key themes that underpin each of the particular positions adopted in respect of the causes and consequences of social control. In addition, there are important contributions to debates about the nature of social control, which do not easily fit into this framework. For example, Zerubavel's (1997) formulation of the workings of 'socio-mental' control and its 'insidious' shaping of social cognition, does not align with the framework and consequently is not discussed further.[1] To re-iterate, the objective herein is to map the dominant ideas in the study of social control, rather than to provide an all-encompassing account.

Although focused upon explicitly theoretical concerns, the discussion at times references developments in control practices, as the theoretical refinements frequently result from attempts to explain developments in terms of how control is being practised at a particular historical juncture. Furthermore, it is also important to note that whilst for the purposes of analytic clarity it is useful to separate out the alternative ideas and theories, in actuality, the development of the idea of social control has involved processes of assimilation, exchange, rejection and agreement across and between the representatives of the different theories. So whilst there is a sense of chronological development of the concept of social control, by focusing upon the underlying themes associated with different theoretical perspectives, the mode of analysis utilized herein is more adept at detailing how different philosophical tenets and values have resulted in alternative ways of understanding social control.

The basic idea

A definition of the term social control was first introduced by Edward Ross in 1901. Effectively, Ross's formulation provided a social psychological approach to explaining the production and reproduction of social order, identifying 23 mechanisms by which social groups influence individuals. However, as Ross acknowledged, the actual term social control was first used by Herbert Spencer some years earlier. The coining of the term social control provided a useful label for a diverse range of issues and problems that had been a focus of attention for political leaders and thinkers since people had established permanent and stable communities. 'The problem of order' was most famously formulated by Thomas Hobbes as part of his reflections upon the proper role of the state in ensuring that the lives of people were more than 'nasty, brutish and short'. But not dissimilar concerns can be identified in Aristotle's writings 'On Politics' and the writings of several other of the great Greek philosophers.

Concerns with how social life is, can, and should be ordered, were central to the seminal early writings of modern sociology by Simmel, Weber, Durkheim and Marx. A key theme of their writings was to illuminate how it is that societies exert control over their members, thereby reproducing a particular form of social order. For Simmel, conflict in a society diffused tensions and thereby over the longer term acted to reproduce social order. For Marx, control was both explicit and hidden, buttressing the operations of the conflict ridden capitalist system. Whereas for Durkheim, social order was based upon the institutionalization and ritualization of traditional moral values, some of which were codified into laws. In contrast Weber saw the 'iron cage of bureaucracy' as representing a rationalized logic of social ordering practices, which would, he believed, increasingly constrain and mould the physical and subjective qualities of individuals. We can see then, that although not explicitly called 'social control', there are an array of concerns predating the introduction of this term, that today we would be inclined to understand as part of these debates.

Mannheim's (1935)[2] discussion of the need for social control as a precondition of complex, democratic 'planned' societies, co-opts dimensions of the various approaches outlined above. His conceptualization of social control as a form of influence that can be used by governments to pressure and persuade individuals and communities in a top-down fashion, but also as a mechanism by which these latter groups can exercise a degree of democratic control over elite groups, is a multifaceted attempt to analyse how societies can and should seek to resolve conflicts of different kinds.

It is widely recognized that the authors discussed above were amongst the key figures in the formulation of the most important traditions in social thought. And indeed, a key concern throughout the development of sociology has been with matters of social control. However, the problem of social order and the conduct of social control has been conceptualized and thought about in different ways by some of the leading theoretical perspectives in the social sciences.

Communication and irony: the symbolic interactionist perspective

The development of the early concept of social control and its instantiation in sociological thought owes much to the work of the Chicago School of sociologists, who were themselves influenced by the American Pragmatist tradition of philosophy. They took Ross's formulation, reworked it and in the process demonstrated the degree of analytic purchase it provided in respect of a number of social problems. More latterly, this approach to social control has been integrated into the concerns of Symbolic Interactionist sociology and developed by Labelling Theory in criminology. Discussions of social control from this perspective have tended to gravitate around three key problems:

1. Processes of control in democratic society;
2. The role of social interaction in the manufacture of self-control;
3. The role of social controls in the production of deviant behaviour.

As such, this pragmatist formulation of social control tends to emphasize the role of processes of communication in the production and enactment of social control, and the ironic consequences that frequently flow from control efforts.

The development of the social sciences in America has been strongly influenced by the Pragmatist philosophical tradition, a set of ideas which directly informed the Chicago School of Sociology, and subsequently Symbolic Interactionist sociology (Rock 1979). For John Dewey, one of the central figures in early Pragmatist philosophy, the key problem for students of society at that time was to understand how societies based upon democratic principles, rather than traditional values and structures, could develop systems for ensuring social order. As Joas (1993) details, the solution he proposed is that communication is required for processes of collective problem solving in order for democratic institutions to operate effectively. The theme of control through communication is even more evident in the work of George Herbert Mead. But whereas Dewey was concerned with political philosophy, Mead was focused more upon matters of social psychology. He described how tacit processes of communication that took place in social interactions, resulted in an almost unconscious, self-regulation of behaviour by those involved. As he put it:

> . . . social control depends . . . upon the degree to which individuals in society are able to assume the attitudes of others who are involved with them in common endeavour.
>
> (Mead 1925: 275)

This notion has been pivotal to the concerns of Symbolic Interactionist sociology, in that transposed to a societal level, it suggests that through participation in social life individuals are induced into a form of 'collective self-control', wherein competent engagement in social actions inherently involves a form of self-control. As Cooley (1902) described, the social self was cast as inherently 'a looking glass self', shaped and moulded according to the reflected sense gained through interactions with others.

The twin themes of democratic communication and collective self-control directly shaped the work of the Chicago School of sociologists, and in particular the work of Robert Park. For Park 'All social problems turn out finally to be problems of social control' (Park and Burgess 1924: 209). As Turner summarizes in his introduction to Park's 'On Social Control', 'The social order is governed by communication, directed by the conceptions of the self and other which the members develop as social beings' (Park 1967: xxvii–xxviii). In his famous essay 'The City', Park (1925) clearly identifies the importance of communication in processes of social control, where he considers the ways in which 'social advertising' functions as a set of elaborate techniques for the control of public opinion. Here then we can see an explicit connection drawn between the role of communication and Dewey's earlier concern with the workings of democratic governance, a theme that was reworked subsequently by Herbert Blumer in his reflections on the problems of maintaining civilian morale during the Second World War (Lyman and Vidich 2000).

For the members of the Chicago School, the rapidly evolving city of Chicago was their social laboratory, providing an opportunity to study the impact of processes of urbanization and the connected problems of 'social disorganization'. Study of successive waves of immigrants into Chicago seemed to suggest that they brought with them attendant social problems, such as crime, disorder, vagrancy and alcoholism. But rather than explaining such problems as symptoms of an individual or group pathology, Park's explanation centred upon a notion of what I would term 'control deficit'. He argued that the ongoing influx of immigrants into the City resulted in the erosion of community stability by destroying or preventing the growth of social institutions that ordinarily provide collective values and shared norms. It was thus the lack of collective norms and controls that created the conditions for 'social disorganization'.

Whilst these theories were popular up until the 1930s, they fell out of favour with the rise to dominance of functionalist sociology. However, in the late 1950s and 1960s, stimulated by a reaction against functionalism, and increased interest in Blumer's (1969) Symbolic Interactionism and the related 'Labelling Theories', there was a revival in the fortunes of some of the themes found in the work of members of the Chicago School. In particular, Edwin Lemert (1967) and Howard Becker (1963) are recognized as introducing a new perspective to the study of social control.

Labelling theory inverted the criminological orthodoxy that control was a reaction to deviance. Both Lemert (1967) and Becker (1963) showed how it was the imposition of control that in essence 'caused' deviance. For Lemert the apprehension of an offender by an authority figure and the imposition of punishment could, in certain circumstances, invoke a form of stigmatizing communication causing the individual to refigure their sense of self, encouraging them to assume a deviant identity and as a consequence engage in more deviant acts. More fundamentally, Becker argued purely and simply that deviant acts did not share some inherent quality or characteristic. Rather they were simply acts that were labelled as deviant, and as such, it was acts of control and the application of the deviant label that separated deviant from non-deviant acts. This 'ironic' approach to the study of social control underpinned a number of studies that sought to unpack the symbiotic relationship between control and deviance.

An interesting application of these ideas concerning the unintended consequences of social control is Ditton's (1979) concept of 'control waves'. Developing the implications of a number of the key themes of labelling theory, he argues that apparent rises (or falls) in crime levels are often better explained by changes in the enforcement practices of agents of social control, than actual shifts in the amount of deviance or number of deviants in society. The irony that the concept of 'control waves' points to is that, by focusing upon a particular kind of deviance, police, other enforcement agents, or journalists, are more likely to discover instances of this deviance occurring that otherwise would have remained undiscovered, thus giving the appearance that the problem has got worse, thereby justifying calls for more or better forms of social control of the apparently worsening problem. It is an approach that has similarities to Cohen's (1980) notion of 'moral panic' and ideas concerning 'deviancy amplification' (Wilkins 1964; Young 1971).

A more recent continuation of the theme of the ironies of social control is provided by Gary Marx (1995). The 'maximum security society' he describes, composed of the engineered, dossier, actuarial, suspicious, self-monitored and transparent societies, has increasingly sought to develop and integrate 'soft' forms of social control (Marx 1988; 1995). The result though has not simply been one of more control, but a dialectical spiral of violations, social engineering responses, new violations and new responses (Marx 1995). In essence, Marx argues that the attempts to solve particular social problems through control oriented methods have tended to create pressures for more controls.

These discussions of the manufacture of social control differ according to the intellectual and practical contexts in which they are situated, in that they have been shaped both by what has preceded them, and also the prevailing concerns of the particular moment in history. Despite these important differences, what unites them, and casts them as belonging to a particular perspective, is a shared emphasis upon the role of communication and the ironic consequences of control efforts. In particular, communication is central to the production and reproduction of forms of collective self control.

Normative controls: the functionalist tradition

An alternative understanding of the nature, production and uses of social control can be found in the Functionalist tradition. Here, reflecting some of the central concerns to be found in the writings of Durkheim, control is held to be founded upon a shared normative order, preserved and reproduced through traditions, collective representations and the presence of social institutions.[3]

The sense that normative control is a pivotal facet of Durkheim's work owes much to Talcott Parson's (1949 [1937]) reading of Durkheim's formulation of the causes of 'anomic' normlessness described in *Suicide* and *The Division of Labour in Society*. According to Parsons (1949: 386) '... Durkheim had been preoccupied with the problem of control'. In analysing Durkheim's contribution to understanding how moral orders become, through processes of institutionalization, systems of 'normative controls', Parsons makes the important observation that '... unless in "individual" desires there were this inherently chaotic "centrifugal" quality the need of control would not be present at all' (1949: 377–8). Thus for Durkheim, the functions of normative controls were to constrain the asocial qualities of individuals through the enforcement of rules of conduct. Certainly in the way that Parsons describes it, Durkheim provides a sociological supplement to a Freudian schema.

For Janowitz (1975), Parson's work in and around the concept of social control is important because he made a distinct contribution to 'narrowing' the sociological definition of the concept. Prior to Parson's intervention, many formulations remained ill-defined, being applied to a wide range of circumstances, referring, in effect to the collection of processes that today we would term socialization. However, as Janowitz (1975) implies, although it was Parsons who started to focus the definition of social control upon reactions to deviance, the basis of this narrowed conception can be traced back to Park and Burgess's usage.

Durkheim famously sought to understand the role of collective ceremonies and rituals in the maintenance of social order. He argued that such forms of group enactment were important in symbolically restating the collective values of the group, thereby reminding the individual members of their shared bonds. A particularly interesting and important development of this dimension of Durkheim's theories relates to Halbwachs's (1992) concept of 'collective memory'. Halbwachs was concerned to document how the sense of a shared collective history is actively constructed via participation in ceremonies of remembrance, ritual commemorations and the display of symbolically loaded artefacts. He maintained that a belief system in the present shapes how the past is remembered. The outcome of which is to preserve and reproduce a sense amongst individuals of them having a shared past and intertwined interests, thereby developing a notion of collective identity in the present circumstances. For Halbwachs, the symbolic construction of the past was a product of a social order, but in turn it served to reinforce the order. In this sense we can detect a degree of overlap with Mead's (1932) theory of the past.

For my present purposes though, we can use Halbwach's concept of 'collective memory' to develop an important insight into the nature of social control. That is our remembrance of the past is frequently actively controlled and shaped in an attempt to exert control in the present. By constructing symbolically loaded collective memories, people are encouraged to believe to a degree in traditional values and ways of doing things. Perhaps one of the most vivid historical examples of the use of deliberately manufactured collective memories to enhance levels of control relates to Stalin's Russia, where history was deliberately rewritten to legitimize and create the conditions for a particular style of rule. Similarly, in Nazi Germany symbolism and stories from the past were invented to support the activities of the regime of the time. More recently, Cohen (2001) has applied similar analytic logics to the role of the Truth and Reconciliation Commissions of post-apartheid South Africa. These examples are perhaps rather extreme, but all states and all collectives draw upon shared remembrances of the past to establish or preserve a sense of shared identity and a collective belief system.

A coherent approach to understanding the functions of social control for collective life is to be found in Erikson's (1966) discussion of the social control of witchcraft in seventeenth-century New England. Erikson shows how the trials and punishments used in attempts to control the activities of alleged witches, functioned to reinvigorate the normative order at a time when the community was under pressure from wider structural changes in society. As Downes and Rock (1988: 103) expound, Erikson, by focusing upon this particular example, is looking for 'a deep structure of deviance and control' that is a fundamental property of social organization. A similar aim can be detected in Mary Douglas's (1966) anthropology, where she demonstrates how cultural orders necessarily provide ways for their members to distinguish between 'the pure' and 'the dangerous'. The implications of her study are that whilst different cultures define good and bad things in different ways, such systems of classification are always present. Classificatory systems of the type Douglas describes, are important because they identify what is viewed as contrary to the social order and thus should be controlled, as well as indicating an appropriate mechanism for carrying out this control.

Parsons's contributions to the functionalist emphasis on the importance of normative controls and in particular his work in narrowing the definition of social control is especially apposite for the criminologist Travis Hirschi's (1969) social control theory of deviance. Focusing specifically upon criminality, Hirschi sought to develop an answer to the conundrum of why it is that some people commit crime, whilst others do not. In constructing his answer he in effect inverted the problem and said that the question that needed answering is not, what are the causal factors that make some people commit crime, but why don't we all commit crime? His answer was that through processes of socialization and civic engagement we are subject to differential levels of social control. The greater our attachment, involvement, commitment and belief in society, the more controls we are subject to, and thus there is a reduced risk of us committing crime.

One of the criticisms that is often made of Functionalist theories is that they tend to assume that everybody accepts the norms of society and is equally committed to the established social order. Although, in Parsons' treatment of Durkheim's writings, recognition is given to individual desires as a source of conflict in social relations, ultimately the consensual orientation of functionalist theorizing tends to see the suppression of these conflicts as comparatively unproblematic. As a result, there is little sense provided of how and why conflict should emerge in a society. This is particularly problematic for a discussion of social control as one of its primary functions is the resolution of conflict. In contrast, Marxist and Marxisant theories stress the sources of conflict and the use of an array of control strategies in response to such frictions.

States of control: the legacy of Marx

For theorists of social control drawing upon a radical perspective, the capitalist order is an unstable order. As a consequence, in capitalist systems social control enacted by the state is intrinsic to the operations of political economy, due to the ways in which capitalism inherently generates conflict. For Marx himself, under such conditions the state played a role in quashing any threats to the capitalist order through the use of coercive force. Subsequent reworkings and developments of these themes have tended to elide the subtle and nuanced ways in which conduct is controlled through various capitalist institutions. As Turk (1982) describes it, minimal control strategies and tactics seek to perpetuate power structures, but their optimum aim is to transform them into authority structures. Such accounts have emphasized that although 'hard' forms of social control are designed into the capitalist framework, the vast majority of control is of a 'softer' kind.

One well known example of this 'soft social control' is Gramsci's (1971) concept of hegemony. Gramsci argued that the effective control of the proletariat relied not simply upon repression, but the establishment of a perceived legitimacy for the capitalist regime through the control of the dominant ideas and values in a society. Similar themes can be identified in Louis Althusser's (1971) discussion of the role of 'the ideological state apparatus'. For Althusser, whilst the power of the state and thus the capitalist system is buttressed by the presence of a 'repressive state apparatus', the more subtle, pervasive and effective mechanisms by which control ordinarily takes place are embedded in institutions of education and the welfare state. The control of the dominant ideas in society works to regulate people's beliefs and desires, thereby functioning to reproduce the overall domination of society by capitalist elites.

The idea that the provision of welfare benefits by the state was not simply benign humanitarianism, but an act intended to extend the penetration of the state's social control apparatus has emerged as a key theme in a number of analyses of this hue. For example, Ginsburg (1979), Gough (1979) and Offe (1982; 1984) have all respectively sought to show how, what on the surface seem to be caring activities that alleviate poverty, actually work to enhance the control of what are seen as potentially troublesome sections of the citizenry. Relatedly, Andrew Scull's (1977) work shows how oscillations in the economic cycle structure the state's understanding of social problems and thus the approach to control that is adopted.

The welfare state is held to be a key component of how capitalism ameliorates its inherent contradictions and conflicts. As will be discussed in more detail in Chapter 4, a similar latent function is often attributed to media organizations. Media provide an opportunity to control the circulation of dominant ideas and they are, according to certain versions of radical theory, routinely co-opted by state agencies in the fabrication of hegemonic crises, manifested as 'moral panics', which establish the conditions for the extension of the social control apparatus by the state (Hall et al. 1978).

More recently, the direct influence of Marxist inspired discussions of social control, centring upon ideas of coercion and ideology, have waned in popularity. In their place have emerged a number of what, for want of a better label, I will term post-structuralist theories of social control.

The dispersal of discipline: post-structuralism

What separates the post-structuralist theories from the radical theories is a different conception of the nature of power. Whereas concepts and theories of social control that take their lead from Marx see power as a monopoly possession of the state and the owners of the means of production exercised in a top-down manner, the post-structuralists see power as more decentred and dispersed throughout society. Therefore, rather than seeing power as emanating solely from the state, the post-structuralist imagery of power is more akin to a network of multiple, nested, power centres that are distributed at strategic points throughout societies. The state is still important in the conduct of control activities, but the role of the state itself has been transformed and there are other important actors whose roles need to be recognized.

The central figure in the development of this approach to the study of social control and social order is Michel Foucault. In an effort to circumvent the problems associated with the concept of social control, resulting from some of the issues reviewed earlier, Foucault only rarely used the term itself. Rather in his work he makes use of a range of concepts such as discipline, panoptic surveillance, governmentality and bio-power, in an effort to understand the different dimensions of how power is enacted and control exercised in different settings, in respect of different problems.

Nevertheless, one of the abiding themes underpinning much of his work is an attempt to unmask the varied range of controlling technologies and practices that societies use in respect of deviant acts and to induce conformity. Indeed, for Foucault, perhaps the defining quality of modern societies was the development of powerful disciplinary technologies, that sought to control both the body and mind of all subjects. In this sense, he was interested in the production and reproduction of what in relation to the pragmatist perspective I labelled 'collective self control'. For Foucault (1988), collective self control resulted from the strategic deployment of specific 'technologies of the self', which were themselves generative of and generated by a particular rationality of government, or what he termed 'governmentality'. The 'art of government' as Foucault saw it, especially in his later works, was the development of mechanisms of security that regulated relations between citizens, between the sovereign state and citizens, and between sovereign states (Gordon 1991). Thus although there are compatibilities in the analytic focus of his work with aspects of that of Mead and his followers, Foucault understands the production of collective self control in a very different manner.

Foucault saw control efforts as being directed ultimately by a concern to effect 'normalization' over different forms of deviance. His discussion of the practices of incarceration illustrates this theme. But importantly, Foucault argues that projects of normalization were themselves dispersed throughout the operations of a range of social institutions, founded upon bodies of knowledge that facilitated classification and definition of different forms of deviance. He thus implicates the human sciences in the development of the apparatus of modern forms of social control. It was knowledge generated by disciplines such as psychology and criminology that was intrinsic to the refinement of the methods for identifying, classifying and responding to different types of deviant behaviour, thereby creating the possibility of a rationalization of the imposition of power and control (Pasquino 1991).

This critique of the role of the social and human sciences in the development and refinement of the apparatus of social control is a key theme in the work of Stan Cohen (1985). Cohen identifies a pivotal role in the development of control strategies for the discursive classificatory frameworks employed by professional practitioners, who are directly involved in the design and implementation of specific interventions. His work is seminally important, because in developing the work of Foucault, and moving beyond it to trace some of the current 'master-patterns' in the development of social control, Cohen maps the outlines of a theoretical framework that has been developed and refined by the contemporary post-social control perspective.

Beginning in the 1960s, Cohen argues that there has been a process of destructuring, wherein the monopoly of state bureaucracies in the business of controlling deviancy has been increasingly eroded. As he terms it, there have been concurrent moves: 'away from the state'; 'away from the expert';

'away from the institutions'; and 'away from the mind'. The 'profound destructuring impulse' that he describes had its roots in a radical and progressive move to restrict the use of some of the more coercive elements of the control system. What Cohen shows though, is that although motivated by good intentions on the part of the reformers, the ironic and unintended consequences of these reforms were to develop new forms of control, refine the logics of those already in place and extend the reach of the state – providing a deeper penetration and permeation of control into the lives and routines of communities. As he puts it:

> The benevolent-sounding destructuring package had turned out to be a monster in disguise, a Trojan horse. The alternatives had merely left us with 'wider, stronger and different nets'.
>
> (Cohen 1985: 38)

Cohen is a key figure in contemporary debates on the logic and conduct of control. In developing aspects of Foucault's historical works, and articulating the trajectory of the destructuring impulse, he bridges the divide between the post-structuralist and post-social control theories. It is Cohen who effectively identifies a number of key themes that have emerged as central to the latter position. First, he recognizes that although Foucault's historical analysis of the 'disciplinary society' identifies some important and relevant trends, the contemporary situation is not simply continuous with them, particularly with regards the role of the state. In addition he notes that one of the most remarkable shifts has been a shift of focus in control efforts, from individual deviants, to whole populations and environments. Critiquing the rise of what he labels 'the new behaviourism', he recounts how the guiding logic of 'community control' has been replaced by the 'control of communities'. Connected to which he explains that the master-patterns of social control in late-modernity have involved a gradual expansion and intensification of the system, and an increasing invisibility of social control as it increases its degree of penetration into the social body.

Post-social control

As outlined above, the ideas of Foucault and Cohen have been highly influential in shaping what Hudson (2002) labels the 'post-social control' perspective. It is 'post' social control, because, heavily influenced by Foucault's efforts to develop a new language for talking about such processes and problems, some advocates of this approach have increasingly sought to construct their arguments in a way that does not rely upon the social control concept. This is best exemplified by Johnston and Shearing's (2003) recent attempt to formulate a theory of the nodal (or networked) governance of security.

In setting out their approach, Johnston and Shearing argue that in the contemporary context the concept of social control should be avoided for several reasons. First, they maintain that it prioritizes the notion of 'the social', which following Rose (1996), they believe is an increasingly problematic concept.[4] According to both Rose and Johnston and Shearing, the generalized notion of 'the social' as a 'governing rationality' (that is as a mechanism of and target for governmentally based interventions) has been progressively replaced by a more fractured and decentred notion of heterogeneous community based interests. As part of this pattern of development, they maintain that the power of the state to deliver security has been reduced, and across many situations the state is now simply one amongst a host of actors whose activities are directed towards this outcome. A further justification that Johnston and Shearing (2003) provide for avoiding the language of social control, is in order to separate their work from what they see as the unwarranted tendency amongst many recent social control studies to identify the dispersal of social control technologies as a negative development.

In addition to Rose's (1996) obituary for 'the death of the social', Hudson (2002) identifies two further contributions that have made pivotal contributions to the formulation of the post-social control perspective. She notes that Foucault's later work on 'governmentality' has supplied a general framework for rethinking the role of the state and other institutions in relation to the inculcation of discipline at the level of the individual. Importantly though, Hudson argues that whereas for Foucault the principal objective of the various 'theatres of punishment' was 'normalization', for those who have latterly drawn upon his work this aim is no longer recognized as being central. Rather, concern has focused upon risk calculation and risk management. Feeley and Simon's (1994) notion of a new rationality of 'actuarial justice' exemplifies this, where they argue that the dispositions of both criminal justice and welfare agencies has shifted to the predictive identification of, and response to, risky behaviours and individuals. It is an approach that is more 'managerial' than 'transformative' in its outlook, seeking to reduce exposure to 'problem' people, rather than attempting to reform or rehabilitate them (Sparks 2001). For Hudson (2002), the increased prominence of actuarial justice is both a reflection and constitutive of a more profound decline in a collective willingness to share exposure to collective risks (see O'Malley 1992; Rose 1996). In sum, this post-social modality of control involves technologies of prediction and risk management, where those people who are adjudged to be dangerous, are increasingly excluded from situations where they threaten the prevailing social order.

Although utilizing slightly different terminology, Castel (1991) has argued that we have started to see the emergence of 'a post-disciplinary order', wherein individuals are 'assigned' to 'different social destinies' on the basis of profiles constructed for them. He posits that it is increasingly the case that the social system is providing some people with enhanced opportunities for self-actualization, whilst the life-chances of others are artificially restricted. People are being locked into 'circuits of inclusion and exclusion' (Rose 2000), and control in late-modernity adopts what Young (1999) evocatively dubs 'cannabilistic' and 'bulimic' strategies, depending on who and what is the object of control. Some forms of actual or pre-dicted deviance warrant an attempt at reform of the transgressor, but for others, exclusion is held to be the only acceptable and practicable response (Crawford 2000). This latter approach stems from a growing belief that changing the 'disposing dispositions' of potential deviants is difficult and frequently unsuccessful, and therefore it is better to alter aspects of the situations that they inhabit. Indeed, this idea of 'situational control' is one of the defining characteristics of late-modern social control strategies (Garland 2000; Hope and Sparks 2000).

This notion of a post-disciplinary order echoes Deleuze's (1995) con-tention that we are now living in 'control societies', wherein enacted social control is more fluid and permeating than it was previously. For Deleuze, disciplinary societies were founded upon fairly distinct and separate systems of social control. But increasingly, the boundaries between controls and control systems have been eroded, and so different types of control flow into one another, overlap and intermingle. A not dissimilar idea is promoted by Haggerty and Ericson (2000) in their discussion of the 'rhizomatic' expansion of surveillance assemblages.

On talking about control?

The post-social control perspective is a complex and emergent perspective. There is some important and innovative work being done that attempts to capture the changing logics and practices of contemporary control efforts. Nevertheless, there are a number of problems that can be identified with it that need to be acknowledged. First, whilst it captures some of the important changes that are occurring in relation to how social control is both imagined and delivered, some of the accounts fail to acknowledge the extent to which these new practices and logics co-occur with some more established and continuing modes.[5] There is not a wholesale change throughout the entire social control apparatus, rather parts of it have continued using established scripts, whilst other components have been reconfigured.

The issue of terminology is also important in two different respects. Johnston and Shearing (2003) drop the term social control altogether from their analysis, in an effort to avoid some of the problems that they identify with it. In so doing, whilst this move does allow them to conduct a sophis-ticated and complex analysis of current patterns, there is also a sense in which much of what they have to say about governance, nodes and security, is simply a rephrasing of themes that others have opted to put in the language of social control.[6] Further to which, work that has manifest affinities to that of Johnston and Shearing, such as Rose (1999; 2000) and Deleuze (1995), continues to pivot around the central concept of 'control', rather than governance. At present then, the overall picture is one of terminological confusion, with different (and sometimes similar) concepts frequently being used to diagnose similar conditions and problems.

Despite this ambiguity about the concept of social control, in trying to capture and articulate some profound shifts in the constitution of late-modern societies, I think the post-social control perspective provides an important challenge to the established conceptualization. In arguing that in late-modernity the dominant logics of social control are increasingly less focused upon either deviance or deviants, and that everyone's behaviour is to a greater or lesser extent subject to control, as a result of the ways in which controls have permeated all our institutional forms, this body of work suggests a need to rethink how social control is defined. In effect, it posits that social control is no longer comprised solely of organized responses to deviant behaviour, but must include the plethora of behaviour modification technologies that routinely alter people's non-deviant behaviour in some subtle and not so subtle ways.

I will return to this theme in the final chapter, where I will outline an approach that integrates such changes within Cohen's established definition of social control. For despite the disagreements that can be detected concerning the most appropriate language via which to describe the current situation, there is broader agreement that can be identified in terms of the form that some of these changes are taking. Most commentators agree that the control apparatus is both intentionally and unintentionally expanding in some areas whilst contracting in others. This is perhaps best captured by a notion of a process of 'control creep', wherein the reach and/or intensity of different components of the control apparatus are incrementally, and often in isolation from each other, being extended. The overall effect being that control progressively extends and expands.

As part of these processes of control creep, the reformatory principle of the 'normalizing' impulse identified in Foucault's 'histories of the present', where through subtle, yet fairly pervasive, technologies of power, individuals subject to a regime were simultaneously persuaded and coerced into reforming their thoughts and conduct so that it conformed with 'normal' models of appropriate behaviour, has increasingly been foregone. In its place, is a more instrumentally based and future-oriented logic that aims at prevention and harm minimization (Johnston and Shearing 2003). Accompanying such shifts there has been a blurring in terms of how social control is enacted, who it is performed by and when, and why it is conducted. The widespread pessimism that Cohen (1985) identified with state based social controls in the 1960s was thus transformed in the context of the late-modern crime complex, and became part of a logic that positively encouraged the development of new controls in, of, and by communities. These new modes of control supplemented and augmented the existing modes, some of which continued as before, whilst others were retooled and reworked to give the appearance of innovation. Frequently such reconfigurations were in the form of making them more explicitly coercive or punitive.

Over the past two to three decades the social order of late-modernity has created forces which have pushed forward these changes, at the same time as the institutional order has sought to accommodate and reconfigure itself in light of the ongoing transformations of social life. One particularly important symptom of which has been the blurring of the public and private spheres, and the increasing penetration of private interests in the delivery of control. This in turn has further promoted the commodification and fetishization of security, reinforcing and amplifying the dominant trends (Spitzer 1987).

The different perspectives on social control outlined previously are, as I have intimated, closely allied to some of the key theoretical positions in the social sciences. The epistemological and ontological standpoints associated with these theoretical frameworks effectively provide alternate lenses through which to view, understand and thus talk about issues of social control and relatedly social order. Thus what has been revealed are not incompatible and irreconcilable features, but rather different dimensions of how social reality can be understood.

Furthermore, thinking in particular about the Interactionist, Functionalist and Marxist perspectives on social control, it should be evident that over time there have been revisions in the dominant ideas espoused, and consequently different positions put forward representing permutations of particular core notions and values. Therefore, before I move on to a more detailed discussion of social control practice, I want to conclude this discussion of the idea of social control by analysing how the various theoretical perspectives are related and how they have mutually influenced each others' development. Because, whilst separating the different conceptualizations as I have done above allows us to identify the key issues in terms of how different theoretical perspectives approach the problem of explaining social control, in actuality, the relationships between them have been more complex than such an approach might be taken to imply. The various approaches to the study of social control have not developed in isolation. Rather, they have reciprocally shaped and guided the development of each other. This has largely taken place in two different ways. There has been a process of 'incorporation', where ideas originally associated with one perspective are taken on board and developed by a subsequent perspective. Alternatively, subsequent perspectives have clarified their position by a reaction against and rejection of the ideas associated with earlier theories.

As an example of the process of incorporation we can examine the links between labelling theory, grounded in a tradition of pragmatist philosophy, and the Marxist inspired radical criminology theories. Labelling theory identified that the imposition of control could promote deviance. This fundamental rationale was incorporated by subsequent more radical theories that used it to argue that the state should curtail its activities in attempting to control crime. The relationship between these state centred theories and the post-structuralist orientation provides an example of how a reaction against established conceptualizations can stimulate innovation. As previously documented, the post-structural approach to social control rejects the notion of an overarching framework of power possessed by the state. Instead it recognizes that the power to exhibit control in different domains is dispersed and pluralistic, taking on different forms according to what is being regulated and by whom. The implications of this dispersal have been worked out by the advocates of post-social control perspective.

Summary

To summarize then, over the course of approximately a century writing on and around the topic of social control it has been studied at micro-, meso- and macro-levels (Blomberg and Cohen 1995). Over this period two key changes have occurred. First and most importantly, the concept has been refined and increasingly narrowly defined. Secondly and relatedly, it has become more complex. Each subsequent theoretical formulation of the processes of social control has tended to both incorporate and reject elements of the variety of theories that preceded it.

This history of the concept provides important background information in terms of explaining the complexities surrounding contemporary debates about social control and why some favour dropping the term altogether. However, I have started to set out an argument that suggests that if we look at the substantive content of these different theoretical debates, there is seemingly a broader sense of agreement about the nature of contemporary control than the terminological disputes might imply. In an effort to further develop this position, having looked at the history of the idea of social control, in the next chapter I will focus upon a history of how and why control practices have altered and adapted.

chapter three

A history of social control practices

A social history in fragments
  The penal-welfare nexus
Rationalization and the administrative apparatus of control
Juridification
Turning ourselves outside-in and inside-out
Summary

In the previous chapter, I traced a history of the concept of social control in the academic literature. In this chapter I will again adopt a historical perspective, but this time focusing upon the development of practices of social control, my aim being to describe how the conduct of social control has developed over time, related to wider changes that have taken place in liberal democratic capitalist societies. I am especially concerned to map out how practices of social control have been shaped by the prevalent social context in which they are situated, and how, in turn, the conduct of social control has been central to the reconstitution of this context. The analysis presented herein, will address how the contemporary situation described in the opening chapter came into being. It will not describe contemporary practices of social control in any detail, as that is the focus of other chapters.

All historical accounts have to strike a balance in resolving the tension that exists between focusing upon the continuities that can be identified across different historical periods, and emphasizing the changes that take place between eras. This history is no different. What will become evident from the ensuing discussion is that there is no master-narrative, no sole overarching pattern presented to explain how and why social control practices have been constituted in their present form. This is because in complex societies there are complex forces at work consisting of sometimes convergent, at other times divergent patterns, distributed across various domains of social, political and economic life. To argue that there is a cohesive unifying logic that explains the ways in which social control is practised is to oversimplify what is a messy and somewhat confused state of affairs. Any such account necessarily glosses over the contingent and contradictory trends involved. Thus in order to avoid any such over-simplification, in what follows I simply try to identify some of the more important trends that have shaped and guided the development of social control practice. Therefore, I provide a selective account of changes and continuities in the conduct of social control in modern societies. It is not exhaustive, rather it seeks to shed light on some of the key occurrences that have served to shape more contemporary control practices. The opening part of the chapter seeks to describe the key historical moments where fundamental changes in the logics and practices of social control occurred, thereby providing a somewhat discontinuous history. In the latter half of the chapter I seek to identify some of the longer-term trends that are apparent.

A social history in fragments

Today's media are replete with stories where someone expresses anxiety about the state of society and the sense that life has become increasingly dangerous. But as Geoff Pearson (1983) has shown through his historical analysis, such concerns about the degradation and dissipation of society and social order seem to be a common feature of modern life. Indeed, surveying society over a longer time-frame, if anything social life has become progressively more ordered. In his theory of the 'civilizing process' Norbert Elias (1994) famously describes the long-term process by which norms, traditions, morals and customs have been adopted, adapted and agreed upon, to provide enhanced regulation of individual and collective conduct. From medieval times onwards, there seems to have been a gradual pacification of social life, wherein the definition of deviance and its control has become increasingly specified and effective.

This is not to imply that prior to the development of the modern institutions of social control that there was no social control; for as many legal and social anthropologists have shown, all forms of social organization require mechanisms to ensure that the behaviour of individuals accords with the norms and expectations of the wider group. Anthropological accounts make evident the fact that all social orders necessarily involve classificatory schemas to identify those facets of the world that are held to threaten their continued existence (Douglas 1966; Needham 1979).[1] Furthermore, it is apparent that although such groups do not have formalized systems of law, or formal mechanisms for the enforcement of their socially maintained rules, there is nevertheless social control in action. In effect such groups are self-policing, utilizing informal mechanisms of social control to enforce a particular social order.

This notion of communities being self-policing was the principal way in which social order was maintained and social conflict resolved throughout pre-modern forms of social organization. The vast majority of the problems of order were dealt with by local communities, and indeed, the expectation was that communities themselves would be responsible for the identification of deviance and the maintenance of order. There was a rudimentary system of justice to supposedly support them in this, but it was somewhat haphazard in its coverage and was employed only in respect of the more serious transgressions. As the forms of social organization became more complex, serious problems of public order which occurred periodically were dealt with by the application of coercive force delivered by the army and militia. As Rock (1983) identifies, even by the end of the seventeenth century, although there was a rudimentary system of policing in place in England, some areas remained unpatrolled and unpatrollable. Thus even at this stage many communities remained effectively self-policing and the basis of social control was decentralized.

When crime occurred, the absence of a regular specialized constabulary meant that the identification and capture of the felon relied upon the efforts of the adult male population of a parish. Through the 'hue and cry' the population of the parish was supposed to perform formal social control functions as and when required. The participation of citizens in such activities was encouraged through methods of exhortation, bribery and coercion. For instance, those members of a community who failed to muster to a hue and cry could be subject to punishment. Under legislation introduced in 1691, the state introduced rewards payable to those persons who successfully prosecuted individuals for certain offences. The offences that came to be covered by this principle included burglary, highway robbery and horse-stealing.

Provision of state sponsored rewards served to initiate a transformation in the basis of crime control, it was turned from a communal obligation into an entrepreneurial activity. This trend was emboldened by the standard practice of victims of crime offering rewards. The reward system formed the basis of the English thief-taker system of the eighteenth and early nineteenth centuries, where thieves and receivers of stolen goods were effectively employed by the state to catch criminals, thereby earning the reward monies. The most (in)famous of the thief-takers was Jonathan Wild who established an organization that at the same time as it tracked down criminals, itself engaged in robberies on commission, whereby goods would be stolen by an associate of Wild, who would then return the goods to the owner thereby earning a reward for their safe return. Although, by the end of the eighteenth century the role of thief-taker had fallen into disrepute, in effect it was the real predecessor of the Bow Street Runners, who in turn formed the basis of the Metropolitan Police (Emsley 1991). And, of course, the practice of paying informers for information to assist in the detection of crimes continues to this day.

The motivation for supplying rewards was less about making crime control a business, than encouraging people to inform about the criminal activities of others. In the absence of a systematic approach for the prevention and detection of criminal and deviant activities, the encouragement of informing became a central component of social control strategy. Informing was done not just for monetary rewards though, arrested suspects or convicts could earn a pardon by informing on the activities of others (Rock 1983).

The widespread use of impeachment to encourage informing is indicative of the extent to which legal and control practices at this time were almost wholly dependent upon negotiation and collusion. For example, those sentenced to imprisonment could purchase comparatively limited punishments if they had sufficient wealth to do so. Of course, the ability to engage in such negotiations was premised upon the social status of the individual concerned, reflecting the distribution of power in society. Indeed, the whole system of control was based upon a clear demarcation between those groups who were understood as part of society and the large numbers of marginalized people, on the periphery of society (Neocleous 2000). These liminal groups were believed to be less than human, posing a continual danger to the existing social order. The members of the included groups could act with a fair degree of impunity from the systems of control, whereas socially excluded persons could expect only harsh and brutal treatment.

The story then is of a messy and confused approach to the provision of social control. The boundaries between legality and illegality were blurred, with some comparatively powerful groups fairly immune from the controls of state, whilst at the same time encouraging the patchwork and arbitrary system of controls to punish harshly the activities of the poor and marginalized.

The penal-welfare nexus

It is widely recognized that by the end of the eighteenth century the effects of the linked processes of urbanization and industrialization were placing the extant institutions of government under increasing pressure. Urbanization and industrialization caused new social problems which if not addressed, it was felt, threatened the stability of the nascent liberal-capitalist social order. It was thus no coincidence that in the 1830s in Britain there were important changes both in the state's response to poverty in the Poor Law Amendment Act, and in the 1829 inception of the 'new police'. Taking the former reform first, the establishment of the workhouse system to provide for the poorest sections of society was motivated by a desire to provide a degree of social care, but also to effect control over potentially destabilizing sections of the populace (Neocleous 2000). Furthermore, the ethos of the workhouse with its principle of 'less eligibility' was deliberately designed to reinforce the work ethic amongst those living outside of the workhouse regimen.

The progressive development of modern welfare systems was of vital importance in transforming the fundamental bases of social order. It functioned to modify attitudes, behaviours and practices in relation to work and the family (Bauman 1998). It is well documented that changes in the political constitution of liberal-capitalist societies and especially the progressive extensions of the electoral franchise were driving forces in the movements for welfare reform. But democratization was in turn dependent upon the transformations occurring in the state's approaches to the conduct of social control. A working democracy is, according to Melossi (1990), a political form that has an elective affinity for social control. For it is the latter, that induces a degree of 'cognitive consensus' and 'co-orientation' towards shared objectives.

The establishment of a full-time professional police force, albeit on a limited scale, was also symptomatic of the start of a shift in the position of government in respect of the production and reproduction of social order. For what we see subsequent to these developments is the gradual, yet progressive expansion of the role of state agencies in respect of both the provision of welfare and the control of crime. This brought into being a penal-welfare nexus where the causes of a number of social problems were addressed via proactive forms of welfare intervention, and the consequences of these problems were dealt with through the criminal justice process. For example, in the latter half of the nineteenth century, there were several legislative reforms which established that the state had a role in areas such as education, the protection of children and public health. At around the same time there were important developments in policing and the prison system.

Once these principles were in place, then economic imperatives and those of national security served to reinforce their salience, and created pressures for an expansion of state interventions to address an increasingly diverse array of social problems. From the point of view of this analysis though, the significance of such developments is their role in facilitating new opportunities for social control.

Garland (1985) argues that this shift in governmental rationality wrought a change from what he terms 'Victorian penality' to 'modern penality'. Critiquing and refining elements of Foucault's (1977) genealogy of incarceration, Garland identifies a fundamental transformation in the strategies of punishment and control at the very end of the nineteenth century. He describes a move away from the Victorian model of a calibrated, hierarchical structure of punishments, including fines, incarceration, corporal punishment and death, to modern penality, founded upon a discourse of penal-welfarism where the system is:

> . . . an extended grid of non-equivalent and diverse dispositions into which the offender is inscribed according to the diagnosis of his or her condition and the treatment appropriate to it.
>
> (Garland 1985: 28)

As part of such manoeuvres, the aims of punishment by the state were recast from 'blind repression' to an attempt to reform and 'normalize' the deviant individual. This reformatory principle was tied into the development of an investigatory and diagnostic form of knowledge and apparatus, whereby the defects and deviations of the individual were to be ascertained and acted upon in order to discipline and normalize them.

The important point about Garland's analysis and that of Foucault before him, is the sense in which they connect transformations in the penal realm with wider currents in society at that time. They show that the inculcation of discipline and the attempts at normalization were not techniques restricted to incarceration, but were integral to the role of state interventions. For example, Donzelot (1979) describes the ways in which social workers and those involved in the protection of children employed similar rationalities and strategies in their work. Over the course of the first half of the twentieth century there was a marked development of the state's capacity and desire to be involved in the delivery of social control. Through expansions and diversifications in fields such as policing, welfare and punishment, involving new forms of expertise and new agencies, the state increasingly became routinely involved (as opposed to a more exceptional role) in social control work.

There are of course other developments which will be filled out in more detail in subsequent chapters, but the next significant transformation to be discussed here concerns shifts in the logics of control that took place in the 1960s. For Cohen (1985), the 1960s witnessed the ascendance of the profound 'de-structuring impulse' detailed in the previous chapter, composed of a number of interrelated ideologies including decarceration, diversion, decentralization and decriminalization amongst others. The implementation of reforms informed by these logics was justified on the basis that they would prove to be more effective and efficient, more humane, and less stigmatizing. But as Cohen documents, the unintended consequences of the resultant turn to community-based controls was the development of a new form of subtle and amorphous discipline, that would in time create the sufficient and necessary conditions for what, in the concluding chapter, I have termed 'ambient social control'.

Commenting on the Italian psychiatric reform movement and the experience of deinstitutionalization and de-professionalization, that took place at about this time, Offe (1984) notes that the reform programmes that were introduced were somewhat naive in assuming that the familial and community infrastructures of civil society were capable of absorbing a certain range of deviance. According to Offe, as these reforms were implemented it quickly became apparent that the sheer complexity of contemporary communities tends to make them intolerant of deviance. This was reinforced by the fact that through the development of the penal-welfare nexus and the professionalization of responsibility for dealing with social problems, communities had lost the popular knowledge necessary for dealing competently with people who have some form of mental illness. The state's response to the failings of these institutions was to introduce supplementary controls into communities, with the intention that these should enable the social institutions to perform their desired control functions. Thus the unintended consequence of these reforms was to contribute to the emergence of the control logics and practices that are the focus of the post-social control theorists, and which were discussed in the previous chapter.

Rationalization and the administrative apparatus of control

Having provided a history in fragments, seeking to uncover key moments when social control practice was reconfigured, I now want to shift the temper of my analysis in order to identify several longer-term trends that are important in explaining the evolution of control practice. I will start by considering Weber's rationalization thesis and its impact upon social control.

It has become commonplace for those assessing Weber's sociology to argue that his diverse studies were fundamentally about explicating the processes of rationalization that he saw as providing the foundations of modernity (Giddens 1971; Dodd 1999). Whereas Marx saw the engine of history as class conflict, Weber saw the emergence and development of modernity, and indeed capitalistic organization, as the product of rationalization, understood as a form of instrumental calculation and basic belief. The spread of reason was, according to Weber, particularly important in the development of the administrative capacities of the state. The down-side to this was that the spread of bureaucracy as a means for the rational accounting of actions tended to produce the metaphorical 'iron-cage', whereby the citizen of modernity found their ability to act freely increasingly constrained. This dimension of Weber's work is taken up by Dandeker (1990) in his exploration of the expansion of the state's surveillance capacities in modernity. He notes that the underpinning logic of Weber's analysis concerning the institutionalization of rationality is not altogether distinct from that developed by Foucault's concern with the relations between power and knowledge.

Increasing levels of state intervention were premised upon the development of a bureaucratic apparatus, enabling the collection of administrative data that made it possible to identify and map the nature, scale and scope of different problems. As Ian Hacking (1990) explains in his treatise on the rise of probability as a mode of reasoning, and the resultant 'taming of chance', although governments had previously collected data on the populace, in the latter parts of the eighteenth century through into the nineteenth, there was an explosion of interest in Prussia, France, Britain and the rest of Western Europe in the uses to which such data could be put. This was driven by:

... new technologies for classifying and enumerating, and new bureaucracies with the authority and continuity to deploy the technology. There is a sense in which many of the facts presented by the bureaucracies did not exist ahead of time. Categories had to be invented into which people could conveniently fall in order to be counted.

(Hacking 1990: 3)

Thus the collection of data by the state itself promoted an extension of the reach of state power through the development of bureaucratic machinery to collect and process information, and then subsequently to act upon it. Furthermore, the publication of data made available new ways of classifying both oneself and the people whom one encountered, together with different ways of understanding society and its problems. As Foucault (1991) provocatively suggested in his discussion of 'biopolitics', the avalanche of numbers provided the basis upon which the normal could be divined from the abnormal, which in turn established objectives for the strategies of normalization that were imagined by the human sciences and practised by state institutions.

In addition to matters of population management associated with birth, marriage and mortality rates, states began to collect data on problems such as levels of suicide, illness and crime. These analyses served to provide the preconditions for the enactment of more effective social control strategies.

It is important to retain an awareness that, at least in part, these ongoing processes of rationalization have their roots in rather more prosaic and pragmatic concerns. The establishment of large-scale state bureaucracies is grounded in a confluence of interactions between taxation, representation and administration (Ferguson 2001). In order to maintain a bureaucracy capable of processing large amounts of administrative data (and thus rationalizing the conduct of governance) a source of financing this work had to be established by states. This necessitated a more comprehensive and sophisticated regime of taxation to acquire sufficient funds to pay for a professional corps of bureaucrats. In addition to the fact that a more extensive tax system itself required an enhanced administrative apparatus to function, the spread and diversification of taxation was connected to the widening of the electoral franchise. As citizens were increasingly required to participate in financing the activities of the state through taxation, so the idea that they had a right to help determine the nature of these activities through democratic processes was progressively propagated and accepted. Therefore, institutional rationalization, and consequently the ability of the state to exert more control over the lives of its citizens, resulted from a complex of adaptive manoeuvres. It was part of the ways in which the relationship between state and citizen was reconfigured. And it was not necessarily viewed unproblematically. As Ferguson (2001) documents, in Britain between 1690 and 1782, the number of 'fiscal bureaucrats' more than trebled, and in a manner redolent of contemporary concerns about surveillance, the Excise became known as 'the monster with 10,000 eyes'.[2]

The development of the tax system provided a rudimentary example of how states could collect and process data on a comparatively large scale. Over time this system developed, and similar principles were used to collect data about other dimensions of social life. Amongst the most significant developments in respect of this latter aspect was the establishment of mechanisms that allowed state bureaucracies to refine their methods of data collection and analysis, and to shift from the collection of data on aggregate groups to the collation of records relating to individuals. Tax records, police records, prison records, health records and education records were increasingly detailed, but the problem, particularly in relation to matters of controlling deviant and troublesome populations was one of personal identification. That is, in an era before the routine use of photography, how could a bureaucratic organization connect a documentary record of data about an individual to that person? As part of a move to rationalize punishment, records of previous convictions became important in terms of identifying recidivist individuals who should be subject to greater degrees of control, than individuals whose criminal participation was a single aberration. Similarly, problems were encountered by welfare bureaucracies in terms of establishing which individuals were entitled to receive particular benefits. The earliest workable solution to this problem was provided by the discovery of fingerprints as a unique identifier, this provided a form of coding that could be used to link a person to the records kept about them (Cole 2001).

The progressive expansion and refinement of the administrative apparatus was continued by conditions under war-time. In an effort to prosecute war more effectively nation states began to collate increasingly detailed levels of data about combatants, which served to reveal the persistence of social problems especially related to health. But perhaps as important as the content of the data was the fact that the total war philosophy revealed that the state actually could develop bureaucratic mechanisms to collect, process and act upon data on a vast scale (Dandeker 1990).

This was not always to positive effect though. In a counter to discussions of the irrationality of the Nazi holocaust of the Jews, Zygmunt Bauman (1989) has argued that in fact it provides one of the most chilling examples of what can be achieved through bureaucratic forms of organization and a logic of rationalization. The holocaust was a highly organized and systematic attempt to engage in actions that most individuals would find reprehensible. And yet it was able to undertake the task set for it with considerable technical efficiency. The power of 'the machine' overwhelmed any resistance and moral qualms that individuals working in it may have had, providing a type of social control over their actions which enabled them to engage in their work without having to attend to its consequences. Rather than being irrational and anti-modern, for Bauman, the holocaust represents the apotheosis, the ultimate example of what can be achieved if you follow the logic of modern rationality.

Drawing upon techniques developed in advertising commercial goods, war-time governments undertook to manipulate popular morale. Through public information campaigns, governments across Europe and in America sought to shape the public's understanding of the conflict, and to control and manipulate their desires in an effort to retain support for continuing to fight.[3] What was made very evident by such work was that the state did not have to rely purely on coercion, or the threat of coercion, to get the public to conform to desired norms of behaviour. Subtle techniques derived from the principles of psychology and psychoanalysis, directed towards the hidden, often subconscious, desires of individuals and groups, could produce effective results in terms of reducing overt forms of social conflict.

Alongside the social, economic and psychological developments I have described above, there were also important developments in the realm of politics. Not least, there was a progressive widening of the electoral franchise which led to an increasing proportion of the population being possessed of political rights. In terms of the provision of control this meant that its exercise could no longer be undertaken in an arbitrary and somewhat haphazard manner, but rather had to be appropriate, proportionate and legitimate. Moreover, as participants in the democratic state, these groups of people were no longer to be simply controlled. Social control by the state had to take account of their interests if the legitimacy of the government and perhaps even the state itself was to be preserved.

According to Reiner (1992), by the 1920s there was broad acceptance and support for the idea that the state should take the lead role in the conduct of formal social control. Through the police, prisons and other institutions of the criminal justice process, a complex bureaucratic apparatus was established for responding to more serious kinds of deviant behaviour. These actions thus served to support and bolster the informal regulation of deviance taking place within communities. And in the post-war era, the setting up of fully developed welfare state systems continued the established trend for the state to collect data on the condition of its citizens and to use these to design interventions.

Weber's theory of the penetration of instrumental rationality into diverse arenas of social life as being the defining characteristic of modernity, provides a meta-narrative for understanding transformations in a number of areas. In his writings, a central component of rationalization is the role played by the expansion of law and the legal system as a source of authoritative rationalizing principles. It is to this subject that I now turn.

Juridification

Law constitutes one of the primary mechanisms via which social control is enacted. For Black (1976), law is 'governmental social control', being the rules and processes that the state uses to intervene in social conflicts between both organized and individuated interests. According to Black, there is an inversely proportional relationship between law as formal social control and other more informal controls. As a consequence of which, when increases in the formal quotient of law are enacted, there is a corresponding decline in the amount of informal social control in a society. As has been intimated in the discussion contained in the opening two chapters, Black's 'correlated proportionality' thesis[4] has been called into question by theoretical analyses of the late-modern situation, which suggest that there has been a marked and substantial increase in, and interlocking of, both informal and formal modes of social control. This does not however, mean that other aspects of Black's approach do not help us to understand the patterns of development in the exercise of social control in modernity.

The driving logic of Habermas's (1989) analysis of processes of 'juridification' is not that dissimilar to Black's arguments. Habermas uses the concept of juridification to trace what he sees as a progressive expansion of the domain of law as a constitutive development of the modern social system. He argues that reform and development of the legal apparatus has been part of the trajectory of social change in modern societies. In particular, he distinguishes between what he identifies as the 'expansion of law', from the 'increasing density of law'. The former notion referring to the ways in which law has progressively 'colonized' new areas of social life, reshaping how these previously informally regulated domains are understood and thus enacted. In contrast, the idea of the increasing density of law refers to a trend for a movement away from reliance on generalized principles of law, to increasingly tightly defined and specified regulatory instruments.[5] For Habermas, the concept of juridification is useful in capturing the extent to which class conflict has been progressively institutionalized within the confines of liberal-democratic capitalist systems. A similar point is made by Dahrendorf (1985), where he remarks on the fact that in late-modern societies the primary kinds of conflict with which states have to engage, are not the mass conflicts of the eighteenth, nineteenth and early twentieth centuries, but more discrete atomized incidents.

In tracing the development of social control practices then, I will adopt and adapt the concept of juridification in order to capture one of the axes along which the conduct of social control has developed. I stress the need for adaptation of the basic tenor of Habermas's ideas because he provides an overly deterministic account, which fails to acknowledge the extent to which the dynamics of juridification are contextually situated, shaped by different combinations of political-historical-cultural circumstances. This is nicely articulated in Melossi's (2001) comparison of penal trends in Italy and America, where he contrasts the 'soft authoritarianism' and low levels of penal repression typical of Italian approaches to social control, with the tendency in American political culture towards an emphasis upon democratic values and high levels of penal repression. Thus, whilst the concept of juridification captures an overarching trend in the evolution of modernity, there are in actuality permutations of the juridification processes that can be observed. But to argue in favour of the fundamental utility of the concept of juridification, it is first necessary to identify the drivers in terms of how and why the domain of law has increased both in size and density.

Processes of juridification are both mechanism and outcome of the wider social changes that I have identified earlier in this chapter. Law has facilitated the ongoing rationalization of social life, supplying a diagnostic mechanism that can be used to effect decisions on those occasions where individuals and collectives experience divergent interests, and actual or potential conflicts. Furthermore, it also provides mechanisms for the enforcement of such decisions. Legal decision making and acting on the basis of principles determined through the apparatus of law, has reduced reliance on traditionally based moral orders, and thereby contributed to processes of de-traditionalization. In turn, the erosion of a reliance upon traditional mechanisms of social ordering has reinforced the power of law.

The above patterns are also implicated in developments in the conduct of government. There is a burgeoning literature detailing the extent to which there has been a shift in the guiding logics of statecraft from the idea of government to governance. Law has been central to such processes, frequently supplying a regulatory apparatus by which the institutions of the state can 'steer' without 'rowing' (Osborne and Gaebler 1992; Rhodes 1997). Furthermore, a plethora of new legal institutions such as the European Court of Human Rights have been developed which add a new layer of legal authority, effectively providing a form of 'meta-control' over the workings of the legal systems of individual countries.

If we shift from looking at macro-structural changes to those that have taken place at the micro-level, the concept of juridification retains its importance. Both Hobsbawm (1994) and Giddens (1991) amongst others, have forwarded influential analyses which suggest that how we understand ourselves and who we are, is one of the most profound changes in the orienting dispositions of late-modern societies. Law has not been insignificant in such matters. Law has, albeit often slowly, been involved in determining which of these new forms of classifying ourselves have substance, and can and should (or should not) be officially recognized. For example, in South Africa under the apartheid system, law was used to enforce discrimination on the basis of ethnicity. But with the overthrow of apartheid, law reforms have also been used to try and overcome such discrimination.

In discussing the ways in which juridification processes have been imbricated in wider social transformations, it is important not to overstate the reach of the changes that have occurred. In his seminal analysis of the impact of law on society, Galanter (1974) demonstrates why it is that legal systems do not tend to generate radical transformations throughout a social order. He argues that the internal institutional structurings of legal apparatuses tend to reproduce interlocking advantages possessed by certain participants in the legal process, thereby restricting the capacity of the system to function as an engine of social justice.

It is important also that juridification is not equated with an increased punitiveness of the type identified by Downes (2001) as characteristic of late-modern criminal justice systems – for as will be shown, this stems from other causes. Moreover, processes of juridification have also been important for guaranteeing freedoms as well as instigating more social control. Newburn (1992) discusses several law reforms in Britain during the 1960s to 1970s to do with issues such as abortion and homosexuality, showing how relaxing the laws in relation to specific acts was accompanied by a simultaneous tightening of regulation of related acts adjudged to be more injurious. This points to the complexities that attend when attempts are made to legislate in respect of issues of morality (Duster 1971). In such circumstances, the tensions that exist between the complex social realities of conduct and their legal portrayal is frequently reduced by recourse to simplified and essentialized paradigmatic cases, that serve to portray the issues concerned in an unproblematic light. For example, Gusfield (1981), in his discussion of the control of drink-driving through legal instruments, details the ways in which the 'myth' of the drunken motorist is actively manipulated by interest groups in pursuance of their objectives. Such myth-making and myth-manipulating thereby constructs an image of law as a form of public action, operating on behalf of, and in protection of, a unified collective belief.

My formulation and use of the notion of juridification is also sensitive to the fact that just because law is available for the control of a particular domain of activity, this does not mean to say that law is always enforced. Echoing the findings of empirical research on police officers' decision making, both Hawkins' (1984; 2002) and Hutter's (1988; 1997) studies of regulatory agencies in the United Kingdom point to the negotiated character of such work, and the fact that frequently law is enacted only as a last resort when other strategies have failed. This signals one of the most important findings of the socio-legal research literature, that the enactment and enforcement of law depends upon the discretionary, interpretative judgements of individual agents – thus introducing a distinction between the law as stated 'in books' and 'in action'.[6] Consequently, whilst in principle there may be extensive juridification in a society, this may be mediated in practice by the ability, willingness and desire of individual enforcement agents to apply law to specific circumstances. To assist them in deciding how, when, why and against whom to enforce law, legal organizations develop scripts about the 'normal' and abnormal qualities that should inform legal decision making (Sudnow 1965; Emerson 1995). In addition to which of course, powerful interest groups such as multi-national corporations can simply resist and obfuscate attempts by legal agents to control their actions (Hertz 2001).

A further corrective to an analysis of juridification relates to the need to acknowledge that such processes have a situated rationality. In certain contexts juridification has been particularly pronounced, whereas in others it has been less important in understanding shifts in the balance of formal and informal social controls. Kagan's (2001a) analysis of the tendency towards 'adversarial legalism' in the United States as a reflection of wider normative principles and institutional orderings, provides an account of fairly rampant juridification. But this can be counter-posed with Tanase's (1995) account of the comparatively nonlitigious nature of Japanese society.

Kagan argues in support of the juridification concept, stating:

> Everywhere in the modern world legal control of social, political and economic life is intensifying. Law grows from the relentless pressures of technological change, geographic mobility, global economic competition, and environmental pollution – all of which generate social and economic disruption, new risks to health and security, new forms of injustice, and new cultural challenges to traditional norms.
>
> (2001a: 6)

His point though, is to stress that the particular values and principles of American legal culture, interacting with a refracted image of those of the political system, produces a situation wherein recourse to law to control the activities of others is an accepted part of the American way of life. This sense of the need to situate a legal apparatus in a wider institutional framework in order to understand its operations and orientations echoes, to some degree, the approach suggested by Nonet and Selznick (2001). But whereas they argue that the shaping of legal arrangements is largely the result of forces extraneous to the system itself, Kagan (2001a) stresses the need to recognize that the system participates in such processes, recursively and reflexively generating internal pressures to the reproduction and development of a particular approach.

Analysing the operations of adversarial legalism in America, Kagan (2001a) maintains it is an approach that has both negative and positive aspects. The negative effects are that it is comparatively costly, inefficient, punitive and unpredictable. More positively though, it tends to be quite open to new kinds of justice claim and new political movements. As a consequence of this, American courts, lawyers and litigation serve as mechanisms of social control over the activities of government and other powerful agencies (such as corporations), constraining their potential for corruption and arbitrariness.

Various examples can be marshalled in support of this argument. For example, Kagan (2001b) notes that for 10–15 years after 1963, American legislatures undertook significant legal reform in areas such as race relations, the control of pollution, accident prevention and the regulation of big business. And that between 1960 and 1980, the number of civil rights cases against the government in the federal courts increased from 290 per annum to about 27,000. Other examples of the use of law to control the activities of the powerful might include mediated 'spectacles' such as the Watergate scandal and the aftermath of the Rodney King beatings in Los Angeles.

But here again I must inject a note of caution and thereby render more complex my argument. To argue that the American system offers greater potential for the social control of powerful actors is not to say that it is always successful in achieving this. In their detailed analysis of the *Iran-Contra* hearings, where members and associates of the Reagan government administration were investigated about illegally supplying arms, Lynch and Bogen (1996) dissect the ways in which the charges were negated and undermined. In this instance, the potential of the American legal system to exact control prior to the powerful protagonists engaging in their actions, or indeed after they had done so, was revealed as fairly fragile.

Lynch and Bogen's (1996) analysis is interesting because, although it is not directly about the workings of law or legal proceedings, it reveals a number of deeper qualities about the social functions of law. In discussing the performance of Colonel Oliver North who emerged as a key actor in the *Iran-Contra* hearings, Lynch and Bogen seek to elucidate the parameters of 'ceremonials of truth' and 'truth-finding engines'. The former concept is used to capture the ways in which legalistic, and legalistically styled proceedings can be understood as rituals for the production of an authoritative account, where there is a disputed understanding as to the reality of what has taken place. In a similar fashion, Rock (1993) in his study of an English Crown Court and Innes (2003) in studying police murder investigations, record how the establishment of 'facts' and truths in law is a pragmatic accomplishment, informed by particular understandings, values, principles and techniques.

Lynch and Bogen describe the workings of 'the truth-finding engine' of interrogation in law, and its immanent, dialogical and discursive properties. The importance of their analysis is in documenting the ways in which the truth produced via legal performances is not restricted in its effects to that social occasion. They show that, in deciding upon what is and what is not to be accepted as 'truthful', formal legal interactions are involved in the production of history. Particularly, in respect of high profile trials and hearings, where the occasion is a dramaturgic performance relayed to the outside world by journalists, the production of legal truth frequently provides the materials for the construction of a 'collective memory'. This will shape how the event is publicly remembered (Cohen 2001; Innes 2003).

The establishment of such collective memories can 'fold back' upon the system that produced them and thereby be consequential for processes of juridification. In recent times, high profile serious cases such as those involving Polly Klass and Megan Kanka in America, and in Britain Sarah Payne and Stephen Lawrence, have functioned as 'signal crimes' that have resulted in either campaigns for, or actual, reforms of the law (Innes in press).

Turning ourselves outside-in and inside-out

As identified briefly in the earlier discussion on the emergence of the state's administrative control apparatus, an important element of modernity has been the production of new forms of knowledge about populations. The knowledge and techniques associated with discourses of the human sciences, and in particular what Rose (1998) labels the 'psy' disciplines of psychology, psychiatry and psychotherapy, produced new ways of 'making up people',[7] together with new classifications of deviance that required control, new ways of thinking about who and what we are, and the problems we experience.

The 'psy' disciplines constitute a further dimension in terms of the diverse ways in which modern and late-modern societies conceive of deviance and organize responses to it. The metaphor of turning ourselves outside-in and inside-out, attempts to capture the ways that forms of expertise have been established that cast troublesome behaviour as an index of 'inner' deviance. Furnished with specialized discourses and epistemologies, these therapeutic versions of control are based upon the diagnostic principle that it is possible to interpret actions and conduct as performances or instances of 'acting out' deeper problems. Once the cause(s) of this inner deviance are divined, then therapeutic controls can be directed at 'the flawed' self, in order to return them to a more normal state.

According to Rose (1990), although our personalities, subjectivities and relationships feel like private matters, they have become socially organized and managed in minute particulars. This management of the self is part of the wider logic of 'governmentality' described by Foucault, wherein it has progressively been enlisted into the aims and objectives of ruling authorities. The desires, wants and needs of individuals are integrated into the political machinery of governance, co-ordinated by the practitioners of 'psy', who are nothing less than 'engineers of the human soul' (Rose 1990).

The inculcation of this form of collective self-control has, though, contributed to a multiplication and diversification of the identifiable and treatable forms of deviance. It has produced a state of 'normal deviance', wherein it seems that any form of inappropriate conduct, by anyone of us, can be explained and accounted for by reference to our emotional or psychological biographies. We are persuaded and cajoled that these forms of normal deviance can be addressed through the application of expertise, knowledge and therapeutic control techniques derived from the psy disciplines.

Given the focus of this book, the importance of the rise to prominence of 'psy' discourses is not simply the ways in which they have contributed to a revitalized emphasis on the inculcation of self-discipline and self-control, but the ways they have blended with legal discourses. As remarked upon previously, for Cohen (1985), one of the most important developments in the trajectory of social control has been the blurring of the boundaries between the therapeutic and the disciplinary. For example, psychiatric and therapeutic discourses are now routinely employed in managing prison inmates. They are also often used by the courts, as part of a sentence imposed upon an offender to be served in the community. But these forms of therapeutic-disciplinary controls are not restricted to the harder parts of the system. Rather they exist on a continuum that extends from the most serious kinds of criminal deviance through to the milder, even trivial forms of normal deviance that we all experience.

This blending of therapeutic and disciplinary forms of control can itself be understood as connected to a wider phenomenon of 'medicalization'. This term refers to circumstances where a 'medical frame' is utilized in responding to different forms of deviance (Conrad 1992). Alongside mental illness, medical social control is commonly to be found in responses to problematic drug and alcohol use, sexual matters and homelessness. But reflecting my earlier comments about the continuum of therapeutic-disciplinary controls, we are all targeted by such controls. For example, through health promotion campaigns that urge us to eat, smoke and drink less, whilst getting more exercise.

Conrad (1992) identifies five primary species of medical social control. The first is *ideological* where a medical model is applied to a problem because of the accrued social and ideological benefits of doing so. The second is *collaborative* where medical professionals act as information providers, gatekeepers or technicians for other social control agents. By administering drugs, performing surgery and providing forms of screening, a third *technological* form of medical social control is enacted. Professionals working in health-related arenas frequently provide a *surveillance* function, where certain conditions or behaviours become perceived through the 'medical gaze'. Finally, there is a reflexive form of *professional self control*, where professional medical associations seek to exert control over the activities of their members.

It is developments such as these that create the conditions for the ongoing contemporary reconfigurations that I outlined in Chapter 1 and will return to in the final chapter. Tracing the histories of the conduct of control serves to make evident the ways in which developments tend to correspond to a combination of reforms, and innovations emanating within social control systems, and adaptations and adjustments to external social forces. Therefore, in seeking to understand the patterns of development in terms of how control is practised, it is important to account for both internal and external factors.

Summary

The aim of this chapter was to provide an overview of how social control practices have changed over time in liberal democratic capitalist societies, and the relations that exist between these changes and the social contexts in which they are located. The story told was of the development of the role of the state in the provision of control as its capacity to do so was progressively rationalized. Central to this pattern of development and a trend that continues into the present day, is the process of juridification, whereby law and legal reasoning is increasingly relied upon to shape and constrain behaviour. A second significant trajectory of development has been the new knowledge and technologies emanating from the 'psy' disciplines.

In undertaking this historical analysis, my account was split between an emphasis upon moments of reconfiguration and tracing out the underlying forces that were involved therein. This approach thus establishes a framework for the analysis to be provided in subsequent chapters, providing a sense of the continuities and discontinuities that exist between contemporary arrangements and those that preceded them.

chapter four

Everyday order

Interaction orders
Gendered orders
The family
Education
Ethnicity
Social ordering and mass media
Summary

In tracing the historical ontology of the concept of social control, I identified that Cohen (1985) and Black (1976) amongst others, have sought to
generate a greater degree of analytic precision for the term by distinguishing it from more generic conformity inducing and socializing processes,
and the notions of social and psychological influence that were a feature of
its earlier formulations. Although still relatively flexible, this definition
tries to establish a degree of separation and fairly firm boundaries between
what is, and what is not, deemed to be an instance of social control. But as
was discussed in relation to the post-social control perspective's emphasis
on control as behavioural modification, maintaining a clear distinction
is increasingly difficult because deviance, either actual or potential, comes
in many different forms, and in studying social reactions to various
behaviours, one is struck by the variety of control-like conduct that is
frequently invoked. This is further complicated by the fact that, as discussed in earlier chapters, community institutions have increasingly been
colonized by the formal control system. Therefore, in this chapter my focus
is upon what, in the opening chapter I defined as social ordering practices
and in particular how they are enacted in everyday life. But in addressing
this theme, the discussion is alert to the ways in which social ordering
practices in late-modernity are increasingly engaged to perform social
control functions. As such, the definitional boundaries between social
ordering practices and social control practices are neither fixed nor stable,

varying across time and space. Nevertheless, the distinction between them emerges as central, providing a way of distinguishing between reactions to deviance, and more general ways in which social order is produced and reproduced, influence exerted and conformity induced.

I will focus my discussion on five key themes. First, I will discuss the interaction order, to look at the ways in which people when they are co-present, make use of what are often seen but unnoticed actions to co-ordinate their encounters, and to influence the direction of the interaction. Having looked at the embedded tacit rules of social engagement, I will then turn to consider how issues of gender and ethnicity shape the ordering of everyday social interactions, and the ways that welfare agencies function in the production of social order. I will conclude by looking at how the proliferation of media has impacted upon the constitution of everyday social order.

Interaction orders

In his now infamous set of 'breaching' experiments, Harold Garfinkel (1967) encouraged participants to deliberately disrupt the established social norms of everyday interaction. In one experiment, students were encouraged to act as if they were boarders in their own homes, conducting themselves in a formal and polite fashion. In four-fifths of the cases, the family members reacted with astonishment, irritation, anxiety and anger. Garfinkel designed these experiments in an effort to demonstrate the extent to which ordinary conduct depends upon quite a sophisticated and complex amount of background knowledge on the part of the actors involved. Without the presence of shared norms of conduct, even the most mundane and routine forms of sociality would rapidly descend into chaos. Similar themes can be identified in the sociology of Erving Goffman.

Across a number of studies, Goffman developed a sophisticated understanding of how social interactions of various kinds are managed and ordered by their participants. He understood social interaction as predicated upon shared norms, conventions, and rituals, which enable individuals to anticipate how others will react to their own actions, and therefore to select lines of action in accordance with these culturally embedded expectations. This tacitly shared knowledge allows all socially competent members of a culture to share expectations about the appropriate modes of conduct across a range of social situations. In his early work for example, he draws a famous distinction between front-stage and back-stage behaviours (Goffman 1959). In so doing, he illustrates that social actors are routinely required to engage in 'front management', in order that their behaviour coheres with the expectations of 'the audience' about the appropriate style of deportment and address given a particular setting. However, these same people, who are expected to act a certain way when in public view, may exhibit vastly different behaviours when they are 'off-stage' and it may be normal for them to do so. The situation or setting for an encounter is thus crucial for Goffman, in that what is and what is not deemed normal behaviour, will depend on the context in which it takes place. In his discussion of mental illness Goffman develops the radical implications of this position, when he constructs a theory of mental illness as a form of deviancy dependent upon the inability of a person to match appropriate conduct to the situations in which they find themselves. It is these 'situational improprieties' that are read by professional diagnosticians as key symptoms and thus indicators of the presence of a mental disorder (Goffman 1961; 1963b).

Embedded within Goffman's work there are then a number of important messages for our understanding of social control. This was something that Goffman himself came to recognize as he reflected upon the ways that:

> The modern nation state, almost as a means of defining itself into existence, claims final authority for the control of hazard and threat to life, limb and property throughout its territorial jurisdiction. Always in theory, and often in practice, the state provides stand-by arrangements for stepping in when local mechanisms of social control fail to keep breakdowns of interaction order within certain limits. Particularly in public places but not restricted thereto. To be sure, the interaction order prevailing in most public places is not a creation of the apparatus of a state. Certainly most of this order comes into being and is sustained from below as it were, in some cases in spite of overarching authority not because of it.
>
> (Goffman 1983: 6)

In contrast to many accounts of social control that tend to concentrate upon the role of the state and its agents, for Goffman, the foundations of social order are located in the conventionalized and institutionalized rituals and norms of social life. This image of social control operating 'below' the state, as a continual and ongoing part of social life, flowing through social interactions and social situations, provides an important corrective to those perspectives where discussions of social control are equated solely with actions based upon legal authority. The approach adopted by Goffman sees the more formal instances of social control being enacted to cope with those situations when the routinized and informal mechanisms are not sufficient for the task in hand.

Running throughout Goffman's work we can detect a concern both with the social control of deviance, and also, the social ordering of human conduct. Of course there is a problem with Goffman's deployment of the term social control, in that it often takes on a loosely defined form, of the type derided by Cohen.

But what Goffman does provide is an insightful understanding of the workings of the micro-orderings through which people are able to perform everyday routine tasks in such a way that they feel everyday and routine. This is perhaps best illustrated by his studies of various dimensions of co-present interaction. As he shows, the co-ordination of conduct between strangers, and between intimates, frequently presumes the presence of situated interaction rituals, which allow the actions and interactions that constitute the encounter, gathering, or whatever, to be carried out in an orderly fashion. Each participant engaged in performing a role within an interaction, bases their performance upon expectations about the motives of the other person (or persons), given the situation in which they are located. In essence, each of the parties signals to the other both a reaction to any previous moves that they have made, as well as indications about what the subsequent response might reasonably be expected to be. There is then a succession of moves and countermoves as each participant negotiates their way towards an end-point. These manoeuvres may be cynical if the motives for interaction of one of the parties are strategically oriented, or they can be enacted for the benefit of a wider audience. However, what Goffman consistently conveys is the sense that interactants are concomitantly controlled by, and controlling of, their fellow participants in the passage of an interaction. Thus what might be termed self-control is socially grounded. Individuals regulate even their most ordinary conduct in order to fulfil the expectations that others have of their actions.

As Randall Collins (1980) notes, by blending elements of symbolic interactionism with a Durkheimian sense of the centrality of moral order to social life, Goffman's focus upon 'interaction rituals' seeks to elucidate the ways in which the entire structure of society rests upon these moral and standardized ritual orders. Competent participation in these arrangements is dependent upon processes of socialization, that provides the individual with experience of dealing with participants of various kinds, together with an array of cultural assumptions that are presumed to be shared (Goffman 1983). Thus he acknowledges a degree of historical and cultural specificity in the customs and conventions that guide interactional life, remarking that '. . . across quite different societies the interaction order is likely to exhibit some markedly different features' (Goffman 1983: 4).

In attending to the ordering of routine conduct, Goffman is aware of the often fragile and contingent nature of social order. This is exemplified in his study of stigma, where, by focusing upon the methods which those possessed of an evident physical 'stigma' seek to manage their 'discreditable identities', he seeks to make a number of broader points about social reactions to deviance (Goffman 1963a). As he puts it, the point of the discussion is less to do with 'uncommon deviations from the ordinary, than for ordinary deviations from the common' (p. 152). Stigmas come in many different forms, they can be existential or physical, and many of us carry stigmas, which we continually seek to manage as part of our presentation of self to both intimate and non-intimate colleagues. For the most part, in our everyday lives we manage to successfully 'cover' or 'pass', allowing only a few to be 'wise' to these things which have to be incorporated within our self-identity. In this sense, many of us are, in Goffman's terms, 'normal deviants'.

Gendered orders

Goffman's work on social order clearly illustrates the necessity of ritual and order in everyday life. It is a 'lubricant' that oils the processes of living together. But although he makes allusions to the fact that the gender of interactants can shape what is, and is not, considered to be 'normal', he never really develops this, despite the fact that he did discuss aspects of gendered identity in his book *Gender Advertisements* (1979). To a large degree, his comparative neglect of gender in the interaction order is merely symptomatic of the period in which he was writing.

Gender is important to discussions of social control in that it is widely recognized that for much of the history of Western societies, women have often been subject to different and in many ways more intense forms of control than men (Carlen 1995). However, in many standard accounts of social control, the ways in which gender shapes and interacts with the imposition and experience of different modes of control has been comparatively neglected.

One reason for this neglect is the fact that traditionally women have been found to commit less crime than men, and given the explicit connection between crime and social control in much of the literature, the reasons for such a bias are self-evident. However, research has shown that when women are the subject of formal social controls it tends to be in a different way than for men. Women labelled as deviant are more likely to be dealt with through systems of social control based upon a welfare or medical model and the regimes to which they are directed tend to combine a doctrine of control with one of care (Carlen and Worrall 1987). Added to which, there is evidence to suggest that the conduct of young women, when compared with that of young men, is more explicitly governed by informal social controls from an early age. Processes of gender socialization tend to encourage young men to develop autonomy and risk-taking propensities, whilst young women are 'chaperoned' according to fairly traditional values (Wilson 1980). These explicit and informal social controls have been shown to continue over the life-course in different social arenas, including the home and workplace (Hutter and Williams 1981), serving to internalize gender codes that function to regulate behaviour (Gelsthorpe 2002).

Thus, whilst it is appropriate to argue that for men the criminal justice process is the key formal social control that they experience, a cogent argument can be constructed that many women's experiences of social control are more related to the workings of welfare agencies interacting with the institution of family. Williams (1989) suggests that the combined effects of women's experiences of family and the welfare state, is to induce a form of subordination and financial dependence, that serves as an effective regime of control over many women.

When they are subject to social controls imposed through the auspices of

the criminal justice process, the sanctions imposed upon women tend to
be either more lenient or more severe when compared with men. The key
explanatory variable for such trends is whether the woman concerned con-
forms to traditional stereotypes concerning femininity and appropriate
gender roles. Women who appear as vulnerable or victims, more often tend
to receive sentences which offer help alongside attenuated punishments
(Hudson 2002). Whereas those whose behaviour or appearance does not
cohere with the 'feminine ideal', may be punished quite harshly for being
'doubly deviant' (Heidensohn 1985). Any such formal controls may be
informally reinforced by local gossip, as a form of 'reputational control',
especially in close-knit communities (Merry 1984).

Notions of the feminine ideal are intimately connected to questions of
sexuality and indeed, much of the literature on the social control of women
has been concerned to shed light on the ways in which the control of
women has gravitated around the control of sexual behaviour. Foucault's
(1980) histories of sexuality report how, in the Victorian age, there were
repeated and somewhat hysterical concerns about the needs to regulate the
sexual behaviour of women, tied to a wider discourse of biopolitics. For
Smart (1981), law has played a crucial part in the reproduction of such
patriachal discourses, reinforcing a gendered political economy of power,
where men tend to dominate women.

But at the same time, law is also an engine of change in the field of gender
relations. A particularly prominent example of this phenomenon has been
the moves to use law in an effort to reduce instances of sexual violence
against women. There have been a number of legislative reforms over the
past 30 years, which have sought to effect a greater degree of regulation
of sexual relations in order, ostensibly, to afford protection to female victims from male violence. But one of the key issues in respect of such
reforms has been that although public debates about such issues often
gravitate around incidents involving strangers, in actuality, the majority
of such crimes occur between people who are known to each other. For
example, in relation to fatal violence it is well known that a significant
proportion of all offences are 'domestic homicides', involving current
or former partners (Polk 1994; Websdale 1999; Innes 2003). There is a
similar pattern in relation to rape and many other of the more serious types
of offending where women constitute the majority of victims. Seeking
to both prevent these types of incidents from occurring and/or improve
the effectiveness of enforcement responses to these types of crime, has
necessitated an extension of the role of state social control further into the
traditionally private spaces of the domestic sphere. In an effort to engage
with the causes and consequences of the kinds of serious offences that
women are particularly at risk of, police and social work agencies have
had to develop monitoring and intervention strategies, premised upon the
regulation of interpersonal relationships.

In her study of the policing of domestic violence, Hoyle (1998) illustrates
some of the complexities of the engagement of authoritative social control

strategies in personal troubles. As her empirical data from Thames Valley show, women who were being abused by their partner and called the police, typically did not want the offender to be subject to punishment, nor were they seeking an end to their relationship. Rather they needed someone to intervene in the short term to stop the violence that they were experiencing. Moreover, Hoyle shows that in many cases the police officers were not arresting suspects in order to prosecute them, but indeed to accomplish the aim of bringing a cessation to the physical violence. As she identifies, they were engaging law in order to bring about 'social service' ends.

It would though be a mistake to infer from these changes that law is solely an instrument of protection for women. For although it has been used to try and afford a greater degree of protection, there remains a strong normative component to it, in terms of enforcing gender roles.

The family

The increased penetration of law into family life has not though been solely concerned with the protection of women. At least as important as these moves, has been an increasing concern with the protection of children. For just as much as the abuse suffered by women occurs in the context of an ongoing relationship, the vast majority of children are harmed by parents, or those responsible for them. In Britain, since the 1973 case of Maria Colwell,[1] there has been an almost constant stream of high profile public inquiries where various failures of public authorities to protect children from their parents have been revealed.

In response to these failures, the trend in child protection has been to develop increasing powers to monitor those families where children are felt to be at risk and to implement allegedly more sophisticated procedures to identify them in the first place. But as was demonstrated by the now infamous Cleveland child abuse cases in 1987, there are questions that can be raised concerning the accuracy of the diagnostic tools utilized to identify who is considered to be at risk by professionals engaged in child protection work.[2]

The area of child protection is especially important, because, as is the case with domestic violence, it provides an example where control strategies are performed by multi-agency partnerships involving police and other welfare bodies, in what are commonly thought of as private spaces. A further relevant link between women and children is that the ways in which judgements are made concerning the degree of a woman's deviancy and thus any punishments to which it is deemed they should be subject, tend to be contextualized by the woman's role in the family. As is made clear by Donzelot (1979), the formulation and imposition of punishment of women is explicitly structured by considerations of the harm that this may entail for any dependent children. This reflects a more profound point, in that, according to Donzelot, from the eighteenth century through into the nineteenth, there was a subtle shift from 'the government of families to government through family' and women were crucial to this strategy (although as I have documented above, the family is currently once again established as an important site of control). As mothers caring for children, women were increasingly targeted by a 'tutelary complex' whereby they were instructed and judged about the quality of the pre- and post-natal care they provided to their young. Motivated by concerns about children in danger and dangerous children, the formerly private sphere of family life was opened up and subject to a form of disciplinary gaze encompassing medical and religious discourses of 'social hygiene' (Donzelot 1979; Rose 1990). Mothers, and by extension families, were the targets of advice, guidance and therapy, intended to ensure that the institution of the family functioned properly in its role of inculcating discipline.

As such, the family is simultaneously a site for the internalization of self control; a mechanism of informal social control; and itself the object of control efforts. Over the past two decades, there has been a particular focus upon the family as an object of control because of the popular concerns relating to physical and sexual abuse discussed previously. But also, due to fears that the family's effectiveness as a mechanism of informal social control is waning. The dramatic rises in recorded crime between the 1960s and mid-1990s were causally attributed to the increase in number of single mothers and families without fathers, by politicians who, for ideological reasons, found this a more palatable explanation, than to look at the structural inequalities caused by their liberalization of free-market mechanisms (Mooney 1998).

Education

The growth of state interventions directed at monitoring and regulating family life is frequently attributed to the investment that a society has in developing self-control amongst successive generations (Rose 1990). This is also reflected in analyses of the role of the education system as an agent of primary socialization, second only in importance to the family.

Those who have drawn upon the work of Marx in studying the education system, have repeatedly suggested that schooling needs to be understood as a de facto component of the ways in which the state seeks to generate social control in a capitalist system. This position is based upon the premise that education is a key mechanism for instilling a belief in the legitimacy of social inequalities and hegemonic consensus concerning the dominant ideas in society. Both Willis's (1977) and Corrigan's (1979) analyses of schooling emphasize the moves and countermoves made by pupils and teachers in a dialectic of order/disorder, the ultimate outcome of which is the reproduction of capitalist social order.

A particularly sophisticated analysis of the role of education vis-à-vis the social order is provided by Bourdieu and Passerson (1990). They maintain that the teacher–pupil relationship functions as a conduit for the transmission of the norms and knowledge held by a culture. Pivoting around a concept of 'pedagogic actions', they theorize that teaching is not simply about the transfer of knowledge, but rather is involved in and founded upon the transmission of a whole universe of cultural knowledge. Bourdieu and Passerson extend their analysis to show that, in actual fact, through the engagement of pedagogic actions, schools and families are engaged in a broadly similar function – the reproduction of power and thus social order.

As part of the institutional order of society, in many ways, the operations of school systems mirror the dominant currents in the logics of social control. Many schools enact punishment through exclusion, and they use experts such as educational psychologists to conduct assessments and classify 'problem' children determining how they are treated. But in America the notion of the school mirroring the societal control apparatus is even more explicit. Large numbers of schools have invested heavily in surveillance and other control technologies, and have police officers stationed on site, in an effort to control the behaviour of pupils.

Ethnicity

Bourdieu and Passerson's account of the reproduction of culture, points to some of the subtle and often unnoticed ways in which social order is made and remade across generations. In his study of a Pakistani community in Edinburgh, Wardak (2000) presents evidence of how traditional cultural norms and patterns of organization were reinvented by the members of a 'closed community', having faced experiences of exclusion and rejection from wider Scottish society. As a result, the family and parental authority function as the most important agency of social control for members of the Pakistani community. These are buttressed by the 'Biraderi': a close and complex network of reciprocal relationships; and communally maintained notions of 'izzet' (honour) and 'bizati' (dishonour), that serve to bind individuals into the moral order. Recourse to such informal institutions of social control reflected the attenuated connections that the minority community felt to formal institutions of social control, believing them to be biased against their interests. Certainly there is much empirical data that shows that many people from minority communities believe that they are systematically under-policed as victims and over-policed as suspects.

Experience of overt and covert forms of bias and discrimination by state agencies has eroded the legitimacy of the state social control apparatus for many people from minority ethnic communities. Such problems have been exacerbated by the ways in which these agencies respond to the problems that are brought to them by these communities. For example, Bowling's (1998) discussion of the process of racial victimization maps out an important disjunction. He shows how the police and other agencies work around the notion of incidents, conducting their tasks on a discrete case by case basis. However, this is not how the victims frame their experiences. Being the victim of racial discrimination, threats or actual violence, tends to be experienced as a process. Individual incidents are not separated out by victims, rather they are overlaid, and perceived in a continuous and synchronous fashion. This suggests why, even when they are able to get police to listen to their problems and to take action in respect of them, many victims of racialized violence remain unsatisfied with the outcome. They feel as if the law has failed to protect them.

Importantly though, there is concern that the failings of the criminal justice system to provide criminal justice for minority ethnic community members is mirrored by the failure of welfare systems to ensure social justice for these groups. Cook (1993) is clear that such forms of discrimination are institutionalized throughout both the welfare and justice systems.

Legitimacy, is then, an important issue. But it is not just in relation to formal social control that such concerns are merited. In his discussion of the situation of America's black ghettos, William Julius Wilson (1996) details the ways in which the operations of an economic system based upon free-market principles has entrenched and reinforced a grinding form of racialized poverty. His qualitative account of life in American inner cities records a potent mix of poverty, lack of economic opportunities, crime, drug abuse and 'fading inner-city families', where informal neighbourhood controls have more or less evaporated. And in response, formal controls have become increasingly militarized and punitively oriented (Parenti 1999).

For conservative commentators, the sorts of conditions that Wilson compassionately describes are held to constitute the basis of an 'underclass' (Mead 1992; Murray 1994). But for Bauman (1998) this label is indicative of a sensibility that conceives of these groups as people who are outside of the class system and thus the value structures that most 'normal' people share. Such imagery enables the development of discourses of control through exclusion. It identifies these groups as suffering as a result of their own fecklessness and indigence. Moreover, it portrays them as wholly dangerous because they do nothing else. As such, they are construed as suitable subjects for the imposition of a highly coercive regimen of control. As a consequence, control, rather than alleviation of the structural causes of the entrenched poverty, becomes the preferred policy solution.

Social ordering and mass media

So far, the discussion in this chapter has reflected upon a variety of ways in which social order is produced and reproduced through fairly ordinary, everyday routines. I have sought to show how a number of familiar social institutions can be understood as contributing to the construction of social order and the performance of social control. I have also discussed the ways that constructed classifications such as gender and race may interact with these other factors. To conclude this chapter though, I want to consider the influence of a factor that has served to shape the very constitution of social order – mediated communication.

The impact of media on social life has been diffuse and multifaceted (Briggs and Burke 2001). From the point of view of this book, its especial significance is that the proliferation of media of communication has changed both what people know and how they come to know it. Mass communication through television, newspapers and radio allow people to know (or at least have an approximation of knowledge) about events that they have never, and possibly will never, directly experience. They create the sufficient conditions for what Marshall McLuhan famously dubbed 'the global village'. That is socially and temporally distant individuals can hold knowledge in common, as a result of the ways in which these media of communication transcend time and space (Thompson 1995).

In so doing, according to Meyrowitz (1985), the proliferation of media has altered the very nature of contemporary social order. He maintains that the transfer of information provided by media, as channels of communication, facilitates an awareness of issues and problems that we might otherwise remain ignorant of. The crucial impact of mediated communication is the progressive erosion of the boundaries between public and private. Coverage of stories by journalists and other media workers routinely transform private troubles into public issues.

The fact that media can function in this fashion has sometimes been mistaken for the idea that it always works in this way. A number of over-simplified analyses have cast media as an explicit mode of social control. Indeed, just such an approach was a feature of many early forays by social scientists into discussions of media effects. In various guises and under a number of theoretical frameworks, early studies often identified media as a primary form of social control, directly determining the responses of audience members. But to conceptualize the workings of media in this way misses the more subtle and nuanced ways in which it works. It is for this reason that I have argued above that media is best understood as a social ordering mechanism. This is not to say that mass media are never used to generate social control, but more often in late-modernity, media are important not because they determine what people think, but because they shape the issues that people think about.

It is an established orthodoxy of studies of mediated factual communications that one of the primary functions of news organizations is to select which events become news. They function as bureaucracies, utilizing institutionalized criteria of 'newsworthiness' to select events which they believe will cohere with the interests of their target audience (Rock 1973; Altheide 1976; Gans 1979). Pragmatic imperatives are thus central to the selection of events for coverage – for example, can a reporter and if necessary a camera crew get to the location in time? News is often time dependent and news organizations view themselves as being in competition to 'break' new stories. Moreover, news has to have a sense of 'newness' about it, there are thus pressures to maintain a flow of potentially interesting stories, which often establishes a form of 'symbiotic' relationship between reporters and their key sources of stories (Chibnall 1977; Innes 1999a). From such arrangements, journalists obtain access to a succession of potentially interesting stories, whilst the suppliers of the stories are provided with an opportunity to engage in a form of 'impression management', promoting a positive image of themselves to the public (Schlesinger and Tumber 1994).

This selection effect may be significant in as much as it may contribute to the definition of what are the kinds of issues that members of the public come to be concerned about and thus which incidents control agencies focus their attention on. Moreover, in certain circumstances, it has been suggested that media become more explicitly involved in the conduct of control. In his discussion of the dynamics of 'moral panics', Cohen (2002) shows how the reportage of events can, if the prevailing social conditions are right, institute a process whereby isolated events are constructed in a fashion that they demand a coercive law enforcement response and become a 'politicized' issue – what Manning (1996) has latterly dubbed 'an axial political event'. The processual qualities of a moral panic, as identified by Cohen, show how journalists' reporting of events can enhance the law enforcement apparatus of the state. By reporting events that key into people's fears in an emotionalized tone, and by focusing upon particular types of issues, news media contribute to defining what problematic issues the public are thinking about, channelling their insecurity and guiding demands for enhanced control (Altheide 2002).

A recent example of this phenomenon in both America and Britain over the past decade or so, has been the social construction of the problem of child sexual abuse and paedophilia. Through a comparatively small number of serious crimes against children, such as the cases of Megan Kanker and Sarah Payne, which have received 'saturation' media coverage, the idea of child sexual abuse, and fears about predatory paedophiles has emerged as a key social problem. In both America and Britain, governments have introduced measures to increase the surveillance of children and to control the activities of those who are thought to pose a risk to children's safety. This has emboldened the processes of encouraging welfare agencies to become involved in social control work, as described above. The small number of serious crimes against children which have been extensively reported by media organizations have been central in creating popular fears which have been translated into politicized demands for the expansion and intensification of the control apparatus.

By focusing upon and disseminating the details of a small number of especially dramatic, but fairly rare crimes, journalists construct these events as forms of signal that the public interpret in making evaluative judgements concerning the state of society. These signal crimes have a profound impact upon how individuals and communities appraise their levels of perceived security and risk (Innes in press). The stories that media tell about what are effectively personal troubles, provide the kinds of details that help people to articulate and warrant their desire for improvements in the application of social control strategies.

Media is thus an important constitutive component of contemporary social ordering practices. It is also significant in terms of its role of providing a degree of exposure to a range of social problems, and thus directing public and political attention to matters over which control may become desired. However, media is also increasingly utilized directly as a mode of social control, providing a form of surveillance over the activities of powerful actors – a topic discussed in more detail in Chapter 8.

Summary

Notions of social control and social order are closely related. In this chapter I have sought to focus on the latter, in an effort to show how and why it needs to be considered as distinct from the former, but also to illustrate the ways in which social ordering practices and social controls sometimes connect up, and overlap. By looking at aspects of co-present interaction, gender relations, racialized discrimination and mediated communication, I have been concerned with uncovering some of the subtle and elliptical ways in which human behaviour can be altered and modified. As will be discussed in the final chapter, the nature of these connections reflects the ways in which social ordering practices are increasingly being reconfigured in an attempt to make use of them in enhancing levels of social control. The fact that this is happening is itself a reflection of the fact that the boundaries between how a society responds to deviant behaviour and the more generic ways that it induces conformity are neither firm nor distinct. And it is for this reason that, revisiting some of the themes from Chapter 2, defining social control as actions intended to change people's behaviour may be increasingly attractive in the current context. As such, there remains a tension about whether it is appropriate to define social control solely in relation to deviant behaviour, or whether it needs to account for more general behavioural modification processes. I have tried to resolve this tension by classifying the sorts of issues that have been addressed in this chapter as social ordering practices. In what follows I will focus more directly upon modes of social control concerned with deviance.

Policing

The concern of the state with social control is perhaps most visibly and dramatically embodied in the figure of the police officer. As a uniformed, hierarchically organized bureaucracy, the police constitute one of the key ways in which the liberal state seeks to intervene in and shape the ongoing social order. However, somewhat contrary to popular wisdom, all policing is not conducted by the police, but in fact relies upon, and involves, a diverse range of agencies and organizations. Therefore, in this chapter I will examine the role of the police in policing, and how this contributes to and is shaped by wider patterns in the conduct of social control. In tracing the development of several contemporary policing strategies, the discussion is intended to elucidate some deeper themes in terms of how social control practice is being reconfigured.

Police and policing

In their everyday talk people tend to use the terms policing and the police more or less interchangeably. However, as Robert Reiner (1997) describes, the words actually refer to two separate things and equating them is a symptom of the 'police fetishism' to which our culture tends to be subject. The police is a specific, modern organization, endowed with the state's legal authority to use physical coercion or the threat of it, to enforce the law in pursuance of the maintenance of social order. In contrast, policing refers to a diverse range of ordering and controlling activities, performed by a wide range of agencies. The latter definition could thus potentially encompass the activities of private security firms, locally based community organizations, local government environmental health inspectors and a host of other additional agencies.

The 'fetish' that Reiner describes results from what Manning (1997) has termed 'the mythology of policing'. According to Manning, since its inception and throughout its history, the police have relied upon strategies of impression management to overcome resistance, and to engender popular support for the task of enforcing law and enacting social control. This mythology provides a symbolically loaded version of reality that portrays policing as a dramatic and dangerous task, thereby conveying the symbolic message that the police are the embodiment and upholders of a basic moral consensus about good and bad, right and wrong (see also Loader 1997). A key component of the police myth is its emphasis upon crime control work as the central focus of police activity. Police officers, media representations of policing and the public tend to focus upon the investigation and detection of criminals as the primary function of what it is that the police do. And whilst crime control is certainly an aspect of the police function, it is not the only thing that they do. Perhaps the key finding of academic research on the police has been to demonstrate that the involvement of the police in policing necessarily requires them to engage with a diverse range of issues and situations, only some of which are directly concerned with crime control.

In what is now widely accepted as the standard definition of the police role in society, Egon Bittner (1974) identified that what unites the diverse range of tasks which the police are called upon to perform, are that they involve 'the emergency maintenance of social order'. That is, the police act in those situations where social order is either going to, or has been breached. This generic order maintenance work reflects the ability of the police to invoke legally sanctioned coercive force to manage a variety of problems.

Discussions of the enforcement of law by police officers have demonstrated the gap that exists between the content of law 'in books' and 'in action' (Dixon 1997). As gatekeepers to the criminal justice process, police decisions in terms of when, why, how and against whom to enforce law are especially consequential in determining which deviant acts are defined as criminal and thus subject to formal social control. Numerous studies of police law enforcement work have documented that the police's legal decision making is framed by extra-legal factors. Amongst the most significant of which are the values of police occupational culture (Reiner 1992;

Chan 1997). As discussed in the section on juridification in Chapter 3, law is the principal mechanism through which sovereign states intervene in the lives of the citizenry, and the police and other policing agencies are central in directing its application and enforcement. But it is evident that their actions in this respect are shaped by a range of factors.

Thus in an effort to better define what it is that the police do, we could perhaps identify three main roles which account for the majority of their work[1]:

1. *Crime management*: as detailed above, a key aspect of the police's role relates to the prevention and detection of crime. Significantly, given the argument that I will develop during the course of this chapter, social research evidence suggests that police have only a limited ability to prevent and detect crime (Ericson 1993; Innes 2003; Maguire 2003). Most crime is not solved and when it is, this is often the direct result of information provided to police by members of the public. Thus whilst a significant proportion of formal social control pivots around the prevention and detection of crime, the impact of these efforts on levels of crime is limited.

2. *Order management*: much of the day-to-day work performed by the majority of police officers relates to the resolution of fairly low level conflicts and maintaining social order. This involves 'policing the dross' of society (Choong 1998), what Reiner (1992) dubs 'police property' – those groups of the population whose activities others find detrimental to their quality of life. It also encompasses policing public order demonstrations.

3. *Security management*: the previous two roles feed into the more generic police function of security management. Security is a 'presence in absence'. By this I mean that it is defined by the absence of risks and dangers in relation to a social order (Spitzer 1987; Crawford 1997).[2] Therefore, the notion of a police security management function refers to their role as the visible manifestation of the state's authority over a territory and population. In performing this role, the police are involved in restricting the exposure of members of the public to an array of material risks and dangers, alongside a more subjective reassurance function, that should the need arise, there is someone charged with exerting control over a troublesome situation. As an element of police practice, it pivots around strategies to neutralize risks, loss prevention, as well as the more nebulous task of mediating threats posed to subjective feelings of safety. Neocleous (2000) identifies that from its early formulation by Colquhoun, the police were envisaged as a form of state power directed towards 'securing the insecure' (p. 59). Significantly, in contemporary writings on policing there has been something of a revival of interest in the concept of security and the role of police and policing agencies in its manufacture (see Ericson and Haggerty 1997; Johnston 2000; Johnston

and Shearing 2003), largely because there is a feeling that the role of the public police in this area has been usurped by the activities of private policing agencies.

These three dimensions of the police mission are important because, in addition to describing what many people feel that the police should do, they also relate to a number of the defining tensions within the police role in recent years. As the police have come under political pressure to be more cost-effective and at the same time to improve their measurable performance in relation to these three functions, tensions have arisen in terms of whether the public police should retain a commitment to providing the more general order maintenance and security management functions, or whether they should become more focused, specializing in crime management work. In addition, conflicts have arisen in terms of how these different aspects of police work should be addressed.

As a consequence of this tension, there are currently several different policing perspectives being espoused and practised by different police organizations around the globe. Amongst the more prominent are community policing, zero-tolerance policing, and intelligence-led policing. At an analytic level, each of these contemporary versions of policing can be seen to be composed of four components. First, there are a set of ideas and intentions, which suggest a vision of what policing as a mode of social control should aim to achieve, and how this can be accomplished. More often than not this vision is constructed in relation to a definition and diagnosis of a problem, or set of problems, that is perceived as needing to be addressed. Then there are the programmes, which are how the ideas and intentions are actually translated into a set of practices and interventions, and thereby enacted. Thirdly, there are the evaluations of the programmes and the assessments of how effective the practices are in achieving the more abstract ideas and intentions. Finally, there are the explanations that are provided to account for any disjunctions between programme and idea or intention. Aspects of these components will be evident in the ensuing discussions and I will return to discuss them in more detail in the concluding chapter as a generic model of social control. But for now it is sufficient to remark upon the fact that the selection and implementation of a particular perspective by a police organization tends to be shaped by several factors, including: the past history of the organization concerned; the social, historical and political context of the area and community being policed; as well as the nature of the current problems to be tackled.

I will now briefly discuss each of the contemporary perspectives in turn. In so doing, I will use the discussion to illustrate how in their respective differences, each of the perspectives references some wider concerns about the state of society and how control should be enacted. It should be noted that in what follows my aim is not to provide a comprehensive discussion of all of the variants and permutations pertaining to each of the perspectives, but rather to map out the key ideas and practices associated with each of them.

Community policing

Community policing is arguably the most significant of the contemporary policing philosophies. Community policing programmes have been implemented by a large number of public police agencies, in a variety of ways, in a diverse array of contexts. In order to understand how and why this vision of policing emerged we must first locate it in a historical context. In his history of the development of the 'new' police, Emsley (1991) describes how, in order to overcome the political opposition to his reforms, Peel deliberately decided that the police should to a certain degree reflect the communities they policed. For Reiner (1992), this ideological notion that the people were the police and the police were the people was crucial to the generation of a growing acceptance and consensus about the legitimacy of the police institution, and thus the 'golden age' of policing that lasted from about 1870 to 1950.

Since this date though, it is accepted by many commentators on policing that the police have become increasingly contentious and that public support for the police, although still fairly strong, is more fragile than it was. Moore (1992) suggests that the problems started around the late 1950s, when the police started to invest heavily in a range of modern technologies, at the same time as police managers began to focus their efforts more explicitly on the 'crime problem'. Whereas previously, crime was a problem to be dealt with alongside more everyday order and security management tasks, under the model of 'professional law enforcement', crime and particularly the more serious types of offence were increasingly identified as an explicit priority. Police organizations focused their efforts upon these incidents, whilst paying less attention to dealing with less serious forms of disorderly behaviour. Although the various reforms that were introduced at around this time were intended to promote greater efficiency, they actually served to increase the distance between the police and policed (Moore 1992).

The early advocates of community policing thus intended to institute a model and philosophy of policing that would re-establish a connection between the police and the community. They justified this approach on the basis that:

- The police should serve the community by ensuring that police activities were driven by responding to the needs and desires of the community, rather than the interests of police managers;
- Developing closer relations with the public would restore popular support for the police;

- Improved public relations would also have the effect of improving the police's ability to control crime, as it would improve the flow of local intelligence that is crucial in solving crime.

Central to this idea of re-engaging with local people and their problems was to be a return to local officers conducting foot patrols in communities, stopping and talking to local people, and keeping a 'benevolent' watch over their beat. This shift in priorities was buttressed by the findings of research that suggested that police strategies for dealing with crime were at best limited in their effectiveness. For example, the findings of the Kansas City Preventive Patrol experiment suggested that uniform patrol had very little impact on recorded crime rates (Kelling et al. 1974). Further to which, studies of crime detection had found that the single most important factor in contributing to whether a crime was solved or not was the quantity and quality of information provided to police by members of the public as either victims or witnesses (Greenwood et al. 1977; Ericson 1993). Fielding's (1995) fieldwork based study identified that one of the primary features of the community policing discourse in the organization he studied, was the connection drawn between engaging with community members and crime control work. This was part of the ways in which the adoption of the model was promoted to officers on the ground, by keying into their traditional cultural concern with crime. But in practice, Fielding notes, much of the work performed was more about local problem solving, thus engaging with the more generalist security management functions identifiable in the police mission.

In Britain, a further key factor in promoting the development and adoption of community policing strategies were the findings of Lord Scarman's 1981 report into the precipitating causes of the 1981 Brixton riots. This suggested that overly aggressive policing of certain sections of Britain's urban communities was contributing to the creation of a deep-seated alienation and opposition to the police. A consequence of which, was that the legitimacy of the police as an institution was being eroded.

Community policing is also important in that it is constitutive of one of the key trends in the reconfiguration of the social control apparatus, whereby the engagement of community has been promoted as a key mechanism for the delivery of enhanced levels of control. As Lacey and Zedner (1995) have identified, notions of 'community' and 'community based controls' have emerged as a powerful rhetorical discourse in the provision of late-modern forms of social control. Attempts to develop mechanisms that provide a form of 'local governance' of crime, through multi-agency partnership arrangements, involving police, other governmental and non-governmental agencies and 'the community', has been a key trend in crime control policy throughout the 1990s (Crawford 1997). Community policing is thus intimately connected to wider developments in the transformation of patterns and logics of social control.

As noted previously, community policing programmes have been introduced into a wide variety of settings in a large number of countries. Although these different programmes are supposedly underpinned by the same key ideas, in practice there are significant permutations in strategy and tactics, reflecting the vast organizational and contextual differences involved. As such, although many police agencies across the globe have claimed to be operating community policing, it is often difficult to identify quite what the different versions have in common. But in part, it was this somewhat 'fuzzy' definition that was responsible for the rapid spread of the community policing philosophy, allowing a wide variety of organizations to see community policing as offering a potential solution to the problems that they were trying to deal with.

The limits of community policing

Although the idea of community policing remains quite popular, it has been somewhat eclipsed by the introduction of several more recent policing perspectives. Having said this though, the ideals and values brought to the fore by community policing can often still be detected in the 'newer' initiatives.

Evaluations of the varied community policing initiatives that have been introduced in both Britain and the USA since the 1980s are mixed (Greene and Mastrofski 1988). According to Reiner (1992), whilst often motivated by good intentions, many such initiatives have suffered from 'programme implementation failures'. This is explained by the fact that in practice the schemes have never been implemented in the ways envisaged at the design stage. There is though a more fundamental limitation in terms of what community policing could realistically be expected to achieve that needs to be acknowledged. Community policing was first introduced in an attempt to halt the decline in public confidence and trust in the police amongst particular community groups. However, this decline in confidence was not simply about police–public relations. It was a symptom of more profound changes in the increasingly complex and flexible structures of communities, and the fabrication of social order, of the sort detailed in earlier chapters in this book. The concerns that the public were expressing were only in part about policing, they also articulated a more nebulous sense of insecurity caused by changing social relations and fundamental transformations of key liberal-capitalist institutions (Johnston and Shearing 2003).

Zero-tolerance

Of all the major contemporary policing perspectives, it is perhaps what is popularly known as zero-tolerance policing (ZTP) that has achieved the highest public profile in recent years. To a large extent this can be explained by both its supposed successes and failures. ZTP has come to prominence largely because of the contribution it is accredited with in the large falls in crime that took place in the mid-1990s in New York City, where between 1994 and 1996 there was an overall reduction by a third of serious crime and a halving of the murder rate. These reductions were directly attributed by characters such as William Bratton, Commissioner of the New York Police Department, and Mayor Giuliani to changes in police practice (Bratton 1998). But public awareness about the strategies and tactics employed in New York has been simultaneously heightened and tinged with concern, as a result of a succession of stories about police violence and routine infringements of civil liberties (Harcourt 2001; Manning 2001).

Drawing upon the logic of Wilson and Kelling's (1982) discussion of 'broken windows', wherein physical and social disorders that are not attended to are held to be generative of further more serious disorders. Supporters of ZTP strategies argue that precipitative police actions in respect of fairly routine and mundane 'quality of life offences' will have an impact upon more serious types of crime. In essence the idea is that, if you control less serious types of criminal and disorderly behaviour, you will also control a significant element of more serious offending. Effective crime-fighting is thus seen to be premised upon the 'assertive' or 'confident' control of behaviours such as loitering, begging, public drunkenness, 'squeegee merchants' and activities which cause a nuisance to other citizens by 'degrading the urban aesthetic' (Stenson 2000). As Harcourt (2001) identifies in his critique of what he dubs 'order-maintenance' policing, central to such an approach is a redefinition of the meaning of such acts. Rather than such incidents being understood as trivial annoyances, they are recast as potential harbingers of more serious problems, and should thus be dealt with quickly and assertively by police.

The purported logic of such an approach is unpicked in Norman Dennis's (1997) three guiding principles for zero tolerance policing programmes:

1. 'Nip things in the bud'; a key concern for police must be to ensure that potentially anti-social elements do not think that they are in charge, by making certain that neglected environments cannot become a breeding ground for more serious and sustained disorders;
2. Make sure control is enacted even against seemingly trivial violations. The performance of control in such situations does not rely necessarily on the imposition of coercive force, but can be low-intensity and humane. The important thing, though, is that control is seen to be present;
3. Reducing petty crime and disorder through the above two approaches will help to prevent more serious offences.

Commenting upon the NYPD's application of these principles, one senior British police officer (Griffiths 1998) notes four key components in many zero-tolerance programmes:

- The collection and dissemination of timely and accurate information;
- Effective tactics;
- Rapid deployment;
- Relentless follow-up and assessment.

Strategies and tactics utilized by police organizations following ZTP are justified on the basis that formal social control is important in terms of creating the conditions where informal social control can develop and thrive.

The limits of ZTP

In the context of a discussion of the nature and conduct of social control in late-modernity, ZTP is central. As Garland (2001a) and Harcourt (2001) amongst others have argued, the discourse of 'quality of life' policing and having 'zero tolerance' for disorder, have become grounding principles for the politics of contemporary crime control strategies. Such discursive frameworks have provided a language and symbolic imagery for the articulation and propagation of the populist punitiveness discussed in the opening two chapters of this book. Manning's (2001) 'dramaturgical' analysis of the NYPD in the 1990s makes clear that the implementation of police reforms in New York during this period was accompanied by a sustained and powerful rhetoric, disseminated by a sophisticated media campaign, that argued that targeted, strong enforcement of the law by police, could make a difference to local neighbourhood order. As such, the importance of the New York story in garnering popular and political support for ZTP approaches cannot be underestimated.

There is however, an increasing amount of research evidence that contests the idea that it was police actions against low-level disorders that prompted the dramatic falls in crime that were recorded. Silverman's (1999) evaluative analysis of the NYPD reforms explains that the falls in the New York crime rate probably had less to do with the nature of the police interventions at street level, than changes in the organization: including a massive increase of 12,000 police officers; improved crime analysis information technology systems relating to COMPSTAT[3]; and changes in the command and control systems, making local police commanders directly accountable for performance in particular districts. To these 'internal' factors Manning (2001) adds a fourth, relating to the ways in which officers were deployed to crime and disorder hot spots, and encouraged to undertake stop-and-searches and misdemeanour arrests as a source for gathering intelligence, which was to be fed back into the bureaucratic system, thereby creating an iterative process of enhancing the organization's intelligence base about local problems.

In addition to the 'internal' reforms listed above, there are a number of 'external' changes that need to be accounted for in understanding the New York situation. It has been noted that at the same time as crime was falling in New York, it was also falling in many other locations throughout Europe and America, including many where ZTP was not in use (Innes 1999b). This suggests that there may be broader structural factors at work. One such factor may be a change in drugs markets, in particular a decline in the supply and use of crack cocaine (Bowling 1999). As part of his broader critique, Harcourt (2001) adopts a 'synthetic', multi-causal explanation, whereby he suggests that the drop in recorded crime in New York is not attributable to one isolated factor, but was the result of the confluence of a number of internal and external factors co-occurring at a particular historical juncture.

Informed by the mediated rhetoric that has accompanied ZTP, one might be tempted to see it as a radical departure from previous approaches to the problems of policing liberal democratic polities. This would of course be mistaken. Similar sentiments to those expressed by many supporters of ZTP can be detected in what Wilson and Boland (1978) had earlier dubbed 'aggressive patrol'. Meanwhile, more recently Choong (1998) has suggested that the enactment of social discipline over marginalized and potentially troublesome people is not restricted to those departments where the ZTP philosophy is purposively followed.

In sum, ZTP maintains that police can tackle and control crime by addressing low-level disorderly behaviours, thereby reinstating a sense of both formal and informal social control in communities. In seeking to understand how and why this approach became so influential in the 1990s, it is important to be aware of the powerful message contained within such ideas. It coheres with a deeply embedded sensibility shared amongst the public and many police officers, that the primary objective of the police is the prevention and detection of crime. In contrast to the more communitarian ethos of community policing, ZTP provides a sense of clarity to police and public alike, that the police both can and should seek to address the crime problem through unambiguous order management work.

Intelligence-led policing

The focusing of police work upon crime control is also a feature of intelligence-led policing (ILP). As Harcourt (2001) suggests, a key explanation for the apparent success of the NYPD's implementation of ZTP has been the emphasis placed upon police–public interactions as an opportunity for garnering intelligence, that can be used to inform subsequent police actions. In Britain, such concerns have tended to be associated more directly with the doctrine of ILP.

The roots of ILP can be traced to two key influences. First, it reworks contemporary discourses on the information age and the implications this has for organizational life and industrial practice (Castells 1996). This is combined with a more internally oriented influence, stemming from the significant rises in recorded crime throughout the 1980s, and the growing feeling that the orthodox crime control strategies and tactics utilized by police were outmoded and ineffective. Such concerns were bolstered by a growing disenchantment amongst many, relating to the fact that community oriented policing initiatives had seemingly failed, both in terms of increasing popular support for the police and in creating the community relations which would result in the continual supply of high quality, crime relevant, intelligence.

Reflecting on these problems, in 1993 the Audit Commission published the findings of a study on the police response to crime. This argued that the traditional approach of 'reactive' investigation, wherein police waited for a crime to occur and then sought to identify and locate a suspect, was inefficient, largely ineffective, and outdated. It was argued that the police should divert far more resources to 'proactive' investigation, that is targeting prolific, recidivist career criminals, who are, after all, responsible for committing a significant proportion of all recorded serious crime. This was to be done in particular, by improving intelligence systems and making better use of informants. The outcome of this approach was what has become labelled as intelligence-led policing.

In effect, ILP's idea of shifting from focusing upon the crime to focusing upon the criminal formalizes and reinforces a trend in police practice over recent years to try and make extensive use of undercover and deceptive methods, including informants, officers going undercover into criminal organizations, and surveillance technologies (Marx 1988). In Britain, the development of this approach has been encouraged by trends at the transnational level, wherein intelligence sharing between European nation states has rapidly developed (Sheptycki 1998). More recently, the introduction of the National Intelligence Model has sought to 'place intelligence at the core' of the policing system, creating arrangements to encourage intelligence sharing between a range of policing and non-policing agencies. Although evaluations have identified a degree of variability in terms of the extent to which this is being successfully accomplished (John and Maguire 2003; Sheptycki 2003).

As such, ILP mirrors, and is part of wider transformations in terms of how social control is imagined and practised in late-modern societies. Specifically, its programmes are based upon strategies and tactics intended to establish a more future-oriented, preventative, risk-based approach to social control (Maguire 2000). Situating such developments in a wider context it is evident that the focus upon intelligence, and the routine collection, analysis and exchange of data as the basis of policing, contributes to the sufficient and necessary conditions for processes of control creep. If police actions are to be based on intelligence, then there is a manifest incentive for welfare agencies, who typically possess a lot of data about potential police targets, to be encouraged to co-operate with police agencies. Thus welfare agencies are increasingly involved in law enforcement type work, supplying the intelligence that the police are looking for in respect of their nominated targets. Similar connections also tend to be fostered between public and private policing agencies (Ericson and Haggarty 1997). It can be seen then that the principles of ILP contribute to the kinds of trends identified in Chapters 1 and 2.

The limits of ILP

On the one hand, recent developments in relation to the use of intelligence suggest that some fairly important changes in the logic of how the police operate may be taking place. On the other though, it seems likely that any such changes will be inhibited by the problems associated with intelligence work, which for the most part the architects of ILP appear to have failed to engage with fully. For example, whilst in theory informants provide a useful, cost-effective investigative resource, in practice informant management is fraught with both ethical and practical dilemmas. The value of an informant to police is frequently based upon their ongoing participation in criminal activities. Moreover, they frequently provide misinformation and disinformation to police, and therefore, there tend to be a lot of 'hidden costs' in routinely using informants in policing (Maguire and John 1995; Innes 2000).

More recently, questions have been raised about the design of police information management systems and whether they can fully support a mode of operation that relies upon the identification, processing and communication of large amounts of intelligence data. This echoes Wilensky's (1967) finding that the causes of intelligence failures are often 'designed in' to the systems of complex, hierarchical organizations. Perhaps the most important criticism of ILP though is its tendency to introduce a degree of 'systemic bias' towards 'rounding up the usual suspects' (Gill 2000). This occurs because intelligence systems are designed to 'target' particular offenders, frequently selected on the basis of which individuals you have most intelligence about – which are, of course, going to be past suspects. And in the process of targeting these individuals, the organization is more likely to generate further intelligence on them, thus justifying their selection as targets both retrospectively and prospectively.

As such, ILP as a fully formed approach to policing, has, as yet, had only a limited impact on police practice. It seems to be more effective for responding to forms of comparatively serious, ongoing and organized criminality. Its utility in terms of responding to more routine and everyday disorder problems has been less evident.

Plural policing

The three perspectives that I have outlined so far relate to attempts to reconfigure the role of the public police. But perhaps the most important changes in recent years in terms of how policing services are delivered, relates to the rapid expansion of the private security sector. Private forms of policing, purchased by individuals, communities and organizations, and supplied by companies who are seeking to make a profit, once again constitute an important aspect of how social control is manufactured. I say once again, in order to remind us that prior to the legitimation of the 'new' public police in the nineteenth century, the private provision of policing services was the norm.

Addressing the contemporary situation, many commentators refer to the emergence of a system of 'plural policing', in an attempt to capture the fact that the conduct of policing broadly conceived, involves a range of public, private and 'hybrid' agencies. The latter term is used by Johnston (1992) to refer to a number of miscellaneous policing agencies such as the Ministry of Defence Police, Atomic Energy Authority Constabulary, the Post Office Investigation Department, and the Health and Safety Executive, 'whose formal status and operating territories cut across the public-private divide' (p. 114).

Mapping the current developments, Loader (2000) argues that changes in the delivery of policing have occurred along a number of axes. He identifies that, in addition to changes in policing by government, there have been four expansionary trends:

Policing through government: where policing services are enlisted by government but supplied by others.
Policing above government: where supranational and transnational policing institutions such as Europol and Interpol have become increasingly important.
Policing beyond government: refers to the expanding and enhanced commercial market in security systems and policing markets that now takes multiple forms.
Policing below government: refers to: activities performed by citizens under the supervision of the state such as neighbourhood watch and neighbourhood wardens; sporadic instances of 'vigilantism'; and the mounting of citizen patrols.

The main consequence of these changes has, according to Loader, been the emergence of a loosely coupled policing network, wherein the activities of the sovereign state constitute one amongst a number of nodes in the plural policing network.

The expansion and enhancement of these various forms of private policing and thus the proliferation of the various pluralistic models of policing has resulted from several factors. First, there has been increased concern about the ability of public policing to provide the levels of security that anxious publics feel that they need. Secondly and relatedly, the rise in crime and the engendering of fear of crime has encouraged people to establish enhanced protective measures for both themselves and their property. The logic of using a competitive market system in the provision of security also coheres with the more deeply entrenched notions of political economy in late-modern societies remarked upon in earlier chapters, which has seen a broad shift from the principles of government to governance (Jones and Newburn 1998; Johnston 2000).

Johnston (1992) identifies that private policing agents engage in a range of activities including: surveillance, intelligence and undercover work; preventative activity; investigation and detection; containment and control in the criminal justice system. Arguably though, the most important is the 'guarding and protection' of property and persons, which is where most of us encounter private policing directly. The protection of commercial, industrial and retail premises is particularly important to our current discussion. The 'normalizing' of 'mass private property' of the type to be found in large shopping malls, and the use of private security guards to patrol them, has resulted in a situation where significant aspects of our lives are subject to the controls imposed by privately employed agents. But what characterizes the performance of all private policing functions is that they provide a particularly 'instrumental' form of social control (Shearing and Stenning 1987). The primary responsibility of the private policing agent is to the client who is paying for their services. Whereas the public police symbolize the presence of law and order, private policing is far more concerned with merely preventing any harm occurring to their clients' interests.

The rapid development of private policing services has led a number of leading commentators to argue that we need to rethink our understandings of policing, in order to account for some of the changes that are taking place in terms of how, by whom and for what purposes policing services are being provided. Proponents of the plural policing model maintain that, in order to describe and understand how policing is being delivered in late-modern societies, we need to examine the activities of private, hybrid and public policing agencies, so as to understand how their work overlaps and interlocks.

Given the focus of this book, the emergence of the plural policing model is significant. First, because it points to the ways in which the monopoly held by the sovereign state in the funding and supply of social control functions has been progressively eroded, to the point where some commentators suggest that state policing agencies could become merely one amongst a mixture of equally powerful, and equally significant suppliers (Bayley and Shearing 2001; Johnston and Shearing 2003). Secondly, the argument that the provision of policing is founded upon a network of private, public and hybrid agencies, coheres with the general tenor of the post-social control theorists reviewed in Chapter 2. For instance, in their 1996 article 'The Future of Policing', Bayley and Shearing argued that the expansion of private policing was a key signifier that the systems of policing in late-modern liberal societies were undergoing fundamental transformation. They saw the sovereign state's monopoly in the delivery of social control being rapidly replaced by a network of private policing, quasi-formal regulatory bodies, and citizen policing initiatives.

The most sophisticated account of these developments is provided by Johnston and Shearing (2003) in their exposition of what they term 'nodal governance'. It is an approach that is part diagnosis of recent developments and part prediction of how the trajectory of these developments might develop in the future. The central idea of nodal governance is that the state's role in the governance of security is fundamentally changing. They suggest that the state's primary function becomes less about the actual delivery of services to the public, than regulating the conditions of the security market and the competition that occurs between providers to supply specific services. In a recent publication for the National Institute of Justice in America, Bayley and Shearing (2001) have argued that, if one takes the ongoing developments seriously, then the next logical step is to de-couple the funding of policing services from their supply. In effect, they suggest the creation of a policing market that is regulated by an outside body, wherein public and private organizations compete to deliver policing services in relation to particular populations, problems and places.

A second, less radical example of how the network metaphor has been employed to understand contemporary policing arrangements is provided by Ericson and Haggerty's (1997) recent discussion of the policing of risk society. They use empirical data to argue that the role of public policing agencies in Canada is increasingly concerned with 'risk communications' to other agencies in the policing network. According to Ericson and Haggerty, the public police function is increasingly that of collecting information from other agencies, processing it and then disseminating it to other nodes in the policing network.

To reiterate, the plural policing perspective is important not just because of the way in which it points to some system-level changes in policing, but also, because of the wider implications that it has for understanding social control. The more decentred and fragmented picture of policing that is painted is directly connected to some of the ideas discussed in relation to the post-social control perspective.

'Control hubs' and 'total policing'

Tracing the ongoing patterns of development in contemporary policing provides a sense of how problems of crime control, order-maintenance and security provision have informed shifts in the key logics of policing. Each of the different perspectives outlined incorporates a diagnosis of the problems of policing a liberal democratic society and seeks to reconcile the demands on policing in different ways. Essentially, the three public police perspectives argue that by targeting police activity in some way, the broader problems can be addressed. In contrast, the plural policing perspective suggests that these reforms have been largely unsuccessful, as a result of which the public have increasingly turned to the commercial sector to meet at least some of their needs.

Issue can be taken with the plural policing models use of the network metaphor to describe the arrangements by which policing is organized. I would argue that certainly in Europe, rather than a network, a more accurate description of the organization of policing may be the metaphor of 'the control hub'. The key difference being that whilst the concept of nodal or networked governance locates the role of the state as simply equivalent to that of all other providers, the notion of control hubs retains a sense of hierarchy in the organization of social control. This is important because although contemporary European styles of policing involve a range of actors and agencies, they are not as yet functionally equivalent. The public police retain greater enforcement powers and when situations become particularly problematic, private agents will frequently call upon the public police to resolve the situation. The majority of private police are poorly paid, poorly trained and have fairly constrained responsibilities. Consequently, the control hub metaphor places the public police at the conceptual centre of the delivery of policing services, but acknowledges that their actions are augmented and supplemented by those performed by communities, private security agents, as well as other public agencies.

This is not to wholly dismiss the utility of the network metaphor in analysing contemporary developments in policing. However, it may be the case that the network metaphor is more applicable to the North American context, where there has traditionally been a more 'decentralized' public policing sector, consisting of a vast number of public agencies. In such conditions, networked approaches to policing are by virtue of necessity the norm. Alternatively, such ideas and programmes may provide a model for those areas of the world where public police agencies do not have a tradition of symbolic legitimation. In Europe though, we have tended to have far fewer public agencies and as such, the metaphor of control hubs may provide a more accurate description of the ways in which policing has developed in this context, and may continue to do so in the near future.

Positioning the public police at the centre of a control hub, supported by the work of private and hybrid agencies and citizens, perhaps provides a better sense of how policing as social control is currently conducted. Furthermore, at a more abstract philosophical level, it retains a sense that policing is, as Loader (1997) has identified a 'public good', the delivery of which needs to be founded upon principles of social justice and democratic accountability, if the fundamental aims of policing are to be achieved. The hub metaphor provides a way of thinking about the activities of diverse policing agents in a way that shows how together they may contribute to tackling crime, maintaining order and providing a sense of security. The participants in the hubs share resources, data and even personnel in an effort to perform their functions, as a result of which the boundaries between the separate institutions are increasingly dissolved. The concept of control hubs also provides a degree of analytic purchase on how policing might develop in the future. What may emerge is a form of 'total policing' system, wherein the police function is focused around tasks of crime control, order maintenance and security provision, but there is a division of labour for these tasks, where they are performed by situated combinations of public, private and hybrid agents.

Summary

As a mode of social control, the logics and practices of policing are shaped by, and shaping of, what Ian Hacking (2000) dubs 'the social matrix' – that is the key social, economic, political and cultural institutions that collectively function to produce and reproduce social order. By tracing the key components of some of the most important contemporary perspectives in policing, what is made evident is the ways in which policing can be used to identify some of the key changes that are taking place in late-modern societies in terms of how social control is conceived of and conducted. Importantly, such an analysis demonstrates that the patterns of development in policing are not all necessarily in the same direction, or wholly compatible. For example, community policing embodies the desire to encourage community participation in crime control, and is thus illustrative of the ways in which one of the key movements in contemporary social control practice is to establish stronger connections between formal and informal mechanisms of social control. Contrastingly, the plural policing perspective perhaps demonstrates the limitations of such attempts – in that private policing agents have increasingly been employed to perform the security functions that public police agencies might have been expected to perform. As such, the development of the plural policing perspective is illustrative of the trend towards the commodification of security and also the formalization of security functions.

Alongside such developments, shifts in the role of the public police associated with ZTP and ILP perspectives are indicative of separate and some might argue contradictory trends. ZTP and ILP respectively embody trends to encourage unambiguous formal social controls of both comparatively trivial disorders (on the understanding that they impact on people's 'quality of life'), and more serious types of crime, respectively. Thus we can see how policing encapsulates trends for intense and systematic forms of social control. It has been directed towards order maintenance and security providing functions, at the same time as being encouraged to tackle more serious types of crime.

Punishing

Punishment, understood as the imposition of some form of censure or sanction in response to a deviant act, obviously constitutes an important mode of social control. As with policing, the most visible forms of punishment are probably those that are enacted by the state through the criminal justice process, but punishing also involves communities and individuals seeking to regulate the conduct of others through more informal methods. Either way, whether we are talking about formal or informal punishments, we tend to assume that the selection of a particular form of punishment will reflect societal norms concerning the perceived seriousness of the deviant act concerned. Thus, in a similar fashion to policing, practices of punishment need to be understood as being imbricated in a social matrix, shaped by and shaping of, wider master-patterns in the conduct of social control.

My purpose in this chapter is therefore to explore how punishment can be understood as a mode of social control, and how, in examining the workings of punishment, the nature and conduct of social control more generally is clarified. In addressing such themes, my focus is principally upon issues of penality, defined as the complex of ideas, institutions, rules and practices pertaining to punishment.[1] I commence my exploration of penality by first providing an overview of the ideas that fundamentally shape how we think about punishment and its aims. Following on from which, I will switch focus to examine some of the key methods by which punishment is performed.

The idea of punishment

Analysing punishment as a mode of social control necessarily involves exploring how punishment should be performed and how it is performed. As Hudson (1996) notes, 'ought' questions are typically posed in jurisprudence and the philosophy of law, whereas the discussion of how punishment is actually practised, is more typically the focus of sociological enquiry. However, what is effectively a technical issue of how to punish, is itself premised upon the more fundamental ethical question of 'why punish?'

The starting point for a discussion of why use punishment as a method of social control, is the often overlooked fact that, aside from a few radical critiques calling for the abolition of punishments imposed by the state, the majority of debates have assumed that some form of punishment for deviant acts is necessary. As a consequence, what has tended to be debated are the aims, justifications and methods to be employed. This signals a sense in which, almost intuitively, we feel that punishment, if it is appropriately designed and implemented, should work. As children we have all experienced being admonished by our parents and other adults, and being subjected to a variety of punishments. Although at the time we may have felt the imposition of punishment to be unfair, and experienced the shame and guilt associated with it. Looking back, most of us would probably identify that the punishments administered to us during childhood are part of the reason we have grown up to be 'normal', socialized, fairly well adjusted adults. Freudian psychologists may go even further than this and argue such early socialization processes are intrinsically necessary for the regulation of otherwise destructive base impulses. From an early age then, we are accustomed to thinking in terms of the social fact that punishment is a way of controlling deviant behaviour and a method for internalizing societal norms as the basis for self-control.

Broadly speaking, philosophical theories of punishment can be distinguished between those that see the primary objective of punishment as being the prevention of future crimes and those that focus on punishing crimes already committed. Amongst the former group are the utilitarian, consequentialist and reductivist approaches. Amongst the latter are retributive and just deserts theory. In essence, the former group of theories argue that the aim of punishment is deterrence, both of the individual being punished, but also more generally, deterrence of potential offenders in the wider population. This deterrence function can happen through prevention or incapacitation, and reform or rehabilitation. In contrast, advocates of a retributivist position argue that punishment is imposed because offenders deserve it. Criticizing the notion of punishment directed by aims of incapacitation and rehabilitation, they argue that such ideas could lead to people being subject to disproportionately harsh punishments on the basis of predictions about their likely future actions. Retributivists maintain that it is important that 'the punishment fits the crime' and that the amount of harm imposed upon the person being punished is proportionate to the harm caused by the offence committed.[2]

Whereas these jurisprudential perspectives on punishment have tended to focus upon issues of morality and ethics, sociological theories of punishment have tended to focus upon the social supports of particular regimes of punishment, and the cultural implications it has for society.[3] Thus for Durkheim and those writing in the functionalist tradition, acts of punishment are not simply a matter of responding to deviance, they are frequently also rituals of order, where a sense of belonging to a particular group and adherence to a belief system is performatively enacted. Punishment is thus identified as a necessary condition of moral order, reinforcing the authority and legitimacy of key social institutions.

Durkheim's account is contested by the conflict theorists writing from a broadly Marxist standpoint. They argue that the how and why questions I posed at the start of this section, can only be addressed by situating the key institutions and practices of punishment in a capitalist framework. For writers such as Rusche and Kircheimer (1939), it is the political economy of capitalist development that determines how and why particular penal regimes rather than others come to the fore. Although now considered outdated, this work subsequently influenced other ideas which cast punishment as a form of ideology engaged in the reproduction of class relations.

Although Weber, as the third key figure alongside Marx and Durkheim in the realm of classical sociological theory did not directly address issues of punishment, Garland (1990) maintains his influence can be detected in a number of key works in this area, including those by Rothman (1980) and Foucault (1977). Weber's rationalization thesis applied to the topic of punishment, points to the ways in which punishment has increasingly been thought of as an administrative undertaking that is managed by a bureaucratic apparatus. As Garland describes it:

> The emergence of a penal bureaucracy as the organizational form through which penal sanctions are administered has meant that an instrumental, formal-rational style has been imposed upon a punitive process which embodies non-rational sentiments and non-instrumental aims. Actual punishments are thus always a compromise formation, being the outcome of these conflicting considerations and objectives.
>
> (1990: 192)

Having all too briefly considered why societies seek to punish, I will now turn to the equally vexing question of how punishments are enacted.

Contemporary punishments take a number of forms, depending upon the gravity of the deviant act that has been committed. They include imprisonment, probation, and parole, through to fines, curfew orders, electronic tagging schemes and community service. But we should not neglect the fact that part of the punishment imposed by these different techniques relates to the stigmatizing and shaming qualities they also frequently incorporate. Given the diversity of punishments available, it is perhaps not altogether surprising, that in trying to understand penality as a form of social control, one is struck by the complexity, ambiguities and array of co-existing trends and counter-trends that are present. Therefore, in order to try and make sense of this complexity, it is perhaps useful to distinguish between punishments that are based upon confinement, those that are served in the community, and the 'hybrid' punishments that lie somewhere between these two positions.

Confinement

As a method of punishment, confinement, most usually through incarceration in a prison, tends to be reserved for what are deemed to be the more serious forms of deviant behaviour, and the more dangerous and problematic offenders.

Over the past three decades the use of imprisonment in Western societies has shown an unrelenting trend towards expansion. As a method of social control imprisonment has become increasingly important. Almost paradoxically though, accompanying this expansion, there has been increasing pessimism about the efficacy of prison as a method of control. Confronted by high crime rates and research evidence suggesting that about two-thirds of those who are imprisoned go on to commit further offences, it has been commonplace to hear popular commentaries that 'prison is an expensive way of making bad people worse', or that they are little more than 'schools of crime'.

The result of this situation has been that the idea that imprisonment can reform or rehabilitate an offender, has increasingly given way to the more modest aim of incapacitation. In effect, the prison as a site of punishment is no longer justified as a means of reform, rather it is portrayed as a mechanism for separating criminals from non-criminals. This reconfiguration has been justified on the basis that, at least by separating criminal deviants from the law-abiding majority, even if it performs no other role, it promotes the security of the latter group.

In what follows, rather than treading the well-worn path of discussing how imprisonment is conducted and managed by the authorities and experienced by inmates, I want to try and show how, by studying this particular form of social control, we can learn much about how social control works more generally. As will become apparent, although the political rhetoric that tends to accompany discussions of the use of incarceration has frequently portrayed it as the ultimate form of social control, in fact, control in prisons is far more contingent and negotiated than these rhetorics imply.

Total institutions?

In liberal-democratic countries incarceration is the key punishment used by the state to respond to serious acts of deviance. But it was not always so. As Ignatieff (1978) explains, prior to the end of the eighteenth century, prisons were somewhat chaotic institutions used to 'hold' deviants until the time when their actual punishment could take place, which tended to be transportation, or some form of corporal or capital punishment. It is important to remember that this confinement function continues to be performed in contemporary penal systems. For example, in the American system, the infamous death row is still used to confine prisoners until the often lengthy judicial appeal process is exhausted and they are executed by the state. Nevertheless, despite the persistence of such practices, most histories of penalty suggest that the transformation of the prison from a place of confinement prior to the punishment being carried out, to the punishment itself, represents a key change in the social functions of imprisonment. There are essentially two interlocking dimensions to punishing through imprisonment. The first is the disciplinary regime of the institution, involving the control of time and space through monitoring and timetabling the conduct of those subject to the regime. The second dimension is the separation from the outside world and all that it involves.

In his history of practices of incarceration, Michel Foucault (1977) traces why the practices of discipline that we associate with imprisonment as a form of punishment were developed and instantiated within the routines of prison life. The sorts of technologies and apparatus associated with the modern prison were, he argued, designed and implemented in order to engage in 'soul training', inducing conformity at the same time as repressing deviant motivations. According to Foucault, the prison was one of a number of institutions that emerged during the modern epoch with the purpose of instilling discipline and thereby producing 'normal' behaviour.

In his study of mental asylums, Erving Goffman (1961) identified that the kinds of 'soul-training' technologies and apparatus described by Foucault, constituted the basis for a number of what Goffman dubbed 'total institutions'. According to Goffman, what these social establishments had in common were similar principles of organization, in that those subject to the regime had their behaviour closely monitored and regulated by the staff of the institution in a systematic and intense fashion. He defined them:

> . . . as a place of residence and work where a large number of like-situated individuals, cut off from the wider society for appreciable period of time, together lead an enclosed, formally administered round of life.
>
> (Goffman 1961: 11)

This approach aims to tease out the common characteristics and features shared by asylums, prisons, some religious orders, schools and some factories. For Goffman, the arrangements in such establishments are deliberately designed to allow for a form of social control that is, at least in principle, almost all-encompassing, or 'total'. The distribution and range of controls in such bounded settings appears on the surface at least to be pervasive, intense and systematic, directed both at the control of outward behaviour, but also regulating the inner-social self. Tellingly, Goffman saw prisons as exemplifying the traits of a total institution.

Although writing from a different theoretical perspective, similar themes to those identified by Goffman are mapped out by Foucault (1977). Foucault argues that the prison constitutes a focused example of how control functions permeate the everyday routines and structures of modern societies. In effect, he uses the prison as a metaphor for wider transformations that he sees as taking place in modern societies. Through his development of the concepts of 'panoptic surveillance' and 'discipline', he details how, within the walls of the prison, pervasive and penetrating regimes for monitoring the conduct of inmates aim to induce a form of reflexive self-monitoring of conduct. These disciplinary technologies and the potential for surveillance that are integrated into the temporal and spatial organization of prison life, provide an almost unparalleled opportunity for exercising a systematized form of control over the regime's subjects. He describes how the inmate's day is structured not according to individual needs or wants, but according to the rhythms imposed by the operations of the social system that is the prison. By charting how control is exacted through the regulation of time and space within the prison regime, Foucault seeks to show how those subject to the unremitting discipline are pressured into conforming to the external demands placed upon them.

There are then, obvious similarities between the accounts provided by Goffman and Foucault, which help us to understand the nature and role of imprisonment. However, Goffman goes further, for as well as seeking to map the practices of the controllers, he also undertakes to explain how these are experienced by those subject to them. Although Foucault's conception of power allows for resistance on the part of inmates, he does little in the way of developing an account of how this is actually done. And, therefore, reading his works, one gets a sense of an almost unchallengeable, penetrating, systematic and intense style of control in operation.

In contrast though, Goffman attends quite carefully to what he terms the 'underlife' of total institutions. What he is able to show is that individuals, even when subject to seemingly all-encompassing regimes of control, are able to actively develop strategies to inure themselves to the regulatory system so as to preserve a sense of self and personhood. Although the system of control may appear seamless from a distance, up close there are cracks and interstices which can be exploited, so that albeit only in small ways, the regime is subverted and resisted.

In developing this theme Goffman distinguishes between 'primary' and 'secondary' adjustments to the control regime. Primary adjustments are those made by the individual in order to meet the demands and expectations of the ordering regime. In contrast, secondary adjustments are the unauthorized habitual adaptations developed to act or think in a way contrary to the regime's expectations. Importantly, there is a distinction that can be drawn between those types of secondary adjustment that disrupt the routines of the organization, and those that become tacitly accepted as part of the normal day-to-day running of the organization. In part, this acceptance or otherwise of secondary adjustments, depends upon the nature of the organization. As Goffman himself notes, the irony is that:

> Establishments that oblige the participant to 'live in' will presumably be rich in underlife, for the more time that is programmed by the organization, the less likelihood of successfully programming it.
>
> (1961: 183)

In the mental institution, inmates facilitated the process of secondary adjustment through the use of what Goffman labelled 'make do's'. These were objects whose use and meaning were transformed by the user to accomplish different ends:

> Obvious examples come from prisons, where, for example, a knife may be hammered from a spoon, drawing ink extracted from the pages of Life magazine, exercise books used to write betting slips, and cigarettes lit by a number of means – sparking an electric-light outlet, a homemade tinderbox, or a match split into quarters.
>
> (Goffman 1961: 187)

The use of 'make do's' in this fashion was, then, a way of accomplishing practical tasks. But for Goffman there was a deeper significance to such adaptations for the person concerned. The refashioning of objects was a form of resistance that signalled that their social self and sense of identity had not been totally lost to the regime. Make do's provided a way of 'doing self with things' in a manner similar to that which takes place outside of such establishments (Perinbanayagam 1990).

In liberal democratic societies imprisonment effectively constitutes the ultimate form of social control that is routinely deployed to control deviant behaviour. What Goffman demonstrates is that even in such circumstances, there are limits to the control that can be exacted.

This theme of the limits of control can also be detected in Gresham Sykes's (1958) classic study of an American maximum security prison. Sykes notes that in such institutions, where all prisoners are working through comparatively long sentences, there are peculiar problems of controlling behaviour that have to be overcome. He was careful to convey the sense in which the social order of the prison was contingent and negotiated between guards and inmates. Control in such establishments is not just formally enacted, but involves the use of informally based rewards and punishments. Prisoners were allowed to participate in various forms of 'minor' deviant behaviours by guards, in return for a 'quiet' institution. In other circumstances though, inmate deviance has been more systematically enacted as a form of political protest. In Northern Ireland, political prisoners engaged in hunger strikes and dirty protests, transforming their bodies and cells into instruments of protest to mark the contested legitimacy of their imprisonment (McEvoy 2001). As Sykes (1995) reflected, a prison is a complex social system, and any such system cannot run on force alone, rather it requires a degree of legitimacy and co-operation from those being ruled over. This sense of negotiated order is also present in Sparks et al.'s (1996) more recent discussion.

The message that comes through from Sparks et al.'s research within British maximum security prisons, is that for the prison staff, the key issue is not that of how to effect punishment over the inmates, but how to ensure the orderly running of the prison on a day-to-day basis. As the authors note, in such establishments levels of surveillance and the managed control of activity is inherently high. Nevertheless, even within this situation where high control is comparatively normalized, 'control incidents' occur, which at least partially or temporarily threaten the established order and as a consequence must be dealt with. In such instances, control ultimately resides on the capability of the regime to exert superior levels and types of physical coercive force to restore order.

A second feature of the empirical findings of this study worth commenting on, is that by contrasting the penal orders in Long Lartin and Albany prisons, the authors show that even within one system of maximum security imprisonment, there are important differences in terms of how order and control are enacted. At a broader more general level of analysis, a similar point is made by David Downes (1988) in his comparative study of attitudes towards, and methods of, imprisonment in Holland and Britain. As Downes shows, the cultural and historical context that surrounds a penological situation manifestly shapes how imprisonment is imagined, practised and justified. This supplies an important corrective to Foucault's influential genealogical analysis of the causes and consequences of carceral regimes.

First, Foucault's account privileges the development of disciplinary practices within carceral institutions. He maintains that the key feature of the development of imprisonment in modernity was the progressive refinement and rationalization of techniques for the structuring and ordering of the imposition of power. This differs from Sykes who maintains that the 'pains of imprisonment' are less to do with the structuring and ordering of space and time, than the physical separation of the deviant from those to whom he or she has emotional bonds.[4] This element of Sykes's account is particularly important in the light of a number of the recent analyses of the master trends in social control, which argue that one of the key ingredients of current social control practices, is a shared orientation to control via exclusion – that is the separation of the law abiding from the deviant sections of the population. For Foucault, the imposition of discipline and the ordering of time-space was part of the orientation to 'soul-training', and the (re-)normalization of the aberrant person. And whilst Foucault doesn't wholly ignore the significance of the sequestration of the deviant individual in practices of punishment, certainly many of the interpretations of his work have seen this as a less significant aspect of his analysis, than the technical qualities of the administrative and regulatory practices.

The second corrective to the Foucualdian literature relates to the Goffmanesque sense that there are limits to the effectiveness of control in practice. Reading passages of Foucault and those who have sought to develop his ideas, one could form the impression that the design of prisons afforded the opportunity for an all-encompassing form of disciplinary control to be carried out. Of course this is not the case. Criminologists, prison governors, prison officers and inmates have long known that there are a lot of criminal acts that take place within the walls of the prison, as well as outside of them. To be fair, Foucault himself recognized the limits of control. Indeed, the notion of 'functional failure' is pivotal to his explanation of how, in failing to rehabilitate inmates, the penal system effectively created the conditions for its own expansion. This system level explanation of functional failure continues to be applicable in the contemporary context and indeed has been deployed in accounts of the contemporary phenomenon of mass imprisonment.

Mass imprisonment

The idea that there are limits to the control that systems can achieve over individuals, even in environments that are characterized by comparatively intense, pervasive and systematic control measures, is further evidenced by the high reconviction rates amongst former inmates. What Foucault demonstrates though, is that historically, the failure to rehabilitate the majority of inmates has not led to the idea that imprisonment constitutes an effective form of punishment being revoked. Rather such problems have been addressed by claims that what is required is a succession of 'technical fixes', slight improvements to the control regimes, which it is posited, will improve the operations of the system. In effect then, the problems associated with imprisonment create the sufficient conditions for the expansion of the penal system.

One of the remarkable features of contemporary society has been that although there is an increased sense of resignation about the fact that, as a method of social control, imprisonment can only be said to be effective in terms of temporarily incapacitating offenders, both Britain and America continue to incarcerate more and more people. In addition to this, there has been the introduction of a wide range of alternative forms of punishment – an issue I will address in due course. But the problem of high imprisonment rates has become particularly acute in America, where the term 'mass imprisonment' has been coined to describe the situation (Garland 2001b). As Tonry (1995) and Mauer (1997) have documented, approximately one-third of all young black males in America are at any one time in prison, on probation or subject to parole.

Simon (2001) argues that mass imprisonment has come about as a result of three key factors. The first is a change in political culture, where what Bottoms (1995) describes as 'populist punitiveness' has become the dominant sentiment. Faced with high crime rates, and a fearful electorate composed of increasingly visible and vocal victims rights groups, politicians have been encouraged to introduce legislation that increases prison sentences for particular groups. Amongst the most notorious examples of this trend is the 'three strikes and you're out' approach. Aimed at recidivist offenders, this law means that if you are convicted of three offences, even if the third is for something comparatively trivial, the courts have the power to sentence the perpetrator to a long period of incarceration.

The second factor that Simon (2001) identifies is the 'war on drugs', where attempts to deal with America's drugs problem through the criminal justice system provided an almost limitless supply of arrestable and imprisonable offenders. The third factor he identifies is the increasing interaction between criminal justice agencies, which in turn he argues, has created strong internal pressures for growth and expansion of the system. For Simon (2001) these three factors interlock and interact, reinforcing each of the individual trends.

The consequences of this situation are, it is argued, potentially profound. As Garland (2001b) suggests, mass imprisonment is not simply a matter of high rates of incarceration, it exists when:

> . . . it ceases to be the incarceration of individual offenders and becomes the systematic imprisonment of whole groups of the population. In the case of the USA, the group concerned is, of course, young black males in large urban centres.
>
> (Garland 2001b: 2)

The normalization of the prison experience amongst this group, may have serious long-term consequences for communities and societies when they are released from their often quite lengthy periods of incarceration. At the moment we can only guess at what form these consequences might take.

More immediately though, Downes (2001) persuasively argues that we need to contextualize the phenomenon of mass imprisonment and in particular relate it to the conditions of late-modern capitalism. Drawing upon a range of evidence, he details how the US prison population amounts to about 2 per cent of the male labour force and has therefore, throughout the 1990s, reduced official unemployment figures by between 30 and 40 per cent. In effect then, not only is a free-market society highly criminogenic, but it exploits this quality to promote an ideology of its apparent macroeconomic success.

Transcarceration

In his diagnosis of the causes of mass imprisonment, I noted that Simon sees a significant factor as being the increased interlocking of the various criminal justice agencies. Mapping the dimensions of contemporary social control though, one is struck that although Simon is correct, he is also slightly restricted in the purview of his analysis. For it is not just within the criminal justice system that there is a broadly integrationist movement. Perhaps one of the most important trends that can be observed is the increasing connections between the criminal justice system and the welfare system.

Clients of welfare agencies are, in many cases, also the offenders and victims dealt with by agents of the criminal justice process. Consequently, through the use of multi-agency working groups, processes of data sharing and reconfigurations of the key welfare agencies, social control functions have increasingly been integrated into the mission of welfare provision. One particular dimension of this has been the increase in 'transcarceration' (Lowman et al. 1987).

Developing the idea that control by exclusion has emerged as a key strategy for controlling economically and politically marginalized persons in late-modern societies, the transcarceration concept aims to capture how particular problem groups are increasingly locked into a cycle of control, shifting between different carceral regimes over the course of their life. For example, an individual may shift from being raised in local authority care, to time in young offenders' institutions, to periods in and out of prison in adulthood, interspersed with spells in hospital for mental disorders.

The idea of transcarceration is therefore potentially useful in terms of how it signals the increasingly blurred boundaries between control functions and welfare functions. Both Scull (1987) and Blomberg (1987) illustrate this trend by reference to the proliferation of 'diversion' schemes that have been introduced over the past two decades. For at the same time as there have been dramatic rises in prison populations, there has been an accompanying development involving the introduction of a vast array of community based correctional schemes. Ostensibly the aim of such schemes is to divert young people, first-time offenders and less serious offenders away from contact with the formal criminal justice system, and the longer-term negative impacts this entails. But the overall impact has been, as Scull (1987) describes, the diversion of people into and within the system, not away from it. It has expanded the reach of the control system, so that interventions now routinely take place not just with offenders, but also those young people who are calculated to be 'at risk' of offending at some point in the future. The result of this is an increasingly decentralized criminal justice network whose controls increasingly penetrate civil society (Blomberg 1987).

For Wacquant (2001), the most important dimension of the development of 'transcarceralism' is that it has become a surrogate policy for dealing with the social problems caused by the racialized and deeply ingrained culture of poverty in many of America's urban areas, described in Chapter 4. That is, rather than tackling the structural and structuring causes of poverty, the dominant policy orientation has been to try and exert increasing levels of control over the destitute and marginalized. In a period of history that privileges the role of the free-market, governments have become increasingly concerned to tackle the problems caused by those whom market systems have failed on the basis that they threaten the system. Thus the value of welfare provision has been increasingly eroded and increasingly it is used as a tool to ensure that recipients do not misbehave. As Wacquant reiterates, the inhabitants of the urban ghettos and the inmates of America's prisons are increasingly the same individuals.

Community based sanctions

Accompanying the resort to the use of imprisonment as confinement, there has been a significant and important growth in the number, range and types of community based sanctions, or what Morris (1995) terms 'intermediate punishments', that are available to control a range of different forms of deviant behaviour. These alternatives to custody include fines, curfew orders, community service orders, treatment orders, electronic monitoring, and intensive probation and parole (Morris and Tonry 1990). Support for these various intermediate punishments is rarely based on the idea that they are better at reducing recidivism rates, the rather more pragmatic claims made are they are cheaper and do not appear to be any worse than incarceration (Morris 1995).

There have always been community based corrections running parallel to the use of imprisonment as a form of punishment. But the development of new alternatives has been emboldened in recent times by the difficulties associated with the economic and social costs involved in building more and bigger prisons to house the increasingly large numbers of offenders sentenced by the courts (Vass 1990).

The effectiveness of intermediate punishments may reflect, as Vass (1990) notes in his study of the operationalization of community service orders, that in practice the day-to-day workings of such punishments are based upon 'toleration'. They necessarily involve a degree of discretion on the part of supervisory officials, which produces a certain degree of elasticity in the enforcement of rules and laws.

Ultimately, the introduction of these measures extends the range of sanctions that are available to the authorities, at the same time as facilitating the penetration of control practices ever deeper into the key arenas of social life. This is because punishment is no longer separated by the prison wall. It is in this sense that the development of these methods of punishment have emboldened processes towards 'decentralized community control' (Cohen 1987).

One of the most insightful discussions of how decentralized community control has developed and spread is provided by Jonathan Simon (1993) in his analysis of the evolution of the parole system in America. Simon explains how the introduction of parole, where a period of incarceration is followed by administrative supervision, was originally based upon the idea that through either the imposition of discipline over, or clinical assistance to the offender, the person concerned should be encouraged to attempt to adjust to 'normal life' after prison. However, increasingly the mission of parole has been subverted by a desire to manage 'problem groups' through a range of disciplinary and clinical techniques. In effect, parole has increasingly been transformed into a comparatively cheap form of punishment, reflecting the wider sense in which both the penal system and the welfare system have been increasingly concerned with 'the government of the poor'.

The 'managerial' parole model that Simon describes as coming into being from the mid-1970s to the present, is increasingly less concerned with what Foucault termed 'normalization' of the deviant. Rather it is based upon the more limited aims of meeting internally set performance standards and targets, which themselves do not aim to deal with causes of problems, but seek to control the effects of these problems as far as is practicable. As Simon explains, the continual measurement of performance of parole agencies induces a 'technocratic rationality' into their work, that tends to transform substantive evaluations (such as is he/she dangerous?) to formal procedures (is his/her drug test positive?). The significance of Simon's argument is that it is not limited solely to changes made in parole, but also describes many of the changes that have occurred throughout the criminal justice and welfare systems.

Restorative justice

Disillusionment with the traditional state-led responses to deviance, and the fact that either intentionally or unintentionally they lead to more and more controls, has led to an increasing number of commentators seeking out alternative methods for developing responses to deviant behaviour. The restorative justice movement has been especially influential in this respect. As a mode of social control, restorative justice is significant in that it deliberately removes the state from the equation. By this I mean that whereas the modes of social control that involve the enforcement of law in some sense pivot around the role of state, restorative justice focuses upon the victim and offender, the harm caused by the incident and how this harm can suitably be redressed – either through an apology or some other form of reparation. Therefore, thought of as a process, restorative justice brings together all the parties directly affected by an incident, in a deliberative and consensual forum, arranged by a third party, in order to establish how to deal with the aftermath of the incident.

At a conceptual level, the idea of restorative justice can be seen to be possessed of a number of features that cohere with Donald Black's 'conciliatory' style of social control, where, '. . . the ideal is social harmony. In the pure case, the parties to a dispute initiate a meeting and seek to restore their relationship to its former condition' (Black 1976: 5). In his early formulation of the principles underpinning the restorative justice movement, Braithwaite (1989) drew a distinction between 'stigmatizing' and 'shaming'. By this he meant to show how traditional penological responses to deviance tended to further criminalize the deviant person and to redress the harm they had caused by harming them. The alternative according to Braithwaite, was that rather than stigmatizing, the goal should be to shame the deviant, but in the process of shaming them provide opportunities to reintegrate them into society. In this sense then, we can detect an echo of the theme of inclusion versus exclusion that is so central to debates around the conduct of social control. Restorative justice schemes seek to establish a form of social control that does not create the conditions whereby the offender is ostracized from the community, rather the emphasis is upon reintegrating the person into the community.

There has been much written upon the topic of restorative justice and many innovative attempts have been made to utilize the principles to engage in problem solving in different situations. However, for the most part, where there are established legal frameworks the impact of restorative justice schemes has, as yet, been fairly marginal, operating largely at the periphery of the highly developed criminal justice system. Where restorative justice as a mode of social control does seem to be potentially more important is in countries where the legal system lacks popular legitimacy, and where there is a deeply entrenched sense of community division and conflict. For example, in South Africa a strong restorative justice movement is emerging alongside the 'retributive justice system' (Skelton 2002). As Roche (2002) describes, in Cape Town, Peace Committees involving appointed members of the local community, have been set up to engage in 'peace-making' and 'peace-building' activities. The former involves the resolution of conflicts and disputes between community members, whilst the latter set of activities is directed more to addressing the structural conditions which are identified as the ultimate causes of many conflicts. As far as Roche is concerned, although there are acknowledged problems with the implementation of restorative justice principles, given the particular situation of South Africa, the Peace Committee approach provides a forum for dealing with a wide range of conflicts and offences by trying to repair the harm caused.

McEvoy and Mika (2002) describe how the principles of restorative justice have been utilized in Northern Ireland, where attempts are being made to use the values and principles associated with restorative justice as an alternative to paramilitary 'punishment beatings'. Here then, community engagement in the provision of a form of informal justice is being employed in an effort to counter the problems caused by a situation where large sections of the populace are highly distrustful of the formal agencies of social control.

What then are we to make of the use of restorative justice programmes in this way, in what equates to a quasi-formal way of delivering informal social control? On the one hand such programmes extend the reach of social control down into communities, in that they enlist community members in the performance of social control functions. But concomitantly, in another sense they also limit the spread of control, by restricting the number of incidents that are dealt with through the formal mechanisms of the state. This reiterates the conceptual concerns about the formal/informal distinctions regarding social control, raised in earlier chapters.

Summary

Punishment is a primary mode of social control. Forms of punishment such as imprisonment, parole and probation directly control the actions of those subject to the regimen. In addition though, the presence of such punishments seek to prevent and deter different forms of deviance. In examining several different forms of punishment I have sought to tease out the analogies that can be identified in terms of how social control works. For example, in discussing the nature and functions of imprisonment, I showed that even in establishments where there is an intense and systematic form of social control, it is a negotiated order. This serves to show the limits of social control in terms of the extent to which a system can totally subjugate an individual.

The discussion of parole was suggestive of the fact that there has been a shift in the dominant orientations of key social control institutions. That is the aims of 'normalization' have been replaced by 'problem management', where the chief objective has been redefined as containment rather than resolution. Running throughout this discussion has been the sense that the boundaries between what were formerly distinct institutions of punishment are becoming increasingly blurred.

The architecture of social control

Amongst the most immediate and obvious ways in which human beings shape and regulate the behaviour of each other is through the construction of physical structures and boundaries. The design of the physical environment is a central facet of how actions and interactions are controlled, and does much to order human conduct. The control functions of architectural design are perhaps most evident in the institution of the prison. As discussed in the previous chapter, the outer walls of the prison quite literally define the boundaries of the prison community and who is subject to its disciplinary regime. Indeed, it is this separation of inmates from the world outside that is held to be a key component of incarceration as a form of punishment. Once inside the outer prison wall though, the layout and physical design of the buildings within, further subdivides the space available, indicating the uses to which the separated spaces should be put. At the same time, as Foucault (1977) recognized, it is this arrangement of space that, to a greater or lesser extent, exposes (or sequesters) individuals to particular control technologies. In this sense, the walls inside a prison function in a similar fashion to those in many buildings.

Whereas the prison wall serves to control troublesome sections of the population through confinement, in recent times, we have seen what amounts to an effective inversion of this logic of control with the re-emergence of 'gated communities'. Gated communities seek to manufacture protection for residents by the use of boundary walls to exclude 'outsiders' and thereby supposedly reduce the risks of disorder within. This development is paradigmatic of a wider movement where the potential social control properties of physical design have been increasingly realized and exploited. Planners, designers, architects and criminologists have all sought to manipulate the physical design of objects and environments in order to enhance the availability of social control.

In this chapter I will look at the role of physical environments in the production of control and order. For the purposes of analytic clarity the chapter will be divided into three main sections. I will start by looking at macro-level issues of urban planning and the make-up of urban areas in order to explore the ways in which such matters relate to processes of social control. Following on from which I will deal with some meso-level issues, focusing particularly on several influential explanations of how the presence of physical disorders undermines social control in communities. Consideration of such issues links with the subsequent discussion of the micro-level logics of specific situational controls, and how they have been integrated into the design of buildings and objects.

Behaviour and environment

The notion that behaviour and environment are interconnected is not a new idea. In his justly famous essay 'The metropolis and mental life' published in 1911, Georg Simmel described how the constant flow of stimuli encountered in modern urban situations produced new forms of social being. He argued urban life induces a 'blase attitude' amongst individuals, where the rush of stimuli are largely screened out in order to prevent them being overwhelmed by their experiences. These processes that are constitutive of the urban condition generates a form of what David Harvey (1990) has latterly termed 'sham individualism', where people reduce each other to little more than the signs they display to denote social status and identity. But for Lofland, this is symptomatic of how the continual immanent uncertainty of living in 'a world of strangers' is resolved by individuals:

> . . . the city created a new kind of human being – the cosmopolitan – who was able, as his tribal ancestors were not, to relate to others in the new ways that city living made not only possible but necessary. The cosmopolitan did not lose the capacity for knowing others personally. But he gained the capacity for knowing others categorically.
>
> (Lofland 1973: 177)

Whereas Simmel and Lofland describe the impact of urban forms on social life, Richard Sennett (1990), in his historical surveys of urban cultures from antiquity to the present day, has shown how the design of cities frequently gives material and symbolic expression to particular dimensions of social life. Thus Simmel and Sennett respectively provide us with insights into the ways that urban design shapes social life, at the same time as it is a product of those selfsame social formations. It is for this reason that the city as social form has frequently been employed as a metaphor for studying the wider social order.

Nowhere is this better illustrated than in Baron von Haussman's redesign of Paris in the nineteenth century, where the tightly packed and winding streets of the Parisian slums were knocked down and replaced with the wide straight boulevards that anyone who has been to Paris will remember well. Haussman's project was not though a matter of aesthetic redesign, it was about the imposition of a sense of order and an act of social control.[1] Motivated by fear of the radical power of the Paris citizenry to overthrow the political order as they had done in the French Revolution, Napoleon III ordered that the slums be removed in order to create the conditions wherein control, if required, could be more easily imposed to overcome the Paris mob. Wide, long, straight streets aided and abetted this project, because they allowed canon to be fired down them from strategic positions, and also cavalry charges could be carried out more easily and effectively than before.

Of course not all cities were as explicit as Paris in the incorporation of social control mechanisms, many others developed in a far less determined manner. Nevertheless, the case of Paris is important because, what the architects of the rebuilding of the French capital city had understood clearly, was that the features of the physical environment could either encourage deviant behaviour, or facilitate control. As will become apparent, these interlinked themes have remained central to work in this area.

Urban studies

Some of the most important studies of the links between deviant behaviour, control and urban life were performed by the members of the Chicago School of Sociology in the early decades of the twentieth century. Through studying successive waves of immigrants into the rapidly developing city of Chicago, the members of the School were able to show that delinquent and disorderly behaviour was not caused by inherent racial or individual characteristics, but was rather better explained as a symptom of the way in which immigration patterns related to the socio-economic organization of the city and a 'control deficit', that was itself the product of social disorganization and a fragmented social bond.

To explain these connections, Burgess (1925) developed his zonal model of the city. He argued that the concentration of criminal and disorderly behaviours in certain areas of the city reflected the fact that these 'zones in transition' tended to have the cheapest rents, and as a consequence, were where new immigrants would settle initially. As these groups of people became more established and settled, they would be able to afford to move to the more prosperous city neighbourhoods. Their places would then be taken by a new group of immigrants. Burgess suggested that these conditions in the transitional zone were inimical to the establishment of the sorts of social institutions that enabled community-based social control to exist in more settled and established communities.

Subsequent work on urban development patterns has sought to refine the potentially overly deterministic interpretations that can be read into the zonal model. For example, Morris (1957) in his study of Croydon, showed that social policy and in particular public housing policy interventions could alter the patterns of crime, offender residence rates and the distances of these from the city centre. Political decision making was also identified as a key factor by Bottoms et al. (1989) in their study of geographic variations in crime and disorder in Sheffield. Although they could not identify the original causes of differences between the crime and offender residence rates of different areas, they did identify that it was local housing allocation policies that had been reproducing the differences.

What these two latter studies demonstrate is that cities are not autonomous social systems, rather the distribution of resources and communities in an urban area, and thus the patterning of social problems, is underpinned by a form of political economy. This theme, which is present in aspects of the Chicago School's studies, has been revived by Logan and Molotch (1988) in their model of urban development as a 'growth machine'. They show how attitudes to different places and spaces are socially constructed according to the political and economic dynamics of development. The implications of urban political economy and its connection to practices of social control in late-modernity is brought to the fore in Mike Davis's (1990) case study of Los Angeles. Through a detailed and theoretically sophisticated analysis of the development of L.A., Davis identifies some broader trends in terms of how urban cityscapes are being refigured, driven by fears about crime and the decline in social order.

Fear and loathing in Los Angeles

For Davis, urban space in Los Angeles has been radically transformed in the latter part of the twentieth century. The key trend he notes is that social control technologies of various kinds have increasingly been designed into urban environments. He describes how, motivated by fears about their risks of victimization, contemporary residents of L.A. have reverted to a 'fortress mentality', erecting walls around their properties, shopping in private malls, putting locks, bolts and bars on their doors and windows, paying for private security guards, all in an attempt to gain an enhanced sense of security. As he describes:

> In cities like Los Angeles, on the bad edge of postmodernity, one observes an unprecedented tendency to merge urban design, architecture and the police apparatus into a single, comprehensive security effort.
>
> (Davis 1990: 224)

It is a trend that he dubs 'the militarization of space'. Not only is there a proliferation of control measures, but many of them are made explicit, clearly signalling their intended function to all who encounter them.

There are two trends driving these processes forwards. First, there is a deeply embedded desire on the part of many citizens to manufacture a sense of security. Confronted with high crime rates and rapid social change, people have sought to manufacture more control by directly purchasing equipment that they believe will reduce their risks of becoming a victim, and by restricting their use of those spaces that they do not believe offer adequate amounts of protection to them (Flusty 1997). Such trends are reinforced by wider shifts in what Davis dubs the 'post-liberal' economic situation where:

> The American city, as many critics have recognized, is being systematically turned inside out – or, rather, outside in. The valorized spaces of the new megastructures and super-malls are concentrated in the center, street frontage is denuded, public activity is sorted into strictly functional compartments and circulation is internalized in corridors under the gaze of private police.
>
> (Davis 1990: 226)

Driven by widespread fears, people are encouraged to increasingly try and insulate themselves from the threats that they perceive to their safety. One response to this is the creation of artificially sanitized space, environments such as shopping malls or gated communities, that are deliberately designed to encourage the trust of users that this is a comparatively safe location. As a consequence, formerly public activities such as shopping, increasingly take place in buildings where those people who are constructed as potential threats to the manufactured social order, such as beggars or tramps, are excluded.

The general trend that Davis identifies for Los Angeles is one of progressive 'enclavization'. The included sections of the population reside, work and take their leisure in highly ordered spaces, founded upon an over-layering of social control technologies. These spaces are both physically and meta-physically separated from the disordered 'badlands', inhabited by the economically and politically marginalized and excluded – the ghettos.

The problem of 'ghettoization', the creation of areas suffering from overlayered and interconnected forms of social exclusion are recognized as being particularly acute in a number of American cities, but this is by no means exclusively an American issue. For as Bottoms and Wiles (1997) note, contemporary debates on the ghettos, re-work the concerns of Victorian city-life and the problem posed by the 'dangerous classes'. As with their forerunners, the contemporary ghettos are marked by high levels of economic deprivation, unemployment and social problems of many kinds, but most significantly, high offence and offender rates. And whereas in previous generations, attempts to control the activities of the residents of socially excluded areas went hand-in-hand with programmes designed to try and improve the situation, in the late-modern social control apparatus the reformist aspirations have now been dropped. The ghettos are subject to highly coercive and militarized forms of social control, which Parenti (1999) interprets as a state of almost permanent 'lockdown'. The efforts of the controllers are targeted towards containment, trying to ensure that problems are restricted to the deprived areas, not leaking out to disturb the activities of the fearful included.

The fears that drive this urban cycle of 'securitization', are not of course wholly unrealistic, Los Angeles is renowned for the problems caused by drugs, gangs and violent crimes. Nevertheless, the outcome of such processes is a 'carceral city', where socially excluded sections are 'locked out' of key strategic public spaces, but at the same time, the wealthy sections of the populace are increasingly 'locked in' these spaces. The wealthy and included engage in a self-imposed form of confinement, in an effort to avoid the risks that they perceive to lie in the areas devoid of adequate security measures.

The key question that arises is whether the fate that Davis (1990) identifies for Los Angeles through his fear-control nexus, is the same fate that awaits all late-modern urban areas. Undoubtedly, we can detect traces of the themes he identifies in Los Angeles in other cities around the world. The spread of mass-private property in the form of shopping malls, the increased use of private security guards to police these areas and the increased use of surveillance systems are recognizable developments in many cities. However, in looking for similarities we must be careful not to ignore the differences that exist between cities. As Body-Gendrot (2000) in her comparative study of European and American cities notes, each city is shaped by the weight of its past. Their individuated histories strongly shape the forms of social control that are exerted in the present. Although the economic, political and cultural forces of globalization produce homogenizing pressures, these are countered by forces towards differentiation. Cities in a global economy are in cultural competition with each other, they grow and develop often by establishing how they are distinct from other nominally similar areas.

Local context matters then, the civic culture, economic traditions, social memories, traditions of community activism and political scene all shape how social control is enacted. Comparing French and American cities in particular, Body-Gendrot notes that in the former there remains far greater support for the use of social welfare interventions to support the urban poor. Relatedly, the degree of 'spatial polarization' between rich and poor is not as intense in French cities, as a result of a combination of history and contemporary welfare policies. The presence of these differences thus manifestly shapes the nature and severity of the problems over which control is sought. Moreover, these matters of context also influence the strategies that are deemed acceptable for addressing such problems. Therefore, whilst American city authorities may turn to coercive forms of social control such as zero-tolerance policing in an attempt to manufacture a solution to what are deemed in political discourse to constitute 'problem populations', in Europe such problems may be addressed by changes in the welfare system.

Nevertheless, although we can use Body-Gendrot's comparative analysis to question the extent to which we will all end up in the carceral urban dystopia described by Davis. Across the Western world, the integration of control measures into urban environments has become ever more commonplace. Having described the macro-level trends present, I will now briefly consider some meso-level concerns about the control of spaces and places, en route to a micro-level examination of the workings of some of the specific control technologies integrated into the physical environment.

Broken windows and community control

In the earlier chapter on policing, I briefly discussed how Wilson and Kelling's ideas about (1982) 'broken windows' have been used to explain some of the more punitive practices associated with zero-tolerance policing programmes. I now want to revisit this argument in order to explore what it tells us about how criminologists have come to understand the links between environment, deviance and control. I view this perspective as important because of the ways in which, at the time of publication, it signalled something of a wider theoretical shift amongst many policy makers and academics from focusing upon the qualities of the deviant actor, to the qualities of the situation in which they are located. A shift which, as has been noted previously, has been profoundly influential in reconfiguring the logics animating social control programmes in late-modernity.

Wilson and Kelling (1982) developed the ideas presented in the broken windows paper in an effort to explain how and why crimes, and disorderly behaviours, tend to cluster in certain areas. In order to map out the fundamental tenets of their argument the explanatory example that they developed was that of the broken window. They maintained that if a window is broken and not repaired, this will encourage the commission of further antisocial behaviours in the area concerned, and over time, the deviance committed will develop into more serious types of crimes. They thus argued that the toleration of even seemingly trivial and inconsequential disorderly behaviours in an area could instigate more crime. In effect the disorder, whether it be physical or social, is envisaged as functioning as a form of signal to residents and outsiders alike. For residents, the presence of untreated disorder indicates that the area is under 'attack' and as a result they should take protective actions, which for the most part involves withdrawing from public space, thereby creating a control deficit. In contrast, for potential deviants the signal is more encouraging, suggesting that this is a location where there are opportunities to engage in deviance with only a minimal chance of control interventions being implemented.

This logic was further developed by Wesley Skogan (1990) and his concept of 'decay spirals'. Using quantitative survey data, Skogan sought to show first that the hypothesized connection between crime and disorder could be empirically validated. Having established a link between robbery rates and disorder he then went on to describe the process by which the occurrence of disorder in even some comparatively well ordered communities, can set off a chain of events that leads to them 'tipping' into high crime rates areas.

Skogan breaks the early stages of the process of a decay spiral developing into three parts:

1. The presence of disorder undermines the mechanisms by which communities exercise control over local affairs;
2. The disorder provokes concerns about neighbourhood safety and 'perhaps even causes crime itself' (1990: 65);
3. The disorder undermines the operations of the local housing market encouraging residents to move away.

A similar notion of 'community tipping' and the undermining of community based social control is to be found in Schuerman and Kobrin's (1986) study. Taub et al. (1984) introduce an important innovation to these arguments in recognizing that a rise in crime and disorder may not have a uniform impact on all residents. For some residents with particularly strong emotional attachments to an area, such as the elderly, or those residents without sufficient economic capital, increases in disorder will not cause them to move. For other groups though, declines in perceived order can provoke a decision to engage in out-migration, thus crime can still function as an engine of community change.

According to advocates of this position, disorder as a cause of crime undermines the informal mechanisms of community social control that are integral to the maintenance of local social order. Under certain conditions, the perceived degradation of the physical environment destabilizes the methods by which communities regulate the behaviour of members and outsiders alike.

In a recent state of the art study, Sampson and Raudenbusch (1999) utilized a multi-method research design to test the links between levels of disorder and recorded crime in the city of Chicago. Although they found that disorder and crime were not strongly correlated, they did identify stronger links with antecedent socio-economic disadvantage and what they term 'levels of collective efficacy'. This latter term being used to refer to the capacity of community members to engage informal social controls in order to prevent crime and disorder, or to mitigate its effects. On the basis of their empirical data they argue that rather than disorder being a cause of crime, both disorder and crime may be caused by attenuated informal social control mechanisms combined with structural disadvantage in particular areas.

A similar sentiment is expressed by William Julius Wilson in his analysis of life in the ghettos where:

> ... what many impoverished and dangerous neighbourhoods have in common is a relatively high degree of social integration (high levels of local neighbouring while being relatively isolated from contacts in the broader mainstream society) and low levels of informal social control (feelings that they have little control over their immediate environment including the environment's negative influence on their children).
>
> (Wilson 1996: 63)

This suggests that different types of social organization and disorganization can co-exist in an area, producing a disposition to suffer from different types of deviance (Bottoms and Wiles 1997).

Thus Sampson and Raudenbusch's (1999) findings provide an analytic connection between the meso- and macro-levels of analysis. There is a link between the operations of urban political economies discussed earlier in this chapter, and the distribution of levels of deviance and control at the parochial community level.

Criminogenic situations

The broken windows concept and the explanations related to it, focus upon the qualities of what David Garland (1996) terms 'criminogenic situations'. That is the features of particular locations that undermine potential social control mechanisms and make them into suitable sites for engaging in deviant acts. But if certain physical characteristics encourage deviance, then logically we might expect that other features can be used to inhibit it or control it. And, indeed, work to develop situational controls has been one of the most important developments in late-modern social control policy. The importance of the situational control movement lies in the ways in which it was adopted and adapted by a number of criminologists in Britain and America (Garland 2000). But in order to understand how it came to achieve such prominence we need to first understand the intellectual background.

By the 1970s, an increasing number of criminologists had become disenchanted with the achievements of academic criminology. People such as J.Q. Wilson (1975) in America, and Ron Clarke at the Home Office in London (Clarke and Mayhew 1980; Clarke and Cornish 1986) expressed the view that criminology had become overly concerned with trying to identify the dispositions or motivations that caused people to engage in deviant behaviours, and had been spectacularly unsuccessful in terms of reducing crime through this approach. They argued that what could be deduced from the failure to reduce crime was that it is extremely difficult to identify a person's psychological motivations and equally difficult to change these in any way. Their argument was bolstered by an increasing amount of evidence from criminological research suggesting the use of imprisonment and other forms of punishment was largely ineffective in deterring people from committing crime, and was also largely ineffective in reforming those who were actually punished.

Therefore, they called for a shift in focus of control programmes. Rather than seeking to change the internalized dispositions of social actors, it was, they maintained, far more practicable and feasible to alter elements of the situations in which they were located. This logic formed the basis for what today are known as Situational Crime Prevention (SCP) and Crime Prevention through Environmental Design (CPED) programmes. These approaches consider the characteristics of different locations and social contexts, and focus upon the possibility of manipulating them to limit the opportunities for committing deviant acts. In turn, these initiatives are part of a wider movement that Jock Young (1994) has labelled 'administrative criminology', where crime prevention and reduction efforts focus upon highly pragmatic 'technical' changes to inhibit deviant conduct. Although proponents of SCP programmes and administrative criminologists more generally typically disavow the need for theory, this is not to say that SCP has no theoretical base. Indeed, it has drawn upon a number of key ideas from Oscar Newman's (1972) theory of 'defensible space' and rational actor theory.

Newman was concerned with some of the impacts of the architectural design of tower blocks upon the behaviour of their residents. In particular, he wanted to understand why it was that tower blocks seemed to be particularly prone to vandalism and more serious forms of crime, when compared with other residential forms. The thesis that he developed was that the design of tower blocks limited the opportunities for residents to engage in the routine informal 'natural surveillance' that was afforded to people when living in more conventional streets. Moreover, the nature of the design of tower blocks disrupted feelings of territoriality, and confused the boundaries between what residents perceived to be public and private spaces. The fact that the physical layout of tower blocks did not afford to residents a sense that they owned the spaces around them, meant that they made little attempt to exert control over the activities that took place in these spaces. On this basis Newman proposed that to make such environments safer, what was required was not more locks, bolts or bars, but to arrange space so that it felt private for residents. The significance of his contribution was therefore, the notion that specific design features could be used to foster social control. This has become the cornerstone of SCP programmes.

The other key theoretical influence that can be detected in the evolution of SCP programmes is that of rational actor theory. Rational actor theory maintains that essentially human behaviour is based upon a model of rational calculation. That is people will perform an act if they think it is going to benefit them in some way. If they can make a material, psychological or emotional gain from engaging in deviant behaviour, with only minimal risks of getting caught, then they will do so (Clarke and Mayhew, 1980). Conversely then, if it is possible to manipulate the environment so as to increase the potential costs to the individual of engaging in deviance, then they would be more persuaded to comply with norms and standards of non-deviant conduct. It is important to recognize that the impact of rational actor theory was not just restricted to the sphere of criminal justice policy. It echoed the logic that was integral to the neo-liberal reshaping of social, political and economic life that commenced in the late 1970s, and whose repercussions continue today (O'Malley, 1992).

By synthesizing elements of these two positions outlined above, a highly influential SCP movement has developed, where control measures are introduced in respect of a range of different situations to try and reduce the opportunities for crime. Situational control measures are increasingly designed into the physical environment, but given the focus of this book, this is especially significant because, due to the nature of the measures concerned, they frequently do not just control the behaviour of potential deviants, they tend to regulate the behaviour of everybody who enters the situation.

Situational control

The basis of SCP is that rather than trying to prevent crime through reforming the criminal it is far easier to modify the situations in which the opportunities to commit such acts arise. Ron Clarke (1995) explains that broadly speaking SCP techniques tend to be based on one of three key logics. Techniques can be intended to:

- Increase the effort required to commit the deviant act;
- Enhance the risks of detection;
- Reduce the value of the reward of deviance.

Amongst the most important measures that are guided by these logics are 'target hardening' efforts. Hardening the target involves reworking the design of a physical location or object, to incorporate aspects which make it more difficult for a motivated offender to engage in their intended course of action. One example of this has been the work that has been done to improve the security systems on cars. Car manufacturers have over the past decade made improvements to the locks on cars to make their products more difficult to steal. Similarly, homeowners have been encouraged to fit better locks on their doors and windows to make their homes more difficult to burgle. Target-hardening techniques frequently feature as important elements of crime prevention campaigns.

Another commonly applied situational control technique is the implementation of access controls. Access controls are designed to make it harder to gain entry to a situation where it is envisaged certain people might wish to commit deviant acts. Examples of the use of access controls include situations where you need to have an identification pass or know the code for the door lock to gain access to an area. These measures, which we have become increasingly accustomed to in our daily lives, are founded upon a notion that opportunities for deviance can be reduced by changing some aspect of the situation.

But perhaps the best example of this integration of control technologies into the fabric of the environment is provided by Shearing and Stenning in their analysis of the social order of Disney World, where:

> Control strategies are embedded in both environmental features and structural relations. In both cases control structures and activities have other functions which are highlighted so that the control function is overshadowed. Nonetheless, control is pervasive. For example every pool, fountain and flower garden serves both as an aesthetic object and to direct visitors away from, or towards, particular locations. Similarly, every Disney Productions employee, while visibly and primarily engaged in other functions is also engaged in the maintenance of order . . .The effect is . . . to embed the control function into the 'woodwork' where its presence is unnoticed but its effects are ever present.
>
> (1987: 319)

Through habituation, embedded controls thus assume something of a seen but unnoticed quality, not unlike the forms of self and interactional regulation described by Goffman (see Chapter 4). Although much of the controlling that takes place is consensual, ultimately it resides upon the availability of a form of coercive power:

> This can be illustrated by an incident that occurred during a visit to Disney World by Shearing and his daughter, during the course of which she developed a blister on her heel. To avoid further irritation she removed her shoes and proceeded to walk barefooted. They

had not progressed ten yards before they were approached by a very personable security guard dressed as a Bahamian police officer, with white pith helmet and white gloves that perfectly suited the theme of the area they were moving through (so that he, at first, appeared more like a scenic prop than a security person), who informed them that walking barefoot was, 'for the safety of visitors', not permitted. When informed that, given the blister, the safety of his visitor was likely to be better secured by remaining barefooted, at least on the walkways, they were informed that their safety and how best to protect it was a matter for Disney Productions to determine while they were on Disney property and that unless they complied he would be compelled to escort them out of Disney World. Shearing's daughter, on learning that failure to comply with the security guard's instruction would deprive her of the pleasures of Disney World, quickly decided that she would prefer to injure her heel and remain on Disney property.

(Shearing and Stenning 1987)

As this perceptive analysis demonstrates, even in seemingly inocuous places, that are supposedly designed for pure enjoyment and fun, situational controls can abound. Equally important though is understanding how this form of 'instrumental control' works. For the most part it is not imposed, but is consensual. Those subject to the control regime are seduced to co-operate by virtue of the opportunities for the consumption of pleasure that are provided. This is indicative of the fact that much of this instrumental control is undertaken by corporations in pursuit of securing their profit margins.

The limits of situational control

The notion of introducing situational controls to restrict the opportunities for engaging in deviant behaviour has been one of the most important developments of recent times. Nevertheless, there are a range of criticisms that can be levelled at the logic of such arguments. First, although some situational controls, such as locks on cars and houses are fairly targeted, other forms of situational control measures are not. Indeed, many of them do not simply control the actions of potential deviants, but either implicitly or explicitly, regulate the behaviour of all users of the location. As such, the proliferation of such approaches signifies the extent to which the logic of late-modern social control has shifted from focusing upon nominated deviants, to a concern with entire populations.

Such movements are, though, indicative of the tensions that exist between some of the key theoretical ideas that have informed the development of current approaches. Risk is based upon the probabilistic differentiation and classification of populations, but rational actor theory problematizes any such epistemology, because it maintains that given the right circumstances and incentives, everyone is susceptible to deviance, thus rendering risk classifications somewhat limited in their purview. This reinforces some of my earlier comments concerning the fact that the forces contributing to the development of late-modern social control, are not necessarily coherent or consistent.

SCP programmes have been dogged by concerns about 'displacement' effects. Because such approaches to control do not seek to engage with changing the motivational dispositions of potential offenders, the criticism has been repeatedly made that they simply result in problems being shifted elsewhere, or simply cause new types of problem to emerge. Some have sought to argue that displacement does not need to be understood as problematic and that in fact it could be used as a tool in a positive fashion. That is if you can displace crimes by hardening the targets in particular locations then it may be possible to concentrate particular problems in defined geographic areas, thereby reducing the nuisance or security risks posed to the vast majority of the population. Of course this hardly seems a just solution for those people who live or work in the areas chosen to 'contain' the problems.

Sennett's (1970) theorization of the consequences that emanate from the ways that public policy is being co-opted into the search for the production of mythologized 'purified communities' points us to the fact that, whilst gated enclaves may provide short-term solutions to popular fear and insecurity, they may be the cause of more serious problems over the longer term. Recent evidence suggests that in fact the exclusion of non-residents from these areas does little in terms of crime reduction, but rather provides an illusion of safety (Minton 2002). The erection of physical boundaries and borders to exclude those elements of the population that are perceived as threatening, is thus primarily concerned with the management of subjective fear.

Criticisms of a different kind have been raised in respect of the kinds of social issues that SCP programmes have demonstrated a tendency to engage with. It has been argued that they have displayed an overwhelming disposition to engage with fairly traditional crime types that occur in public space, but have been of less use in tackling problems such as: the hidden abuse of women and children; corporate crimes; and crimes of the state (Box 1983; Stanko 1990; Hughes 1998). A not unrelated concern is the extent to which SCP can be seen as 'victim-blaming', that is the idea that the victim is at fault for failing to take adequate protection of themselves and/or their property.

I have already implied that many of the key protagonists associated with SCP take an avowedly pragmatic approach to the problem of crime control, eschewing the need for what they see as overly complex and largely irrelevant concerns with theorizing the motivations of offenders. It is perhaps not unexpected then that some of the most important criticisms of SCP and its associated rational choice theory have focused upon its theoretical foundations. Criticisms of these approaches have tended to gravitate around the fact that they fail to adequately explain the significance of history, context, motive and interpretation in the commission of deviant acts. Jock Young (1994) adds a further political dimension to this list of weaknesses, describing how the position taken by advocates of SCP, allows politicians to effectively ignore the issue of how wider social and economic conditions, to do with unemployment and poor housing, shape the crime rate (see also Hughes 1998).

Control signals

The deliberately atheoretical stance adopted by many of the most influential proponents of SCP and its allied approaches constitutes a significant weak point that has led to a condition of 'analytic interruptus', whereby there is, in effect, only a limited understanding of how and why situational controls might work (or indeed, why on some occasions they do not work). In thinking about SCP programmes, the key question is not simply that of whether such control measures work in terms of preventing or reducing crime, but, as Crawford (2000) notes, the potentially more vexing one of explaining how they work and for whom. This is particularly, important given the fact that evaluations have shown vastly differing success rates in terms of introducing the same SCP technologies into different situations.

Somewhat ironically, the theoretical ideas associated with SCP approaches have, for the most part, largely failed to account for the influence that the characteristics and qualities of the situation has in shaping social action. They assume that, by introducing some form of situational control measure into a location, the reaction of all people to this measure will be broadly the same. This approach neglects to account for the fact that if people are to react to situational controls they must first be aware of their presence. This points us to a crucial fact that it is vitally important not to overlook; many situational controls work on the basis that they signal to the offender that their deviant act is probably going to be difficult to carry out, or is likely to be detected. Relatedly, these signals are also intended to reassure users of a space that it is comparatively secure. Many situational controls are deliberately designed in such a way as to display these communicative properties in order to deter potential deviant behaviours. For example, the presence of CCTV cameras on public streets are made fairly obvious in public and mass private spaces, and are frequently accompanied by warning notices that people are being monitored.

I would therefore suggest that the establishment of a 'social semiotic analysis of situational controls' provides the opportunity to help us better understand how and why such control measures work in regulating behaviour. Social semiotics is derived from semiotics, which is the science of signs, and provides an analytic framework for exploring the ways in which human actions and physical objects communicate to people and are thus rendered meaningful.[2] The development of such an approach would allow us to recognize that situational controls work not just by directly shaping behaviour, but also by moulding perceptions about the opportunities for committing deviant acts in a particular location. These control signals function to make potentially deviant actors aware of the restricted opportunities for deviance, they may also though serve to reassure other users of a space about the levels of security provided.

The development of this social semiotics of situational controls additionally promises to provide insight into why particular controls are not always equally effective in different settings. The setting may shape how the control measure is interpreted by the users of a space, including potential deviants. For example the environmental characteristics of an area may determine how noticeable a control measure such as new CCTV cameras are. Attending to the semiotic properties of situational controls thus provides the potential for developing a more sophisticated apparatus for interpreting how and why situational controls work in practice. Such an approach could develop the important work of Umberto Eco (1986), who, despite providing a relevant and interesting semiotic theory of architecture, has been ignored by the policy oriented CPTED protagonists. Eco explores the processes of signification through which buildings communicate subtle messages to their users. He persuasively argues that if we want to understand how architectural design functions, then we need to attune to the subtle ways in which the physical properties of a building can encode culturally embedded meanings, which are 'read' and thereby elide meanings with the intention of persuading those present to use the space in a particular way. This is not that far removed from Oscar Newman's (1972) approach, but the greater level of theoretical sophistication provided by Eco, provides significant opportunities for developing innovative ways of understanding the forms and functions of situational controls.

Summary

The physical landscape of late-modernity has been profoundly reconfigured by the increasing integration of measures designed to control a wide range of different forms of deviant conduct. The design and implementation of these situational controls has been largely premised upon a shift in theoretical focus from the figure of the deviant person to the deviant act. That is, rather than seeking reform of the actor, efforts have been directed to controlling the environments in which such actors are located and exerting influence that way. The dispersal of this logic and its often seamless incorporation into the physical structures of everyday life is illustrative of a key feature of late-modern control. That is its increasing opaqueness and invisibility.

To draw this chapter to a close and echoing my earlier comments contrasting the work of Simmel (1911) and Sennett (1990), the integration of situational controls into the landscapes of contemporary society functions to control the conduct of citizens. But at the same time, such developments also serve to illustrate the centrality that problems of social control and social order have assumed in late-modernity.

Surveillance

Do you ever feel like you are being watched? Well in late-modernity you probably are. The principal logics and practices of social control have been profoundly transformed by the development and proliferation of surveillance technologies. As a mode of social control, surveillance has traditionally featured as part of the work that the police do and how state punishment is practised. But in late-modernity, the conducting of surveillance has infiltrated a variety of public and private situations, via a panoply of techniques and technologies, and is performed with multiple objectives in mind. It is no longer the preserve of formal social control agencies, but in being de-coupled from them, surveillance has effectively been rendered more systematic and intense. As Gary Marx remarks, this has brought to the surface:

> . . . bits of reality that were previously hidden or didn't contain informational clues. People are in a sense turned inside out, and what was previously invisible or meaningless is made visible and meaningful.
> (Marx 1988: 207)

The development and dispersal of technologies for the monitoring of conduct has established surveillance as one of the principal modes via which late-modern societies seek to modify behaviour, regulate deviance, and respond to problems of order. The proliferation of the 'electronic eyes' of CCTV systems in both public spaces, such as town centres, and more private spaces such as workplaces and shopping malls, represents one of the most visible manifestations of the expansion of the 'control net'. But there are a range of less obvious, more invisible methods of surveillance that are currently in use. In many arenas of our social lives we are now monitored in some way or another, with the intention that this should restrict the probability of our engaging in deviant or disorderly acts. As Armstrong and Norris suggest,

> In Britain in the late 1990s it is unlikely that any urban dweller, in their role as shopper, worker, commuter, resident or school pupil, can avoid being passively or actively monitored by camera surveillance systems.
>
> (1999: 42)

In this chapter I will examine a number of dimensions of surveillance, reflecting its multifaceted applications and workings. This will include a review of the two principal alternative theoretical explanations that have emerged from the literature, together with an outline of the practices that they emphasize. Having explored how and why surveillance has developed in the way it has, I will then briefly consider a number of more empirically based studies, and the implications they have for understanding surveillance as a contemporary mode of social control.

A definition

In his book, David Lyon (2001) has defined surveillance as:

> ... any collection and processing of personal data, whether identifiable or not, for the purposes of influencing or managing those whose data have been garnered.
>
> (2001: 2)

Thus surveillance involves the purposive monitoring of conduct to allow for the identification, acquisition and classification of information with the intention of modifying that conduct in some manner.

However, it is important that the current growth of interest in the topic of surveillance is not misinterpreted. A casual observer might be forgiven for thinking that the rapid expansion of the literature on surveillance signalled a totally new movement in the logics and practices of social control, and that we are witnessing the emergence of a new mode of control. This would of course be a false impression. As part of group life, human communities have always developed mechanisms for the observation of each other's conduct. For example, in his accounts of city life in ancient Greece and Rome, Richard Sennett (1990) shows how architectural design was employed to make some forms of conduct routinely publicly visible. Similarly, there are historical records of how during the Black Death, communities were forced to nominate individuals to monitor the population in an area in an effort to identify new outbreaks of plague and thereby limit the dispersion of the contagion. It is a system of surveillance described by Foucault (1977), where the figure of the 'syndic' was appointed from amongst the members of the community to keep watch over its condition and to record the spread of disease within it. In turn, the work of the syndic was monitored by the 'intendants', who reported to the magistrates, who reported to the mayor. More recently, the Stasi, the East German Secret Police, operated a mass informer system as a mechanism via which to monitor the activities of whole communities.

As the above examples imply, the development of apparatus for conducting surveillance over populations was central both to the development of the modern nation-state system and the mechanisms by which fundamentally coercive political regimes sought to retain their domination over the citizenry (Giddens 1987).

What is innovative about late-modern surveillance systems is how the observation is conducted, and the depth and scale that it involves. Therefore we perhaps need to distinguish between the 'old' and 'new', or 'modern' and 'postmodern' surveillance styles.[1]

The first key characteristic of the new surveillance is the extent to which it is embedded within the routines of everyday life. Late-modern citizens have quickly become accustomed to having their behaviour purposively monitored in a range of venues, such as: residential areas; schools; in their cars by road traffic cameras; in car parks and petrol stations; at cash machines; in town centres; in retail and commercial centres; when attending football stadia; at major transport termini. A second key characteristic of the new surveillance is that it tends to be based upon 'remote observation', performed via a mediating technology. As Lyon (2001) argues, it is 'disembodied'. This is encapsulated by the deployment of CCTV cameras in a range of urban and suburban locations. The basic movement has been one where surveillance has proliferated and become increasingly systematized across a range of public and private arenas, as a result of the situating of a variety of technologies with monitoring capacities in these aforementioned arenas. In the process, some surveillance functions have become increasingly hidden, whilst others have been rendered more visible.

The logics of surveillance

Surveillance is then a central issue for those seeking to understand the social ordering practices of late-modern societies. Broadly speaking, we can identify two key theoretical perspectives on surveillance. The first I term 'disciplinary surveillance' theory, which can be counterposed and contrasted with 'liberal surveillance' theory.

Disciplinary surveillance

To date, the most influential theory of the nature and functions of surveillance in late-modernity has been founded upon the work of Michel Foucault, and in particular his concepts of 'discipline' and 'panopticism'. As discussed in Chapter 2, these ideas have been developed in important ways by the post-social control perspective. Running throughout Foucault's 'histories of the present' in fields as diverse as sexuality, madness and incarceration, was a concern to document how the era of modernity saw a transformation in the logics and technologies of power. As Foucault saw it, these logics and technologies were based upon the collection and production of knowledge.

For Foucault, the key transformation wrought by the enlightenment and the naissance of modernity was in the conduct of state power, the 'raison d'état'. Whereas previously the authority of the sovereign state had relied upon coercive force in order to subjugate citizens to its command and control, the modern state developed new technologies of power for the performance of this function, which were progressively dispersed throughout key strategic institutional sites in society. Central to this reconfiguration of power, was the emergence of what he termed discipline. Discipline is a form of automatized power, wherein the subject of the regime is induced to become almost self-regulating, so as to act 'normally'. As identified in Chapters 2 and 3, it is based upon a form of knowledge and allied technologies designed to inculcate within the subject, a fundamentally self-disciplining disposition.

The generation of this reflexive and for the most part unnoticed automatic monitoring of the self was, Foucault argued, based upon the principles of 'panoptic' surveillance. The panopticon was an architectural prison design presented by the utilitarian reformer Jeremy Bentham in the eighteenth century. Bentham's aim in forwarding the design, was to show how the exercise of power within the confines of the prison system could be rationalized, with the intention of improving the reformation of the posited deviant natures of the inmates. By designing the potential for constant surveillance into the architecture of the prison, the inmate would be encouraged to accede to the power of the regime and become 'normalized'.

For Foucault, the significance of Bentham's design was as a paradigmatic example that captured, and in effect embodied, wider and deeper trans- formations in the conduct of governance throughout society at this stage of modernity. The design of the panopticon prison set out the principles for a logic of panopticism, involving the automatization and de- individualization of power through systematic observation. As Foucault notes, this is 'polyvalent in its applications', transforming the functioning of a number of key social establishments and institutions, including prisons, schools, hospitals, asylums, factories and barracks from the eighteenth century onwards.

The progressive dispersal and development of discipline and the principles of panopticism was facilitated by the development of new institutions, but also as a result of the ways in which it infiltrated established institutions, and transformed them from within. This was particularly pertinent to the development of the state's administrative control apparatus, which became increasingly adept at collecting data on various aspects of the lives and work of the citizenry, data increasingly used for the design of more, and more effective, government interventions. As discussed in Chapter 3, this established a capacity to engage in the 'governing of the soul' through the regulation of physical bodies, based upon the continual, and ongoing, management and training of subjectivity, constituting a key shift in relations between state and citizen (Rose 1990). Thus the development of a web of surveillance, permeating the institutional structures of society, was for Foucault both a product of, and productive of, a particular approach to governing. This latter dimension is important to his argument, because for Foucault, the automation of surveillance also occurred in respect of the monitoring technology. Not only was surveillance directed outwards to an external population or problem, but also inwards to reflexively monitor the operations of the 'machine' itself.

Foucault's ideas about discipline and panopticism have been especially important in terms of the influence that they have had upon writers addressing the conduct of surveillance in contemporary society. For although Foucault himself never directly addressed issues relating to com- puterization, many of those writers who have attempted to understand the growth and development of information and communication technologies (ICTs) in the performance of surveillance functions have found in his work, resources to assist them in this area. For example, Mark Poster (1991) talks of the presence of a 'superpanopticon', where ICTs provide capacity for vast amounts of data to be routinely captured and quickly processed, and are thus perfect instruments to accelerate and amplify the conduct of surveillance. Large amounts of data on a large number of activities can be aggregated to a central point and thereby used to monitor how people are acting. This in turn can premise more effective interventions.

Overall, the logic of surveillance propounded by Foucauldian scholar- ship is essentially 'dystopic'. It argues that the era of modernity was based upon the emergence of a mode of rationally oriented power informed by particular discursively framed epistemologies, where subjects were subtly persuaded to control their own conduct. Coercion was no longer chiefly an explicit thing, rather, for the most part, it was implicitly integrated into the routine conduct of everyday life, as the controls became increasingly fine-grained and effective, penetrating ever deeper into the psyche. We are, then, increasingly controlled and regulated.

Liberal surveillance

A more positive account of the logic of surveillance and its relation to late modernity is to be found in the work of David Lyon (1994; 2001). Whilst acknowledging the insights provided by Foucauldian analyses, Lyon argues that the primary stimulus to the expansion of surveillance has been changes in the institutional order of society. For Lyon, the rise and development of surveillance reflects changes in the nature of social order, social inter-action and social relations in late-modern societies. We are, he argues, echoing some of the arguments reviewed in Chapter 3, living in a society that is increasingly mobile, flexible and adaptable. This brings with it changes in economic, political and social orders. To draw upon Anthony Giddens's (1991) notion, society is having to cope with the effects of processes of 'disembedding', wherein routine social conduct and the per-formance of social or economic interactions no longer relies upon co-presence. Surveillance then provides a surrogate mechanism for generating a sense of trust between people who are either engaged in forms of 'action at a distance', or who have not had the chance to develop such social bonds over time in a more organic manner. An example of this would be the ways in which computers are used to identify the traces of 'virtual', or 'de-materialized' social transactions and exchanges, in order to classify them as normal or deviant. A rather different account of the beneficent dimensions of surveillance can be found in the explicitly panoptic design of San Francisco's newest prison. The architectural design has been praised by its inmates because of the way that it undermines the culture of rape to be found in other establishments (Pecora 2002).

But for Lyon, it is the change in the conduct of ordinary transactions and interactions that has created the conditions for the proliferation of surveillance. Surveillance allows for the provision of a sense of trust and security in a society that values freedom, flexibility and mobility in its social, political and economic arrangements. Therefore, Lyon argues, surveillance has two faces. On the one hand it encapsulates a 'caring' sense of watching over and assisting in the manufacture of objective and subjec-tive security, a rhetoric familiar from crime control debates and the claims made for more surveillance. But at the same time there is the potential for a bleaker more pessimistic future, where the positive effects of surveillance systems are eroded, and evolve into an unrelenting and pervasive system of control.

A key facet of liberal surveillance theory is the notion that changes in economic relations, and the political-economic order, have acted as a precursor to the expansion and development of surveillance. This is an idea supported by the empirical work of Coleman and Sim (2002) in their critique of the role of CCTV in the urban regeneration of Liverpool city centre. Writing from a left-of-centre position, they show how the use of CCTV cameras for the performance of surveillance was driven by economic imperatives to attract shoppers and their custom to the area, rather than any metaphysical or physical concern with inculcating self-discipline. It was the desire to establish what Parenti (1999) dubs the 'theme park city', that provided the primary motivating factor for investing in CCTV by the scheme affiliates. For those financing the scheme, the objective was to reassure potential consumers about their security, by utilizing surveillance technologies to assist in identifying, and thus controlling, those groups whose behaviour might upset the economic order and thus inhibit the accumulation of profit. Similar findings are reported in discussions of surveillance programmes in 'mass-private spaces'. Wakefield (2000) notes how the identification and monitoring of potentially nuisance-causing and criminal actors, together with general 'housekeeping' and 'customer care' services, constituted the main activities of the security staff observed.

The political scientist Reg Whittaker (1999) presents a different facet of liberal surveillance theory when he argues, contra the Foucauldian position that there is a certain inevitability regarding the development of a continuous, all-encompassing, all-seeing panopticon. He maintains that, situated in a broader understanding of ongoing developments in key political institutions, what is made evident is the extent to which the emergence of enhanced surveillance capacities is marked by ambivalence. In effect, surveillance as a mode of control necessarily generates meta-controls, which provide a secondary form of control in terms of how, where, when and over whom surveillance is deemed to be legitimate. Furthermore, as well as promising new ways to control behaviour, surveillance also generates new sites and methods of resistance.

Gary Marx's (1988) account of the evolution of the new surveillance seeks to fuse elements of the panoptic logic with a more liberal set of values. As he notes, civic participation frequently requires the democratic citizen to actively participate in and accede to processes of surveillance. Banking services, medical care, insurance, housing, jobs, credit, all routinely involve the individual in a regimen of surveillance. As a result, the records that are kept about different aspects of our economic and social lives become core components of our social selves (Poster 1991). Developing Goffman's (1959) conceit, the presentation of self in everyday life now routinely involves and necessitates the presentation of a 'data self'. As Marx (1988) describes, the ubiquity of data selves opens up new vistas in terms of how both deviance and control can be enacted, but equally importantly it provokes a refiguring of more established elements of the control apparatus.

Despite Marx's attempts at a dialectical synthesis, there is a basic tension between disciplinary and liberal surveillance theories. The former set of studies, pivoting around the panoptic concept, tend to describe a scenario wherein the accumulation of data for disciplinary purposes is conducted almost exclusively by the state and its agencies. In contrast, the liberal perspective more easily accommodates the extent to which much of the growth in surveillance in recent years has been the result of actions taken by commercial and corporate enterprises, who are less concerned with the strategies and technologies of governmentality. This latter perspective, rather than focusing upon the centralizing tendencies of the panopticon, tends to employ the metaphor of the network to describe the organization of surveillance throughout society. And is thus aligned with the central tenets of the post-social control perspective.

Three applications

In order to develop a better understanding of the implications that surveillance has for social control, I am now going to discuss in more detail the impacts that the integration of surveillance technologies has had in relation to three key arenas: crime control; organizational life; and political economy. In considering all of these three arenas, it is notable that a key component of the impacts that have occurred, relate to the potentials offered by micro-chips and computers to collect and process large amounts of data. Essentially developments in micro-chip technology have allowed for the processing of more data, faster. It should not be surprising therefore, that they have found ready use in the conduct of surveillance. The dynamics of development are important though, because the social-shaping of the technology is a significant dimension in terms of explaining how things have unfolded in a particular way.

Crime control work

Probably the most visible and widely known about use of surveillance has been in relation to ongoing attempts to control crime. Particularly in Britain, central and local governments, along with private firms, have invested large amounts of money in developing Closed Circuit Television (CCTV) systems in an effort to control criminal and deviant activities. Indeed, such technologies are now routinely present in both public and private spaces. The introduction of these schemes throughout Britain has frequently been justified on the basis that they are effective weapons in the fight against crime, reducing the levels of risk of victimization of the users of a location. They are held to work by deterring people from engaging in criminal activity in the first place, by increasing the potential offender's perception of the likelihood of them being caught. And then, if they fail in this function and the crime is committed, they may assist police in identifying likely suspects for the crime.

Recently however, an increasing number of evaluative studies have started to question the assumptions that have underpinned the spread of CCTV as a crime control measure. Brown's (1995) overview of three impact evaluation studies, reported that the introduction of CCTV in Birmingham had little impact upon crimes such as robbery and theft from the person. Moreover, he reported some evidence of problem displacement to surrounding areas. As Tilley (1998) has explained, anyone seeking to claim a causal connection between a CCTV scheme and falling crime rates has to be sensitive to a wide variety of factors, that can both individually, and cumulatively, skew that which is being measured. Given that this is so, it is perhaps unsurprising that Norris and Armstrong (1999) report that scientific evaluations of CCTV schemes have failed to consistently produce evidence to support the public's beliefs about the efficacy of CCTV surveillance systems.

Such a situation thus raises an important question about how CCTV systems are being used. In their ethnographic study of CCTV operators, Norris and Armstrong (1999) sought to deconstruct the observational work of those individuals who direct the gaze of the CCTV cameras. Aside from the use of the cameras to engage in sexually motivated voyeurism, Norris and Armstrong elicited a number of working rules that operators use to guide their work. Given the large number of potential targets for surveillance, operators used their own understandings and biases about what constitute signifiers of criminality and trouble to select 'risky' looking individuals for focused observations. Certain behaviours warranted observation because they were disorderly or criminal, but other behaviours were targeted because they signalled the likelihood of crime or disorder occurring. Operators employed cognitive 'maps' or a 'normative ecology' for an area, whereby anything that created a sense of 'dissonance' from the ascribed 'normal' conditions, was likely to attract their attention. Furthermore, operators were socialized to see those who treat the presence of cameras as other than normal, as other than normal themselves. Overall, Norris and Armstrong concluded that it was comparatively rare for a crime control intervention to be made on the basis of the observations being made by CCTV operators.

These findings might be used to suggest that CCTV has more of a symbolic function than a crime control one. When questioned, a significant proportion of the public express support for the introduction of CCTV schemes to reduce crime (Bennett and Gelsthorpe 1996; Ditton 1998). The presence of cameras as a deterrent coheres with popular 'folk beliefs' about crime and criminality – intuitively it seems to make sense that if a location is subject to monitoring it is less likely that a crime will occur there. Therefore, the value of CCTV may be less to do with its crime control functions than the fact that it reassures people about their security in particular locations.

However, the integration of CCTV cameras is not the only way in which surveillance technologies have been used to an increasing degree in pursuit of crime prevention and detection. In his book, Gary Marx (1988) charts the social forces that have been involved in encouraging police officers to utilize human and computerized informants, visual and audio surveillance, and 'personal truth technologies' more often in their work. Significantly, Marx argues, these various mechanisms for monitoring the activities of suspects and targets:

- Transcend distance, darkness and physical barriers: the new surveillance technologies, utilizing as they do infra-red and heat-sensing technologies in cameras and highly sensitive microphones in listening devices, effectively overcome the natural limitations on surveillance imposed by the human senses;
- Transcend time: in that the products of surveillance can be recorded in a form that preserves the material concerned, so that it continues to be available for a long time;
- Are low visibility: the technologies involved make it ever more difficult to establish who is watching whom, miniaturization and remote control amplifies the difficulty of discovering such devices;
- Are involuntary: data can be gathered on a target without their knowledge or co-operation;
- Aid prevention: the incorporation of these technologies tends to push working procedures towards anticipation and prevention;
- Are capital intensive: whereas previous approaches to surveillance were labour intensive, the functions of a number of agents are now effectively replaced by the technological apparatus, although the technology is often costly;
- Are continuous: these technologies encourage a shift from focusing upon specific suspects to categorical suspicion of whole groups;
- Are more intense: the new technologies can probe ever deeper into social arenas becoming ever more sensitive to the clues that can be detected;
- Are more extensive: at the same time as it probes deeper, the new surveillance covers an increasing range of social arenas and population groups.

Thus for Marx, the spread and development of the new forms of surveillance based policing has created the conditions for what he terms a 'maximum security society'. As he suggests, the particular qualities of the new surveillance technologies makes available a never-before-possible combination of concomitantly decentralized and centralized forms of control.

How and why is this disjuncture between public beliefs and actual effectiveness, produced and simultaneously glossed over? As intimated above, popular support for CCTV is grounded in the fact that it coheres with a common-sense logic about crime and criminal behaviour. The 'gaze' of an 'electronic eye' monitoring locations for evidence of deviant behaviour should, according to the culturally embedded, common-sense models of 'rational' human behaviour that we share, discourage criminality. Such rhetorics are performed and reinforced in media coverage of CCTV stories.

Surveillance in organizational life

The increased use of surveillance to respond to crime has been mirrored by changes in its use in the conduct of social control in organizations. Surveillance of workers by management is a key theme in terms of understanding how social control is being routinely conducted in late-modernity. In addressing this issue, care needs to be taken in terms of mistaking technological development for functional change. By this I mean that, whilst the methods for facilitating control may have changed, this does not automatically equate to a new form of control, it may simply be a new way of doing the same things. This caveat is essential given the fact that a precondition for the existence of formal organizations is the ability to monitor, and thereby regulate and co-ordinate, the actions of the organization's members.

Returning to Weber's rationalization thesis and the role of the bureaucratic division of labour in establishing more efficient systems in production, it is evident that social control in organizations has increasingly relied upon the integration of different forms of surveillance system into the work process. Nowhere is this better illustrated than in the doctrine of Taylorism and the idea of 'scientific management' (Whittaker 1999). Braverman (1974) notes that the ideas of scientific management constituted a fundamental break with the traditional basis of delegated control, by shifting the key decision-making functions of the production process away from the workers, craftsmen and foremen, to managers whose specific function was to direct and control the process. Taylor's approach effectively removed the discretion of workers to control their own work. Starting with a systematic analysis of the process of production, individual tasks were separated out and then simplified, thereby minimizing the skills required to perform the particular component concerned. Similarly, the roles of foremen, middle managers and upper-level managers were subject to the same process of analysis, focusing roles around particular delineated functions. The second aspect of scientific management was the reintegration of the production process now divided into components through a division of labour. This control function relied upon processes of planning and surveillance to check that the overall process was running to plan. Hill (1981) argues that the rationalization of work organization along these lines laid the foundations for the greater control of both manual and non-manual labour by management.

The overall trend towards greater control of work processes is continued by many modern writers who have studied the impact of computerization on control in organizations. The general sense that one acquires from these accounts is that computers as well as making work more profitable and efficient, have also created the potential for more intensive and systematic surveillance of workers' activities by management (Zuboff 1988). The example often quoted in support of these trends is the experience of call-centre workers, where performance levels are supposedly routinely monitored on the basis of the number of key strikes made on the computer keyboard over a defined time period. Other organizations who employ not dissimilar forms of electronic monitoring include insurance companies, banks and restaurants.

James Rule (1996) argues though, that in most organizations, the performance of surveillance through monitoring electronic data flows has less to do with the inculcation of worker discipline, than with tracking work processes and ensuring profitability. Based upon empirical data from 181 firms, Rule records that over 60 per cent of the surveillance applications identified were used for analyses of sales, logging and tracking of work orders and monitoring of inventory. For Rule, this demonstrates the limitations of the disciplinary panoptic surveillance theories in terms of explaining how systems are employed in the conduct of social control in contemporary organizations.

Rule has certainly identified a weak point in Foucauldian analyses of surveillance, in that the theory would seem to predict an all-encompassing form of surveillance, subduing workers, and successfully moulding them to the needs of production processes. Whereas, labour relations obviously remain more conflictual than such an account implies. However, Rule's conception is not without problems itself. In particular, what he misses is the sense that, in drawing upon computerized data to conduct organizational control, several control functions can be performed at once. The unique quality of information is that it can be used without being used up. Thus it can be potentially stored for a long time, or used repeatedly, without degrading its original quality. Therefore, data that is collected primarily for the purposes of monitoring work processes, can also be used to discipline individual workers. Moreover, even on the basis of Rule's own interpretation of his data, somewhere in the region of 40 per cent of the systems he studied explicitly contained the potential for worker surveillance. Furthermore, as I have already detailed, a particularly important aspect of panoptic surveillance is that it is not just outwardly directed, it can also be directed inwards to monitor the activities of the supposed controllers.

Consumption

This discussion of the role of surveillance in the workplace and as a tool for performing social control in organizations, points to the extent to which surveillance has become embedded in the very political economy of late-modern societies. This is particularly consequential for the last illustrative example I want to focus upon – consumption. The surveillance of consumers is a vital component of understanding how social control is conducted in late-modernity, especially given that a number of social theorists have argued that the nature of contemporary political economy is increasingly less defined by processes of production than consumption (Bauman 1998).

Perhaps the most obvious way in which surveillance technologies have been employed in this respect relates to our experience of shopping. Many supermarkets have introduced variations on the idea of the loyalty card. The ostensible idea of these is that, in return for doing the weekly shopping at the same store, the customer is rewarded with vouchers towards future purchases. However, far more important from the store owner's point of view is that in participating in this scheme, the customer is effectively allowing the store to 'peak' inside their basket to collect data about purchasing habits in a way that ties them to socio-demographic data. Therefore, on the surface both the customer and the store get a benefit from engaging such a system.

Another surveillance device available to and used by a number of stores for the purposes of trying to enhance profitability are CCTV systems. In a way that exemplifies the 'mutable adaptability' arguments discussed earlier in this chapter, although introduced primarily to try and prevent shop lifting, the cameras have the added advantage that they can be used to reduce employee pilferage at the same time as monitoring worker productivity. More interestingly though, they can simultaneously be used to monitor consumer behaviour. By observing the routes that people take around the shop, what products they stop and look at and which they actually pick up and buy, store owners can gain a sense of how to arrange their products to maximize the number of sales.

In an economic system oriented towards consumption, information about the likes, dislikes, habits and interests of potential consumers, has considerable economic value. In engaging in acts of consumption through the use of credit cards, store loyalty cards, or by making enquiries about certain products, the late-modern citizen routinely leaves traces of their identity and status, which if collated and processed, can be used in a number of ways. When combined through processes of data-matching with other data about financial income, educational status, credit ratings, behaviours and lifestyle, the consumer data forms the basis for detailed predictive profiles. These profiles tend to separate and classify individuals and groups of consumers as part of a process that Gandy (1993) dubs 'the panoptic sort'.

Gandy (1996) identifies three distinct but related operations in the conduct of the panoptic sort: identification, classification and assessment. The need for reliable evidence that a person is who they say they are is part of the trust mechanisms required to enter into a commercial transaction. Proof of identity is required in many settings for the exchange of goods and services where the parties to the transaction may have only weak ties, or indeed may not be known to each other at all. However, increasingly it is the case that personal identification is required not for the purposes of authentication, but to enhance the level of knowledge contained in a consumer record. The acquisition of personal information in this fashion contributes to the performance of Gandy's second function, that of classification.

Assigning people to groups based upon a range of criteria is a way in which commercial enterprises can seek to maintain their profitability. This forms the basis of an assessment about the probability that a particular offer will be met with an affirmative response by the prospective consumer.

The deployment of a range of surveillance technologies to monitor and ultimately shape consumer behaviour reinforces a point made by Lyon (2001), that it is the changes in the economic order of late-modern societies that has created the preconditions for the development of electronic forms of surveillance. Many aspects of contemporary life are regulated by often hidden forms of 'data-veillance', whereby records of economic and social transactions and exchanges are monitored for the purposes of identifying any unusual activity, which might signify some form of deviance. The processing of increasing amounts of data is being aided by the increased automation of 'algorithmic' surveillance systems. These overcome many of the inhibitors caused by human operators, who tend to manipulate systems according to their own biases and judgements, and who also get tired.

Developing some of the themes discussed earlier in relation to intelligence-led policing, the integration of information and communication technologies (ICTs) in the conduct of surveillance has proven to be especially consequential. ICTs allow for large amounts of data to be processed rapidly, in effect serving to extend organizational memories across space and time (Marx 1988). Through techniques of data matching and data profiling, data gathered from a number of separate sources can be collected together and combined to provide increasingly detailed levels of knowledge about the individuals or groups being targeted. Therefore, as well as having a number of potential impacts upon those being watched, the integration of ICT based forms of surveillance has consequences for the organization of the watchers.

The limits of surveillance

So far in this chapter I have discussed the two principal theoretical perspectives on surveillance. Of the two perspectives, the dominant one is the Foucauldian tradition that has focused upon panoptic surveillance and the inculcation of discipline. This position can be contrasted with a more liberal theory of surveillance, which although absorbing aspects of Foucault's approach, differs in a number of important respects from it and seeks to act as a corrective to some of its more unabashed dystopic tendencies. But in addition to these reworkings, there are several further critiques of the concept of panopticism and it is to these that I now turn.

System integration

As a modality of power the panopticon is premised upon a centralizing imperative. That is through technologies of surveillance, data is acquired and collected at a central point, whereupon it is used in the formulation of strategies of action. Haggerty and Ericson (2000) argue that in practice the expansion and development of surveillance in society has been far less centrally directed than Foucault's model implies. They maintain that the expansion of the surveillance network in late-modernity has been underpinned by both government activity and the extensive involvement of private corporations. A sense of this diversity is provided in the ways in which surveillance has developed differently in respect of crime control, in organizations and in respect of the management of consumption. In actuality then, the surveillance map is rather more fractured, decentred and less monolithic than would be in keeping with the panoptic model.

As an alternative conceptualization to Foucault's rationalistic model of development, which, as Dandeker (1990) notes overlaps with Weber's thesis, Haggerty and Ericson (2000) propose a 'rhizomatic' model of development, wherein the processes of expansion are rather more fragmentary in nature, taking place throughout diverse social arenas. The result being complex, layered and nested assemblages, wherein previously discrete surveillance systems are becoming increasingly interlocking. At the same time, social actors are transformed, becoming simultaneously the practitioners and targets of surveillance activities in relation to other components of the assemblages.

The criticism made by Haggerty and Ericson (2000) of the monolithicism of the panoptic model, coheres with one raised by Norris and Armstrong (1999). The latter argue that the concept of panopticon overstates the degree of system integration present. As Norris and Armstrong (1999) show through their empirical data, there are a range of sociotechnical inhibitors, and practical limitations to the development of a fully functioning, fully integrated, all encompassing, surveillance network.

Synoptic surveillance

A second criticism that has been made of the master-concept of panopticism is that it provides a top-down approach to understanding surveillance. That is, surveillance is portrayed as something that is done by the more powerful members of society over the less powerful. However, Thomas Mathieson (1997) argues that the concept of panopticism captures only half of the picture in terms of how surveillance is routinely conducted. Focusing upon the role of media in late-modernity, Mathiessen argues that whilst there has been an increase in the prevalence of top-down surveillance, this has been accompanied by a growth in surveillance from below, where through media channels, the lowly are able to monitor the conduct of their superordinates. He suggests that surveillance is increasingly embedded in a whole range of social relationships and as such the current historical moment is best characterized as a period of 'synoptic' surveillance. By synoptic he means all watching all.

A good example of the trend that Mathieson identifies is provided by Thompson's (2000) book about the dynamics of media participation in political scandals. In effect the fear of those in either politically or economically powerful positions that media interest may unearth potentially damaging information about either their public or private life functions as a form of control over their activities.

Incidents such as that involving Rodney King in Los Angeles illustrate this dimension to the spread of surveillance. Cameras are not just useful in regulating the actions of 'problem' individuals and communities, they can also be used to control the controllers as well. These principles have been employed by Amnesty International to catalogue human rights abuses around the world. Campaigners have been given small portable video cameras to record evidence of the violence and torture performed on behalf of different regimes.

Detecting deviance

A further criticism that can be levelled at the logic of panopticism is the emphasis that it places upon the prevention of deviant activities. The logic expounded is that those potentially subject to monitoring will become more or less self-disciplining because they can never be sure when they are subject to observation. Empirical evidence to support the idea that this is how such systems actually function in practice is far from conclusive. A particularly telling example of this is provided in a recent Home Office systematic review of evidence on the effectiveness of CCTV. Reviewing the findings of 22 studies the authors found that whilst CCTV schemes may have an impact on crimes against vehicles, they had negligible or no effect for most other types of crime (Welsh and Farrington 2002). This is a significant finding because throughout the 1980s and 1990s vast amounts of money were spent by the British government to set up public CCTV systems in most cities and towns.

In practice, it seems that one of the most important functions performed by CCTV systems is not about encouraging discipline, but recording evidence to assist in the identification of an offender, once a crime or other form of deviant act has been committed (Valier 2001). The pictures provided by CCTV cameras are frequently used by law enforcement to assist with the post-hoc detection of offences. Similarly, anyone who drives a car will be familiar with the impact of speed cameras. They do not reduce speeding per se, rather they may reduce speeding in certain locations, where drivers know they are present and thus temporarily reduce their speed.

Surveillance and social control

These three critiques of the logic of panoptic surveillance suggest that at minimum some refinement of this highly influential rationale is required. The need for revision reflects the fact that Foucault's account was primarily historical, uncovering the logic of surveillance as part of the episteme of modernity. Thus, whilst it provides a degree of analytic purchase on some features of late-modern social control, Foucault's theory cannot account for all the features that pertain to the current situation. To a certain degree, Lyon's more liberal theory of surveillance remedies some of the more obvious limitations of the Foucauldian approach.

On the surface then, whilst there are differences between the disciplinary and liberal models of surveillance, I am inclined to see these differences as products of focusing upon different problems, rather than irreconcilable and insurmountable incompatibilities between the two approaches. Fundamentally my argument for a synthesis of the two approaches is this: Foucault's concept of panoptic surveillance retains its utility as a meso-level analytic construct, but not as a macro-level diagnosis of the workings of the social system overall. The liberal model based upon surveillance networks connecting the involvement of public and corporate interests probably provides the more accurate description of the arrangements of the macro-level system, but it does not really describe the operations of the nodes in the network. The nodes seem to work according to panoptic principles, but the objectives underpinning the work performed differ. Some panoptic nodes will be focused upon crime control tasks, whilst others are concerned with maximizing profitability, either by improving the efficiency of the organizational processes, or by shaping potential consumers.

As a mode of social control, the integration of various methods of surveillance is illustrative of a more profound facet of how control works, relating to what Hacking (1990) has termed 'the looping effect of human kind'. Applied to the workings of social control as a form of social action, this recognizes that control never works in an unadulterated fashion. By virtue of its introduction into a social setting, a new method of control changes some facet of that over which control is being sought. This might include the inculcation of discipline for some people subject to a particular mode of control, but it will also shape how, when, why and with what purposes people deviate from socially prescribed norms of behaviour.

Summary

Surveillance as a mode of social control is premised upon the collection of data, with the objective of shaping in some way the conduct being monitored. The development of surveillance programmes, and their integration into a wide variety of different social arenas, to perform a range of alternative functions, represents one of the most significant changes in the social ordering of late-modern societies. The ideas and intentions identified by the concept of panopticism attune us to a number of important contemporary developments in terms of how social control is performed. However, we need to be careful not to overstate or mis-state the changes that have taken place. Certainly, the extent of surveillance activity has increased, but it has not been based upon the development of a single knowledge centre. The ongoing developments have involved an expansion of the surveillance activities of a range of different social actors who have engaged in this monitoring work motivated by a variety of different objectives.

Furthermore, it is important to place developments in surveillance in a broader social context, in order to understand how surveillance relates to other types of social control practice. The danger of seeking to understand surveillance in isolation is that the connections with other aspects of social control will be missed.

chapter nine

Risks, regulations and audits

Risk
   Risk perception
   Risky decision making
Regulation
Auditing
Summary

Surveillance is a mode of social control that has undergone rapid change and development in late-modern societies. But as I have discussed in earlier chapters, changes in the logics and practices of social control are not restricted to surveillance alone. In this chapter I am going to focus upon three modes of social control that have become increasingly important in terms of how societies seek to respond to and deal with deviant behaviours of various kinds: risk management; regulation; and audit. These modes have all had a profound impact upon how social control is both imagined and conducted. Each of the three modes has generated considerable research activity, as scholars from a number of disciplines have engaged with a range of problems and issues. Due to limitations on space, I will not provide a review of the diverse array of debates that have gravitated around each of the concepts, my interest is simply in extracting from these discussions those elements that are useful in seeking to map the dimensions of social control. In particular, I will use them to elucidate aspects of reactions to deviance in and by formal organizations.

The concept of risk has become highly influential over the past two decades. A particularly important theme in the debates on risk has been the fact that it provides a new way of thinking about, identifying and reacting to a range of deviant behaviours. In this sense, the discourses of risk analysis and risk management that have become increasingly prevalent, have important implications for the conduct of social control more generally.

The second mode of social control I intend to explore is that of regulation. Sometimes used in conjunction with the concept of risk, regulation keys us into the ordering and organization of economic activity (Kagan 1978). I will explore the concept of regulation as a mechanism and method utilized for constraining deviance in the operations of markets and other spheres of economic life.[1] The third mode of control that I will examine in this discussion is that of audit. Auditing has become a key way in which control is sought over the conduct of organizations and the conduct of individuals in organizations. As with the previous two modes, by examining the conduct of audits we can obtain a sense of the different strategies and technologies through which social control is enacted.

Risk

Risk is a multi-dimensional concept that has featured strongly across a number of academic disciplines, providing a degree of analytic purchase on a wide range of different issues and problems. In spite of, or perhaps partly because of its widespread use, the study of risk has assumed a compartmentalized and fragmented form (Jones and Hood 1996), with differences in meaning evident in terms of how it is used in 'technical' as opposed to social scientific analyses (Renn 1992). Even within the social sciences the meaning of risk remains hotly contested and debated. Three main conceptualizations can be identified:

1. *Social theories of risk*: Formulated most strongly by Giddens (1990) and Beck (1992), this perspective focuses upon how changes in the macro-structural and institutional ordering of late-modernity shapes the risks citizens are exposed to and the nature of the adaptive responses that are made to these risks. Beck (1992), for example, suggests that modernity is characterized by: a rising intensity in the risks to which societies are routinely exposed; an expanding number of contingent events; more risks stemming from the created environment; an increased use of institutionalized risk environments such as financial markets, which impact on the life chances of millions of people; a well distributed awareness of risk as risk; and a profound recognition of the limitations of all kinds of expertise. In addition to this 'strong' social perspective on risk, there are a range of related positions which reflect other theoretical frameworks, some of which draw on the work of the cultural perspective discussed below.[2]

2. *Cultural theories of risk*: These are founded upon the pioneering work of the anthropologist Mary Douglas (1992) and her collaboration with Aaron Wildavsky (Douglas and Wildavsky 1983). Cultural theories of risk focus upon the ways in which risk represents a secular culture's response to hazards, taboos and dangers. They are concerned to understand the political processes by which certain risks

rather than others become focal points for cultures, in terms of how they understand and respond to the dangers that beset their members. A key finding being that social groups do not respond to potential risks in an objective and rationalistic fashion. Rather what is and is not viewed as risky is a cultural construct.

3. *Genealogical theories of risk*: This approach is based upon and develops aspects of the work of Michel Foucault. It provides what Hacking (2002) dubs an 'historical ontology' of the concept of risk, tracing it back to its emergence in the nineteenth century and the establishment of the state's administrative apparatus. The genealogical approach to risk seeks to demonstrate how the emergence of risk in contemporary society is part of shifts in the logics and practices of sovereignty, discipline and governmentality (Foucault 1991).

It is perhaps worth noting that these perspectives contrast because they attend to different problems, but that does not mean that they are intrinsically incompatible. Indeed, when applied to different substantive problems it is not unusual to observe hybrid formulations, borrowing from more than one perspective.

Cutting across these three perspectives there are some agreed upon characteristics of risk. For example it is established that risk is a future-oriented concept (Douglas 1992; Luhmann 1993). In terms of understanding risk as a mode of social control this is perhaps its most important feature. Translated into action, risk management represents an attempt to predict and thus in some sense control the future. That is, in conducting some form of risk analysis, which seeks to anticipate, recognize and appraise the likelihood of a potential danger occurring and the magnitude of its consequences, risk management seeks to minimize its harmfulness, or, indeed, to prevent it occurring in the first place.

It is this predictive and anticipatory quality that has been identified as the key component in terms of how risk management practices have transformed crime control practices. In their discussion of the incorporation of risk into the penal system, Feeley and Simon (1994) maintain that actuarial justice pivots around practices of classification and prediction. In essence, people are subject to control not just as a punishment or sanction for their past behaviours, but rather because it is adjudged that they represent an unacceptable risk of committing further criminal acts in the future.

Variants of this approach can be detected in a range of crime control institutions. For example, in his account of probation, Simon (1993) details how the risk classification of offenders has been central to the reworking of the objectives of the probation service in America. Johnston (2000) and Maguire (2000) have detailed how risk discourses have been integrated within contemporary policing strategies, encouraging the sorts of changes discussed in relation to intelligence-led policing.

Perhaps the second key feature of risk as a concept, is that it provides a way of thinking about uncertainty, that is, a risk may or may not happen depending on the actions taken in respect of it. Again, this is significant in terms of thinking about the features and dispositions of late-modern social control systems. In adopting a predictive and anticipatory approach to future deviance, risk based social control programmes do not operate on the basis that deviance definitely will or will not happen. Rather, by drawing upon some form of evidence base about past events of this kind, a probabilistic calculation is made as to the likelihood of its occurring. Thus control will be engaged to prevent or reduce the seriousness of events where deviance of some kind is predicted to occur, but it will also be enacted in respect of events where deviance would not have occurred. In effect certain groups of people, or certain situations, will be the subject of more control because they cohere with the profile drawn up about the prevalence of particular types of risk, although they were never going to engage in the acts concerned. This is a central facet of the idea of risk as social control, in that whilst attempting to prevent future forms of deviance, this approach inevitably controls the actions of some non-deviants. Thus representing a profound ethical shift in the make-up of society. For whereas previously controls tended to be more or less targeted on deviant people in an *ex post facto* fashion, in seeking to prevent and predict forms of deviance the 'control net' spreads, classifying everyone and assigning them to a risk profile.

Risk classifications tend to operate at the individual or territorial level (Ericson and Haggerty 1997). The former classes are constructed on the basis that particular personal characteristics can be used to determine the probability of engaging in deviant behaviour. In contrast, territorial classifications are aggregated categorizations that seek to differentiate between areas and localities according to certain criteria. Either way, it is here that risk and surveillance as modes of social control connect up and overlap. For the data trails left by individuals and organizations, as part of their everyday actions and interactions that are collected and sorted by surveillance mechanisms, are used to construct forms of risk classification. In turn these classifications may recursively determine what forms and how much social control the sources of the data and others like them, are subject to. This is especially consequential given that one of the fundamental moves in terms of the logics of contemporary social control is control via exclusion. As Young (1999) has described, those people who are classified as 'unacceptable risks' will find themselves excluded from participation from many of the spheres of social life available to others.

Thirdly, and perhaps equally importantly, the concept of risk as applied to social control is founded upon the sense that to a greater or lesser extent the danger is controllable. That is there are choices to be made which will either increase or decrease the likelihood of a risk materializing. It is here that Mary Douglas's work on the politics of risk analysis and risk decision making becomes especially relevant to understanding risk as a future oriented form of control for dealing with conditions of uncertainty. For analytic purposes, we can identify that Douglas's work identifies two key stages to the politics of risk: risk perception and then risk decision making.

Risk perception

Douglas's theory of risk posits that what we fear is dependent upon our wider shared belief system. People will attend to certain risks, rather than others, because of the pre-dispositions inculcated within them by a cultural frame. That is, our shared ways of understanding both our own behaviour, the behaviour of others and the social worlds that we make and remake, attunes us to certain threats. For example, in a study of how people think about health risks such as smoking and poor diet, Cutter (1993) identified that the majority of people are more likely to change their health behaviour in respect of visible risks than comparatively invisible threats. Moreover, Cutter identifies that when people are confronted by a new risk they tend to simplify any information and do not handle complex or equivocal data well. Overall, people are more responsive to dramatic and high profile events than more subtle ones.

Developing aspects of this approach Slovic (1992) sought to explore how and why different risks may have different 'signal values'. He was seeking to identify what factors it was that caused the public to react to certain threats quite vigorously, whilst in respect of others, which empirical analyses suggest pose the greater objective threat, there could be little or no public reaction. Slovic identified that the 'visual impact' of a threat played a significant part in public perceptions of a risk. That is if the nature of the potential harm could be seen, then it could easily be believed. In addition though, he also noted that risks posed by familiar social systems were perceived as less problematic than those occurring in new or unfamiliar systems.

This approach to risk perception has demonstrated that people calculate their exposure to risks in a subjective fashion, shaped both by qualities of the risk concerned, but also the condition of society and the characteristics of the individual. This has obvious consequences in terms of what dangers people seek to exert control over.

Risky decision making

As might be expected, if the perception of risks is socially shaped rather than purely rationally determined, then the fabrication of lines of action in order to respond to risks is equally complex. Nowhere is this better illustrated than in Diane Vaughan's (1996) analysis of the NASA Challenger space shuttle disaster. By examining an instance where an organization's risk based social control mechanisms spectacularly failed, Vaughan is able to illustrate some of the key features and problems of both risk and social control in organizations.

Contesting the dominant explanation provided by the official government inquiry into the launch of the fated shuttle, that blamed particular individuals for the erroneous decision to launch. Vaughan provides a more subtle and persuasive analysis, which seeks to trace the interactions that took place between the political context of NASA as an organization, the occupational cultures shared by workers, and specific isolated decisions. Central to her account is the concept of the 'normalization of deviance', where she argues that due to the structural conditions in which they were working, potential signals about the risks involved in launching the shuttle were repeatedly redefined by workers in such a way that they were not perceived as risk indicators. Indeed, this status was only evident after the disaster. Importantly though, Vaughan shows how this redefinition of the situation and the neutralization of the risks was not attributable to individual wrongdoing, but was a product of the organizational structures of NASA, which in turn reproduced certain cultural belief systems within the work groups that guided the actions of individual workers. Thus, echoing Douglas (1992), even in an organizational setting where risk assessment was a manifest goal of the organization, and was continuous, systematic, formalized and regulated; how risks are understood and responded to is negotiated and subject to interpretive flexibility.

Risk assessment and risk management have become central methods by which organizations seek to exercise forms of social control both over their workers, but also aspects of their environment. In such circumstances, risk management tools are often presented as amoral calculators that will provide a fairly objective appraisal of potential threats and sources of deviation that may impede the operations of the organization in some manner. What the work of Vaughan and Douglas amongst others demonstrates is that the perception and reaction to potential threats and hazards is inherently a political matter. This reiterates Sparks's (2001) point that in penal control systems, practitioners often do not deploy risk based technologies in a rational and objective fashion, their applications are shaped by subjective, political and emotional concerns.

Regulation

One way in which societies seek to respond to and control the risks produced by organizational actions is through regulation. Regulation involves the use of law to manage those risks that result from aspects of economic life, broadly conceived. It is the mode of social control routinely employed to manage the activities of markets, firms, businesses, corporations and industries. As a mode of social control, regulation serves to clarify a number of fundamental dimensions of how control is enacted, 'The very use of the word regulation signals a toleration of the activity subject to control. Regulation is not an attempt to eradicate risk, crucially it is an attempt to manage it' (Hutter 2001: 4). This echoes a theme from previous chapters, where we have seen that the imposition of social control is always limited. But what is significant about regulation as a mode of social control is that it actively recognizes and signals the negotiated character of the control work that is performed. A further distinctive element of regulatory programmes is that whilst the control enacted by the police tends to be reactive (although as we have seen they are becoming increasingly pro-active), the dominant mode of operation for regulatory agencies is more proactive. Their fundamental disposition is to aim to prevent harms from occurring, rather than responding to them after the event. A disposition it shares with risk.

A further echo of the earlier discussions is that, just as social control involves a range of overlapping and interspersed strategies and tactics, so too does the regulation of economic life. As with the other modes of social control discussed in this book, regulation frequently involves state action, but is not restricted to the activities of the state alone. Traditionally, the role of the state in regulatory activity has been based upon a model of what is known as 'command and control' regulation. This mode of operation involves the state using law and ultimately the threat of criminal sanctions to control organizational actions. The state regulatory function establishes detailed and prescriptive rules and statutes designed to govern the conduct of organizations, administered and enforced by government departments and local authorities.

The foundations of the command and control approach to regulation can be detected in the nineteenth-century penetration of the state into various domains of social life. As part of the generic processes of rational-ization, juridification and formalization of social control that took place over the course of the nineteenth and twentieth centuries, an array of regulations concerned with a variety of different social problems were developed, refined and proliferated. However, accompanying changes in other social and economic arenas, in the 1980s there was a significant disruption to the overarching pattern of development. The neo-liberal governments of the time undertook a programme of deregulation. Conflict theorists in particular had always been sceptical about the efficacy of command and control regulation, as they argued it displays an inbuilt predisposition to 'regulatory capture', wherein the state simply accedes to the wishes of corporations in terms of what regulations are formulated and how they are enforced (Gunningham 1974; Yeager 1987; Slapper and Tombs 1999). However, the deregulatory moves instigated by the neo-liberals were not justified in these terms. Rather extensive regulation was opposed at an ideological level, on the basis that it functioned as an impediment to the functioning of free markets, and thus restricted opportunities for economic development and growth.

However, the lasting legacy of this era is not one of reducing the overall amount of regulation, somewhat ironically it has promoted something of a growth in new regulatory methodologies. This occurred because the neo-liberal reforms stimulated a shift in terms of the governing logics of how regulation both could and should be conducted. In 'rolling back the frontiers of the state' the reforms that were introduced promoted the development of new ideas about regulating, increasingly involving both public and private agencies alongside a growing diversity of available forms of control. Although the political rhetoric of the time emphasized the pre-eminence of free markets, what actually occurred subsequently was the development of a number of diverse, and different, forms of regulatory instruments, strategies and principles. This included the delegation of state authority to non-governmental agencies, the increased use of 'enforced self-regulation', enhanced use of third-party enforcement, and the use of economic incentives to persuade and cajole active participation amongst the regulated.[3] As a consequence, the current situation involves a 'regulatory mix', wherein a plurality of approaches are adopted and utilized in regulating different arenas.

Given this shift in the fundamental practices and strategies of regulation, there has been an accompanying shift in the ways in which regulatory work is conceived of. The command and control model is now understood as co-existing alongside other forms of 'constitutive regulation' (Unger 1975; Ayres and Braithwaite 1992), 'participative regulation' (Hutter 2001), and 'smart regulation' (Gunningham and Grabosky 1998). Constitutive regulation is particularly important due to its emphasis upon the ways that effective regulation is not simply imposed upon an organization, and does not exist outside of the organizational systems and structures. Rather, the introduction of a regulatory programme impacts upon the organization's make-up, and causes changes in its motivations, processes and systems, thereby encouraging it to comply with the regulatory demands. Indeed, there is some suggestion that this constitutive role has been deliberately exploited in the design and implementation of a number of recent regulatory instruments. Organizations have increasingly been co-opted into and actively participated in regimes involving part self-regulation and part external oversight (Hutter 2001). In many ways, these are themes that echo some of the previously noted debates in the social control literature more generally, wherein modes of control are less targeted towards deviance, and work through more generalized processes of behaviour modification.

Drawing upon the literature we can identify that much of the regulatory work that takes place involves internal control systems and processes, where organizations are encouraged to be largely self-controlling. With such approaches the role of external agencies becomes largely one of 'meta-control', that is checking the effectiveness and probity of the organization's internal checking systems, rather than directly regulating and checking the actions of workers. This layered approach to the design of regulatory systems is captured in Ayres and Braithwaite's (1992) notion of 'responsive regulation'. They argue that perhaps the optimum design for contemporary regulatory systems is one where organizations with strong and highly developed internal control systems are subject to only minimal levels of external control, but those organizations with weaker internal control systems are subject to more extensive and intensive external controls. Although there is increasing diversity in terms of the regulatory instruments and strategies available, a survey of studies conducted does tend to suggest a more generic processual quality to the performance of regulatory work. As Hawkins (1984; 2002) has explained, regulatory agents tend to use law as 'a last resort', the majority of their work, and indeed their preferred strategy, involves trying to persuade the regulatees to comply with the applicable standards and laws.

This processual quality of regulation is further illustrated in the work of Hutter (1988; 1997). As she documents, the first stage of any regulatory process relates to 'defining the situation', that is before any enforcement actions are taken, the regulator has to decide whether a rule or law has been broken, or is likely to be broken. If it is decided that some form of action is appropriate, then the next phase of the regulatory process is to decide upon a line of action. Hawkins (1984) notes that the distinctive quality of regulatory actions is that the compliance-seeking strategy adopted by most regulatory agencies, most of the time, uses coercive tactics or the direct enforcement of law comparatively rarely. Most regulatory agencies have been found to adopt an 'accommodative' approach, relying upon persuasion, negotiation, bargaining, education and the offering of advice, as a means to secure compliance with the law. It is only if these approaches fail to yield what the enforcement official deems to be a satisfactory response, that formal action involving the threatened or actual use of sanctions tends to be invoked. The overall aim of regulation is to develop compliance with law. This contrasts with the more traditional orientation of the penal mode of social control that is central to policing, which focuses upon concerns of deterrence and punishment.[4]

The negotiation of compliance is, then, a complex and often intricate form of work. Organizations and individuals may choose to comply or not comply with regulatory standards for a number of often interlinked reasons. One factor that has been identified as frequently inhibiting, but by no means prohibiting the development of compliance, is organizational size and complexity. Thus large corporations may effectively be simultaneously compliant and non-compliant with a particular rule or standard, in as much as certain sections of the organization and particular individuals may be complying, whilst others are not (Di Mento 1986). For example, Hutter (1997) has shown how individual workers within an organization may choose not to utilize safety equipment if they feel it makes their tasks more difficult to perform.

At an organizational level, a key feature that has been identified as encouraging non-compliance is if the financial, political or reputational costs of compliance are viewed as detrimental to overall profitability (Sigler and Murphy 1988). Although other studies have argued that cost considerations only become a powerful explanatory variable when they interact with other factors (Wilson 1980; Di Mento 1986). Of course, another important factor for explaining how and why non-compliance with regulations occurs is ignorance, or a lack of awareness of the risks involved (Hutter 2001).

In late modernity regulation has emerged as an important mode of social control. It represents one of the chief ways in which governments and other agencies seek to exert control over a particular domain of social life. As Braithwaite (2003) notes, many of the key contemporary innovations associated with the social control of criminal behaviour have their roots in the traditional routines and working practices of regulatory agencies. Furthermore, the turn to regulation is both reflective of and constitutive of wider and broader changes in the macro-structures of society. Recently though, there have been a number of events which have effectively served to demonstrate some of the problems and limitations associated with regulation in terms of its efficacy in controlling behaviour.

The accounting scandals in the USA in 2002, involving the multi-national corporations Enron and Worldcom, where it was found that both corporations had systematically misrepresented their financial accounts in their reports, raised a number of fairly fundamental questions about the regulatory frameworks and instruments that were being used. As these cases were investigated, it became clear that under pressure, the firms and their accountants had colluded to mask the true extent of their debts, and lower levels of profitability, seemingly in order to protect their share prices. When the scale of the problems in these two corporations were revealed, there were serious ramifications for stock markets around the world.

This example is symptomatic of a more profound problem for regulation. The fundamental aim of regulation is to get organizations to comply with the rules and laws that should, in principle, govern their conduct. However, when concerned with organizational deviance, rather than the more traditional focus upon individual deviance, it is often problematic to ascertain who precisely should be blamed. As a result, when searching for the causes of organizational deviance, whether seemingly intentional or unintentional, there is frequently a recourse to a politics of blame that identifies individuals within the organization, rather than aspects of the organization as a whole. As Vaughan (1996) notes in her account of the Challenger disaster considered previously, the blame that is cast often tends to be focused upon middle managers, rather than those in overall control. This is in spite of the fact that individuals within an organization can be put under a great deal of pressure by managers, through informal methods, to bend the rules in order to ensure targets are met.

This is indicative of a more deeply embedded issue about the conduct of social control in general. That is blame is intrinsically important to any conception of social control. The attribution of blame to some things, rather than others, will direct where efforts to effect control are focused.

The focus of regulatory efforts or, indeed risk management strategies, will depend upon how consequent effects and antecedent causes are conceived of and understood.

Auditing

Regulation is not of course the only way in which the activities of firms, businesses, corporations and markets are controlled. There has been an equally important growth in the use of auditing to perform similar functions. The particular importance of auditing for this discussion is that what started out as an instrument designed for effecting a particular form of financial regulation has, over the past two and a half decades, rapidly diversified, migrating into a whole range of private and public establishments, in the process mutating into an array of forms. It is now commonplace to think in terms of environmental audit, safety audit, teaching audit, value-for-money audit, management audit, medical audit and so on. There has, as Power (1997) describes it, been an 'audit explosion', wherein a generic methodology for checking and verifying performance has become a normalized component of many social worlds.

At a technical level audit involves the collection of evidence to express a judgement concerning some aspect of the object that is being audited. However, as Power (1997) notes, the significance of audit is not primarily connected to its technical apparatus, but rather what it signals about the condition of trust and social relations in contemporary society. Power argues that what the proliferation of audit technologies reflects, is a need amongst people for mechanisms to replace what Putnam (2000) dubs the 'thick trust' that was available to individuals and communities of previous generations. In addition, following Giddens (1990), the decline in trust of expertise and authority of nearly all kinds, adds further impetus to the creation of sufficient conditions in which a mode of control such as auditing can thrive. In an era when social and economic interactions are increasingly based upon 'weak social ties', audit makes individuals and organizations accountable in some sense for their actions.

But in a somewhat ironic manner, and in a manner redolent of Foucault's 'functional failure' explanation of how and why the use of incarceration expanded in the nineteenth and twentieth centuries, Power (1997) suggests that the audit explosion cannot be accounted for by virtue of a 'trust deficit' alone. He maintains that typically auditing is beset by 'a dialectic of failure', wherein the failure of audits to spot problems that later become evident, rather than raising concerns about the effectiveness of auditing as a regulatory technology per se, tends to establish the preconditions for future expansion, refinement or development of auditing in some fashion.

This notion of the dialectical qualities of functional failure seems to capture a more fundamental and deeply ingrained quality of the politics of social control, in that failure ironically tends to lead to expansion. This explanation thus identifies one of the key dynamics by which Cohen's (1985) 'control net' expands – or what elsewhere I have termed 'control creep' (Innes, 2001). When a particular control strategy fails, the typical response of the agency concerned is to invoke a 'stylized politics of blame' which interprets the failure according to a range of 'techniques of neutralization' or strategies of denial. Thus they may argue that the incident demonstrates that 'the problem is worse than we thought', 'we need more resources', or that 'we need more or better powers to deal with this problem'. Rather than acknowledging that the strategy of control does not work, the inherent tendency is to reformulate it, or to introduce supplementary methods, thereby leading to a general condition by which levels of control throughout society 'creeps' to become more intense and/or systematic.

A second key theme that Power's (1997) discussion of auditing illustrates concerning the process of control creep, is the importance of 'fuzzy' definition. As he describes, part of the power of audit has been its elusive epistemological character. It is the very vagueness of the idea of audit that has enabled it to be easily assimilated within the routines and working practices of a host of diverse organizations and establishments. Moreover, even when there is a suspicion of 'audit failure', the essential obscurity of the fundamental idea means that the attribution of failure can be disputed and contested, which allows the essential premise to be preserved. This is not dissimilar to the ways in which techniques of risk assessment and risk management have been developed in a number of criminal justice institutions.

In a similar fashion to that which I described when discussing regulatory strategies, audit is important not just as a mode of direct control, but also because of its use as a method of meta-control. Audits are often not just about the direct control of deviant activity, they are used to effect control of the controllers. They provide a way of checking the control systems and processes used by particular establishments or organizations. This is significant in that the notion of indirect social control mechanisms is clearly relevant to understanding the ways in which control is enacted in late-modernity.

Summary

The three modes of social control reviewed in this chapter are all indicative of some of the principal ways in which social control is being recast and refigured. Indeed, authors such as Reiss (1984), Hutter (2001) and Braithwaite (2003) maintain that compliance based systems are forms of control that are characteristic of modern societies. Certainly it is the case that each of the three modes simultaneously reflects and constitutes shifts in some of the key institutional structures and orders of late-modern societies. Under a governance oriented system, the role of the state shifts from taking responsibility for many direct interventions in an array of social arenas, to a role where it effectively establishes the framework of conditions under which these interventions are performed by a combination of public agencies, private organizations and public–private partnerships. In this sense, the three modes of social control reviewed herein are important because they point to some of the continuities and discontinuities in terms of how social control is currently enacted, compared with other more traditional modes. By looking at these contemporary modes, we can begin to get a sense of the ways in which some of the fundamental ideas about how social control should be practised, and the fundamental logics and rationalities that underpin such practices, are changing.

A second dimension to this discussion has been that each of the three control modes has been of particular importance to the enactment of control both in and of organizations. As intimated in the earlier discussion of social order, control is both a product of, and producing, forms of organization. The ongoing reproduction of a social order requires some mechanism by which conduct and beliefs can be co-ordinated and established. The integration of risk management technologies, regulatory structures and auditing mechanisms into the routines and systems of many formal organizations signals a deeper trend about how the contemporary logics and practices of social control are evolving. This will be the subject of the final chapter.

Conclusion

The aims of this book have been twofold. First, I have sought to trace the meanings of the concept of social control to show how it can assist us in thinking about social life and how it is ordered and organized. Secondly, and relatedly, I have explored a range of control practices in an effort to describe how social control is enacted in relation to a range of social arenas and social problems. These two themes are connected by a dialectical relationship, wherein ideas about social control and control practices are mutually influencing. In this final chapter, I want to review the argument that has been developed throughout the book, and examine some contemporary problems and issues. My purpose being to demonstrate how and why the concept of social control is still relevant as we enter the twenty-first century, but also, to show how we need to revisit it and reconfigure it. In doing so, we can account for a number of emergent developments in terms of how social order is propagated and conflict managed.

Contemporary logics of social control

Although the concept of social control has always been a core concern for the sociology of deviance, there currently seems to be something of a revival of interest in the idea, in both criminology and the social sciences more widely. This is directly attributable to the ways in which society is developing and the complex ways in which our conduct appears to be increasingly subject to different forms of control. Connections between social control as an object of study for academics, and as practices performed by professionals and ordinary people, can be traced right back to the original coining of the term. The ways in which social scientists have formulated and understood the dynamics and logics of social control have been shaped, both by the dominant intellectual ideas of the time, but also what was going on in society itself. How then can we explain the logics of social control today, how can we make sense of what is happening around us?

We are living through a period of history where the control apparatus is being reconfigured. It is evident that the conduct of social control in late-modern societies is very complex, involving a range of state and non-state agencies, using an array of layered and interlocking technologies, strategies and ideas. There is certainly a sense that overall, the control apparatus is becoming more intense and systematic. But almost counter-intuitively, this is an outcome of the decentralized manner in which innovations in control practice are occurring. In some arenas and in respect of some social problems, the state has sought to enhance its powers, but in relation to many others it has encouraged other social actors to assume responsibility for responding to deviance.

There is an accompanying sense that the reach of social control is extending and the social control network is expanding. Both in the realms of the criminal justice process and in the 'softer' parts of the control apparatus, it seems as if more and more people are subject to some form of control. In part, this reflects a change in some of the orienting logics of social control practice, where there has been a shift from focusing upon individual deviants to a concern with segmenting whole populations and territories. Any such pressures towards a gradual 'creeping' expansion of the control apparatus, have been amplified and reinforced by 'exogenous' and 'iatrogenic' processes (Cohen 1985). An exogenous process involves the ongoing development of new classifications for deviance and the assignment of individuals to them and their allied control regimens. Iatrogenic process is a term used by Cohen to refer to the ways in which control systems increasingly employ several layers of controls. In such a system, those subjects who fail at one level can simply be reprocessed by another, typically more intense form of control.

The feeling that levels of social control in society are expanding and intensifying is in part attributable to the ways that particular technologies and strategies are becoming increasingly sophisticated, enabling social control to penetrate more easily into what were previously understood as private arenas of conduct. As discussed in Chapters 4, 7 and 8, this is also important in understanding how and why much social control is becoming increasingly opaque. The proliferation of situational controls alongside other strategies, makes it increasingly hard to identify when, precisely, control is being enacted. In this sense, contemporary developments represent a continuation of a longer-term trend in the history of social control practices, wherein they have been progressively rationalized through technical and methodological refinements, generating new specialisms and, in the process, new problems to be controlled.

In tracing such developments, the danger is that we automatically assume that we are living in a dystopia, where every sphere of our conduct is subject to control. This is something of an oversimplification, and in reality the situation is rather more complex. First, although parts of the late-modern control apparatus are being reconfigured, other parts are not being revised in these ways – their operations continue according to more traditional scripts. In addition to which, as new practices and concerns come to the fore in control agencies, others are relegated in importance and may become operationalized less frequently. Certainly, whilst the potential for state agencies to exert more social control has been made manifest through technological advances, to some degree, these have been offset and inhibited by financial and resource restrictions that have limited the capability to make full use of the potential on offer. There is an important tension in late-modern social systems between the ideational capacity of what control practices can be imagined, and the material capacity available to carry these out.

Empirical studies of various control techniques suggest that they are frequently less effective in practice than the discourses associated with them would suggest. As was considered in the chapter on punishment, control is rarely ever all-encompassing. Despite all the claims that have been made for new technologies and strategies of social control, it is important to be aware of their comparatively limited efficacy, evidenced by the fact that levels of deviance, in the form of recorded crime figures, remain very high.

In many cases, the very technologies that are involved in new and innovative approaches to social control are also involved in the creation of new forms of deviance to be controlled. For example, the spread of computer technologies have made the theft of computer chips a significant crime problem. Relatedly, the enhanced communication provided by technologies such as the internet have provided opportunities for those so inclined to access a vast amount of child pornography with relative ease, or to plan and co-ordinate terrorist attacks.

But at the same time as they create new forms of deviance, such technologies provide new opportunities for many of us, although, as is becoming increasingly apparent, the ability to access any such opportunities is not independent of levels of social and economic status. This inequality is reflected in the conduct of social control, where there is increasing bifurcation as control practices seek to provide inclusion for some and exclusion for others. Inclusionary strategies aim to re-integrate the deviant into the norms, institutions and structures of society through programmes of punishment or treatment. In contrast, exclusionary strategies are founded upon a logic that changing and reforming an individual's subjective disposition is extremely difficult and ultimately pointless, and as such, it is far better to sequester such persons from opportunities to engage in deviant behaviour.

There is a tendency within much of the academic literature on social control to evaluate changes in practices, of the type described above, in negative terms. It is a disposition that sees any such innovations as indicators of a new, more controlling form of social order. However, we need to be cautious in making any such judgements. For whilst the conduct of states in the delivery of social control can be coercive and oppressive, one only has to look at the conditions of life in communities where there are no developed formal or informal mechanisms of social control, to see the severity of the problems that occur. In conditions of rampant anomie, of the type that occurs after war, or in the absence of a popularly legitimated and properly functioning legal system, the imposition of some control by the state may seem preferable to the endemic violence that occurs between citizens. Just as too much control is problematic for us in the West, we must not forget that in some regions of the world, the problems that are being experienced relate to too little social control.

Describing the contemporary patterns and logics of social control is then a complex undertaking. As discussed previously, it is not simply that old modes of social control have been replaced by new modes. Rather there has been a multiplication in the sites of control, where an increasingly large number of both public and private organizations are engaging in control functions. It is also increasingly the case that these control functions are 'designed into' the operations of social organization and environment. They become formalized and an explicit objective of the work performed, where previously they may have simply been latent functions. Some of these controls are motivated by an instrumental self-interest and a desire to maintain or boost profitability, but, in so doing, they may work for the public good, boosting perceptions of security and order more generally.

Arguably the most important component of these innovations has been the increasing emphasis placed upon the management of risks and the establishment of actuarial control discourses. In shifting to a more pre-dictive logic that seeks to anticipate the occurrence of deviance prior to it happening, a profoundly different approach to the conduct of control is brought into being. This has involved the introduction of some new control practices, at the same time as causing reform of other more established ones. Overall, what seems to be happening is that the boundaries between different sources and sorts of control are being blurred, and as a result, a range of different forms and technologies of social control are increasingly blended together.

The engine for these ongoing developments are the combination of con-cerns about the state of society resulting from the structural and existential conditions associated with life in late-modernity. These are reinforced, channelled and amplified by the problems of persistent high crime rates.

Motivated by popularly shared sensations of material and existential insecurity, control functions are being retooled and reworked. People are less willing to rely upon informal social controls, and have less and less confidence that such arrangements will meet their needs. As a result, new roles, such as community wardens, security guards and so forth have been introduced to perform control functions, and people have appeared willing to finance these controls in an attempt to enhance the perceived security of themselves and their property.

Similar social forces are involved in the development of law as formal social control. There is an ongoing 'juridification' of society as law penetrates and permeates different realms of social life, in an attempt to regulate potential problem areas. Relatedly, technologies of surveillance are used to monitor both public and private spaces, and organizational life is increasingly subject to audits to check on the probity of conduct.

In many respects, through the dissemination of psychotherapeutic and psychoanalytic discourses, deviance has become a normalized aspect of social identity. Now, in discussing normalization here I am not using it in the Foucauldian sense. Rather, I am referring to the fact that many people have been encouraged to think of their lives, identities and/or personalities as being in some way flawed, lacking in some respect, or needing to be worked upon. These discursive frameworks have constructed new classifications of personal deviance to be treated and responded to via an array of possible interventions, subtly inculcating a need for enhanced self control.

It is evident then that the practices involved in the delivery and conduct of social control are being altered. The question then becomes, how can social scientists capture and explain this reconfiguration of social order and social control?

Dimensions of control

In Chapter 5, in the course of discussing policing as a mode of control, I differentiated between four dimensions of social control – ideas and intentions; programmes; evaluations; and explanations – and suggested these could form the basis of a generic approach to social control. I now want to expand on this and suggest that such distinctions may be useful in helping us to think about the ongoing changes in control logics and practices. In addition though, distinguishing between these dimensions may also provide a useful analytical resource in reviewing the theoretical and empirical literature on social control, as it seems that they capture some of the different foci of the accounts that collectively constitute the academic literature.

All social control efforts are based upon a set of ideas and intentions. These ideas and intentions may be more or less explicit, and more or less abstract, and indeed their precise contours may only be established with a degree of hindsight. However, what ideas and intentions do, is to identify and diagnose a problem (or problems) in such a way as to make a claim that the solution is to be found through the manufacture of more/better/different forms of social control. Thus their significance is that they will be translated into programmes, which are composed of the actions and interventions designed to manufacture more or different forms of control. A programme of social control may be enacted by a diverse array of actors, whose motivations for participating may be varied. As such, a social control programme can be composed of a myriad of policies, strategies and tactics, which are provided a degree of coherence by virtue of them sharing a set of ideas and intentions. All control programmes are subject to forms of evaluation. For the purposes of this discussion, the presence of two key types of evaluation can be noted. 'Technical' evaluations focus upon investigating the extent to which a programme is successful in achieving its stated goals, and a particular set of ideas and intentions. Somewhat contrastingly, 'normative evaluations', which have been a core feature of much of the academic writing on the subject of social control, comment on whether the net effect of the programme and its animating ideas is good or bad for society. Finally, there are explanations for the occurrence of gaps between ideas, programmes and evaluations. These explanations frequently account for the problems identified by evaluations, and in particular, why programmes do not seem to meet their underpinning ideas and intentions, as originally conceived. Of course, precisely what has to be explained is dependent upon how social control is defined and, as I have alluded to throughout this book, social control has been and remains a contested concept.

Thinking about control

Over the course of this book I have identified that there are two principal definitions of social control in the literature. The dominant contemporary definition and the one I have drawn upon throughout this book, is that provided by Stan Cohen, whereby social control is defined as an organized response to deviant behaviour, and can be understood as part of the way in which social order is manufactured and social conflicts managed. There is, though, a second approach that conceives social control rather more loosely, as a generalized form of social and psychological influence. In its latest incarnation this more loosely formulated notion of control has been inspired by Foucault's work on disciplinary surveillance, technologies of the self and governmentality. As discussed in Chapter 2, writers such as Nikolas Rose and Clifford Shearing amongst others, have been using a formulation of control that seems to understand it as any deliberate attempt at behavioural modification. This reflects a central theme of their analyses, which is the sense that control efforts are no longer focused upon deviant behaviour or deviant people, rather the logics and technologies that are central to the contemporary control apparatus are all-encompassing. In many ways, this revisionist approach revives the kinds of understanding seen in some of the earlier theorizations of the concept and consequentially is beset by many of the problems Cohen was trying to overcome. My solution to the tension that exists between these two positions has been to propose a number of concepts, including 'collective self control', 'situational control' and 'risk based control', as permutations of social control as a master-concept. These permutations are formulated in such a way as to recognize that the intended consequence of many contemporary control practices (and also the basis upon which they are justified) is to effect enhanced control of deviance, but that in so doing, they also routinely modify non-deviant behaviours. These particular concepts also acknowledge the fact that many control technologies are multi-functional, performing different tasks at the same time. So for example, a camera surveillance system, scanning car number plates to collect revenue for a congestion charging scheme, can simultaneously be used to locate stolen vehicles, or those where the owner has tried to avoid paying car tax. As such, this approach that I am advocating maintains a commitment to Cohen's connecting of control with deviance, whilst at the same time recognizing the validity of more recent arguments concerning the trends to extend and diversify control, which are 'stretching' Cohen's definition.

Retaining a coherent definition is important because analyses of the dynamics and development of social control in society necessitate consideration of a wide variety of issues including: the interaction order; policing; incarceration; social policy; surveillance; psychotherapy; risk management; regulation; target hardening; auditing; architectural design and the law. In one sense, this plurality of issues is simply illustrative of the diverse mechanisms by which, and through which, social actions that are adjudged to be deviant in some way are controlled in late-modern societies. It also reflects how social control strategies have developed, both extending their reach in terms of the range of problems to which they are applied, but also becoming increasingly focused and specialized when responding to particular problems. From an academic standpoint, this diversity is more problematic, because, if we want to construct a map of how social control is developing in society overall, to trace and detect the 'master-patterns', we are faced by the problem of having to cut across a range of increasingly specialized literatures. There are increasingly developed and specialized literatures on all of the areas listed above, and they are all important in terms of understanding contemporary approaches to social control. But they are not always connected up to establish a holistic picture

Therefore, I favour a synthetic line of argument, suggesting we should continue to understand control as a response to deviance, whilst at the same time recognizing that how deviance is conceived of and how it is controlled also changes people's non-deviant behaviour, thereby exhibiting a degree of control over that as well. It is an approach that seeks to identify the different 'species' of social control that are enacted in relation to different social problems and different contexts, whilst retaining a degree of conceptual unity by pivoting around the central concept. This seems preferable to allowing the splintering of the field by breaking social control studies into a number of heterogeneous and increasingly specialist discourses, where it will become increasingly difficult to track developments in the master-patterns of control.

To date, differentiating between types of control has tended to focus upon a distinction between informal and formal social control. The problems with this approach have already been reviewed in this book. In a recent paper, Newburn and Jones (2002) have sought to start the development and refinement of the concept of social control along the lines I am suggesting here. They distinguish between primary, secondary and tertiary forms of social control. Whilst useful, their primary concern is with elucidating changes in policing systems, and as a result their theoretical framework, in aggregating the dimensions of social control, does not convey a sense of the variety of different control mechanisms available and the diversity of uses to which they are being put.

The conceptual permutations of social control that have been identified over the course of this book aim to capture how innovative modes and logics of control now operate alongside and in collaboration with the more established forms previously located in the literature. As such, social control can be understood as a generic 'master-concept', which is comprised of and practised through these different permutations.

In order to develop this position though, I need to introduce three further ideas. First, I would argue that through processes of control creep, and as a result of a number of other trends in control practice, social control is assuming an 'ambient' form. The concept of ambient social control is supported by notions of organic and manufactured control. In proposing these additional ideas, my intention is to establish an analytic frame – a language – for talking about the changes that can be observed in the world around us.

Ambient social control

The argument that has been developed over the course of this book is that social control has assumed something of an 'ambient' form. By ambient, I mean to capture the sense in which it permeates, surrounds and pervades the conduct of individuals, communities and social institutions. The control capacity that was formerly implicit in social institutions and situations, is being formalized. This has involved the introduction of new modes of social control, alongside reconfigured and retooled older modes. The impact of which has been to contribute to a situation where social control appears more integrated, continuous and seamless. There are cross-cutting revisions too: 'hard' and 'soft' controls; reactive and proactive controls; targeted and untargeted controls; systematic and unsystematic controls; and coercive and non-coercive controls.

Ambient social control thus provides a frame in which to locate and connect the permutations in control practice detailed previously. The various types of control, both individually and collectively, contribute to the overall ambient qualities. Particularly important to the development of this complex situation, where a variety of controls overlap, interlock and intersperse are two forms, which I have not, as yet, described: 'organic' and 'manufactured' social controls.

'Organic' social control

As I have intimated in earlier chapters, the distinction between informal and formal social control, although commonly employed, is somewhat problematic. The nature of these problems gravitate around the issue of intentionality. The concept of formal social control tends to be used for instances involving law. This is accompanied by the term informal social control, referring to everything else, and as a consequence, lacking in analytic specificity – it is so loosely defined as to be almost meaningless. In an attempt to rectify such problems I would argue that we can differentiate between informal social control, organic social control and social ordering practices.

With such an approach, informal social control can be defined as planned and intended responses to deviance that do not involve the direct application of legal systems and/or legal authority. Correspondingly, social ordering practices are understood as those institutionalized aspects of social life that contribute to the production of social order and hence social organization. In between these two forms, I would argue, sits the concept of organic social control, referring to those actions or practices that work to change, influence and modify people's non-deviant behaviour in some way, but as a by-product of mechanisms directed towards the control of deviance. To be clear, organic social control is a latent function, that arises from responses to deviant behaviour, whereas social ordering practices are never intended or designed to control deviance. The label of organic is a metaphor for a sense of the 'natural' qualities that the resulting control processes assume. That is people are rarely conscious of the ways in which their conduct is being shaped.

The important thing about organic social control is that it has become a key component of recent approaches to effecting social control. As many contemporary writers have noted, perhaps the single most important quality of social control in late-modernity is its tendency to encompass non-deviant behaviour. The introduction of a concept of organic social control thus enables the resolution of one of the key tensions between the main thrusts of Cohen's (1985) definition and more recent writings.

'Manufactured' social control

The proliferation of organic forms of social control is to a large extent indicative of wider and deeper changes in the key social institutions of late-modern society, where:

> The problem of crime control in late modernity has vividly demonstrated the limits of the sovereign state. The denials and expressive gestures that have marked recent penal policy cannot disguise the fact that the state is seriously limited in its capacity to provide security for its citizens and deliver adequate levels of social control. The lesson of the late twentieth century experience is that the nation state cannot any longer hope to govern by means of sovereign commands issued to obedient subjects, and this is true whether the concern is to deliver welfare, to secure economic prosperity, or to maintain 'law and order'. In the complex, differentiated world of late modernity, effective, legitimate government must devolve power and share the work of social control with local organizations and communities.
>
> (Garland 2001a: 205)

As a consequence of which, there have been increasing moves amongst states and other agencies to embed social control capacities within a diverse array of institutional forms. In an effort to capture these moves I will suggest a concept of 'manufactured social control', to capture the ways in which mechanisms deliberately designed to control deviance have increasingly been constructed and superimposed upon existing forms of social organization (in the process frequently generating organic social control).

Such moves are exemplified in the changes that have been made in recent years to tackle the interrelated problems of crime and fear of crime, where the solution to these problems has increasingly been construed as requiring not just partnerships between state agencies and communities, but rather actively promoting change in the constitution of communities.

In his theory of 'social capital' the American political scientist Robert Putnam (2000) has proposed that the solution to the crime and fear of crime problems is not to be found with the formal agencies of social control. Rather he emphasizes the importance and efficacy of social control mechanisms that seem to exist in communities possessed of high levels of what he terms social capital.

Social capital is conceived of as the 'social glue' that is derived from residents' active participation in local social networks that benefits the whole community in terms of making it a better place to live. Putnam argues that both the cause and solution to the problems of crime and fear are to be found in the state of local communities. In accord with his wider theory of social capital, he presents empirical evidence of an erosion of civic participation and engagement in late-modern life, that has, over successive generations, culminated in a deficit in the amount of social capital available in many American communities, with a multitude of deleterious effects. Putnam argues that, if you can generate more social capital in a community (that is social trust, neighbourliness and so on), this will cause a reinvigoration of social control mechanisms, thereby producing falls in crime levels, reductions in fear, and promoting a greater sense of well-being and security amongst residents.

Putnam's theory has been seized upon by a number of academics and policy makers, including the Blair government in Britain. In a growing number of publications, the idea that crime and fear can be reduced by encouraging and revitalizing local community networks, thereby fostering enhanced levels of social capital, can be detected. By way of illustration, in a recent report on social capital, the influential Performance and Innovation Unit at the Cabinet Office noted that social capital may affect levels of crime in a number of ways. In particular by:

> . . . strengthening community ties social capital may provide sanctions for those who transgress accepted norms of behaviour e.g. through shaming and interventions by neighbours in the precursors of crime.
> (Performance and Innovation Unit 2002: 22)

The report concludes that there is:

> Strong evidence of the impact of social capital on crime at all levels and especially on violent crime. Multiple pathways are operating, but especially 'social control' through the internalization of values through social networks.
>
> (p. 28)

Underpinning these ideas seems to be a notion of 'manufacturing' social control through purposively changing the make-up of community organization.

In Britain, a significant amount of attention is currently being given to the ways in which 'active communities' can be encouraged and generated through governmental and non-governmental actions, with the intention of thereby impacting upon levels of material and existential security. Whereas previously, the emphasis was upon police and local authority partnerships, with the community as a subordinate partner, this logic has now been effectively reversed. With the focus upon the benefits that will accrue from deliberately manufacturing social control, the emphasis is upon the conditions of the communities and citizens, and what can be done by local authorities and the criminal justice system to them, in order to propagate conditions for enhancing levels of social control. Governmental policy and actions in this area are directed to mould and shape communities to encourage the development of 'local' solutions, rather than addressing the problems directly themselves. Community is no longer identified as an end in itself, but is a mechanism for the achievement of enhanced levels of order. Of course we can be somewhat cynical about whether such a strategy can be successful in artificially inducing the creation of effective social control. But in some ways the success or otherwise is less important than the logic that is revealed. What we can see is an attempt to construct community life in such a way as to encourage the development of mechanisms that might promote social order.

The concept of 'manufactured social control' keys us into how new and innovative attempts are made to establish more/better/different ways of controlling behaviour that is defined as deviant. An important aspect of the concept is the ways that the control measures that are manufactured as part of a response to what is identified as a pressing and urgent situation, also facilitate the control of other problematic situations, where, in ordinary circumstances, it would be politically unpalatable to introduce such measures. An example of this process relates to the aftermath of the attacks in America on 11 September 2001.

When three airliners crashed into the World Trade Center and the Pentagon in America on the 11 September 2001 (9/11), a 'new' problem for the key agencies of social control was made plainly and dramatically evident. In the latter three decades of the twentieth century, political and popular concerns with social control had focused upon the control of crime. During this period, terrorist campaigns and actions had been problems to a greater or lesser extent for all nation states, but these had been largely subsumed by concerns about crime. However, as we enter the twenty-first century it seems likely that, at least over the short- to medium-term, these trends and developments are likely to be emboldened by the introduction of new controls and the augmentation of already established control mechanisms aimed at the control of terrorism.

By June 2002 the President of the United States had announced the establishment of a new multi-billion dollar funded agency for Homeland Security, whose role is to ensure better integration of the established intelligence agencies. A few months later, news organizations revealed that the American government was to invest a massive amount of resources in a programme called 'Total Information Awareness', the aim of which was to significantly improve the capability of the American government to monitor and analyse data flows, although this programme was quietly 'dropped' later on. In Britain, the government sought to significantly extend the ability of a range of government departments to conduct surveillance of electronic communications. Under the Regulation of Investigatory Powers Act, many government departments are to be allowed to demand records of individual citizens' phone and internet communications. Publicly the extension of surveillance powers was justified by these governments on the basis that it would assist in combating the 'new' terrorist threat and serious crime.[1] But in reality, extending the powers of surveillance of electronic communications was as much concerned with curtailing fraud in the welfare state and increasing the effectiveness of tax collection, as with controlling criminals and terrorists. And although such programmes are likely to be limited in their impacts, they are interesting in terms of signalling how governments increasingly see the solution to various social problems as requiring enhancement of the social control apparatus.

In this sense, the reactions to 9/11 and other similar events, continues a process of 'control creep' whereby developments in the social control apparatus do not take place in large leaps, but in a slower more incremental fashion. New forms of control and new discourses tend to emerge bit by bit, as technical refinements to a diverse range of control problems.

Increasingly important in such processes of development have been a small number of high public impact 'signal crimes' that 'dramatize evil'. A signal crime is an incident that generates a public reaction and concern, thus creating a demand for enhancements of the control apparatus. It may not set off the process of events described in Cohen's (1980) theory of moral panics, but these events are nonetheless important in signalling to the public the presence of a particular type of problem, over which some form of control is desirable (Innes in press). The occurrence of signal crimes frequently creates such levels of insecurity amongst the populace, that governments, in order to be seen to be acting, will make short-term decisions to invoke more control. In some ways, the efficacy of any manufactured control measures that are introduced is secondary to their political symbolism. Anyway, if an initiative does not work as expected then the argument can be made that more control is required because the problem is worse than actually thought. Somewhat counter-intuitively then, under the right conditions, failure breeds expansion, and control creeps.

Summary

It is likely that, in the near future, such trends in the development of a mixed approach to social control will continue. There are, though, significant developments whose impact it seems more difficult to forecast. The human genome project may well provide the sorts of knowledge that constitutes the basis for radically new approaches to controlling human behaviour. It does not require that much imagination to conceive of a situation where the genome of future generations is manipulated as part of attempts to promote socially desired physical characteristics and to remove perceived 'flaws' and 'imperfections' from our species physical make-up – thus providing a rather different example of controlling deviations. At the other end of the scale, transformations in the conduct of geopolitics will undoubtedly necessitate new controls both of citizens, but also by citizens.

Without resorting to unrelenting pessimism it thus seems probable that the social control apparatus will continue to become more elaborate, more systematic and more intense. The challenge for social scientists is to keep track of these changes and to develop the conceptual tools that will enable us to understand how social control is changing and why it is changing in this way. My attempt to contribute to this enterprise has been based particularly upon seeking out areas of complementarity in the works of Erving Goffman, Stan Cohen and Michel Foucault. For between them, they serve to illustrate the varied nature of social responses to deviant behaviour, and the complex and subtle (and not so subtle) ways in which human behaviour is influenced. Equally importantly, each of them transcends disciplinary boundaries, drawing upon a range of materials and ideas in developing their arguments. This is an approach that is increasingly necessary in studying social control. For there is a real danger that an increasingly atomized and specialized approach to the study of various dimensions of social control is allowed to continue to develop, without people being in a position to conduct synthetic and multi-dimensional analyses that seek to identify and unpack the common trajectories in the development of social order.

References

Altheide, D. (1976) *Creating Reality: How TV News Distorts Events*. Beverly Hills: Sage.

Altheide, D. (2002) *Creating Fear: News and the Construction of Crisis*. New York: Aldine de Gruyter.

Althusser, L. (1971) *Lenin and Philosophy and Other Essays*. London: New Left Books.

Armstrong, G. and Norris, C. (1999) *The Maximum Surveillance Society*. Oxford: Berg.

Ayres, I. and Braithwaite, J. (1992) *Responsive Regulation: Transcending the Deregulation Debate*. New York: Oxford University Press.

Bauman, Z. (1989) *Modernity and the Holocaust*. Cambridge: Polity.

Bauman, Z. (1998) *Work, Capitalism and the New Poor*. Buckingham: Open University Press.

Bauman, Z. (2000) *Liquid Modernity*. Cambridge: Polity.

Baumgartner, M. (1984) Social control from below, in D. Black (ed.) *Toward a General Theory of Social Control: Fundamentals*, Vol. 1. Orlando: Academic Press.

Bayley, D. and Shearing, C. (1996) The future of policing, *Law and Society Review*, 30(3): 585–606.

Bayley, D. and Shearing, C. (2001) *The New Structure of Policing: Description, Conceptualization and Research Agenda*. Washington: National Institute of Justice.

Beck, U. (1992) *Risk Society*. London: Sage.

Becker, H. (1963) *Outsiders*. New York: Free Press of Glencoe.

Bennett, T. and Gelsthorpe, L. (1996) Public attitudes towards CCTV in public places, *Studies on Crime and Crime Prevention*, 5(1): 72–90.

Bittner, E. (1974) Florence Nightingale in pursuit of Willie Sutton: a theory of the police, in H. Jacob (ed.) *The Potential for Reform of the Police*. Beverly Hills: Sage.

Black, D. (1976) *The Behaviour of Law*. New York: Academic Press.

Black, D. (1984a) Social control as a dependent variable, in D. Black (ed.)

Toward a General Theory of Social Control: Fundamentals, Vol. 1. New York: Academic Press.

Black, D. (1984b) Crime as social control, in D. Black (ed.) *Toward a General Theory of Social Control: Selected Problems*, Vol. 2. New York: Academic Press.

Blomberg, T. (1987) Criminal justice reform and social control: are we becoming a minimum security society?, in J. Lowman, R. Menzies and T. Palys (eds) *Transcarceration: Essays in the Sociology of Social Control*. Aldershot: Gower.

Blomberg, T. and Cohen, S. (1995) Editorial introduction, in T. Blomberg and S. Cohen (eds) *Punishment and Social Control*. New York: Aldine de Gruyter.

Blumer, H. (1969) *Symbolic Interactionism*. Berkeley: University of California Press.

Body-Gendrot, S. (2000) *The Social Control of Cities*. Oxford: Blackwell.

Bottoms, A. (1995) The Philosophy and Politics of Punishment and Sentencing, in C. Clarkson and R. Morgan (eds) *The Politics of Sentencing Reform*. Oxford: Clarendon Press.

Bottoms, A., Mawby, R.I and Xanthos, P. (1989) A tale of two estates, in D. Downes (ed.) *Crime and the City*. London: Macmillan.

Bottoms, A. and Wiles, P. (1997) Environmental criminology, in M. Maguire, R. Morgan and R. Reiner (eds) *The Oxford Handbook of Criminology*, 2nd edn. Oxford: Oxford University Press.

Bourdieu, P. and Passerson, J.C. (1990) *Reproduction in Education, Society and Culture*, 2nd edn. London: Sage.

Bowling, B. (1998) *Violent Racism*. Oxford: Clarendon Press.

Bowling, B. (1999) The rise and fall of New York murder: Zero tolerance or Crack's decline, *British Journal of Criminology*, 39(4): 531–54.

Box, S. (1983) *Power, Crime and Mystification*. London: Routledge.

Braithwaite, J. (1989) *Crime, Shame and Reintegration*. Cambridge: Cambridge University Press.

Braithwaite, J. (2003) What's wrong with the sociology of punishment?, *Theoretical Criminology*, 7(1): 5–28.

Bratton, W. (1998) Crime is down in New York City: blame the police, in N. Dennis (ed.) *Zero Tolerance: Policing a Free Society*. London: IEA.

Braverman, H. (1974) *Labour and Monopoly Capital: The Degradation of Work in the Twentieth Century*. New York: Monthly Review Press.

Brewer, J. (1989) *The Sinews of Power: War, Money and the English State*. London: Unwin Hyman.

Briggs, A. and Burke P. (2001) *A Social History of the Media: from Gutenberg to the Internet*. Malden, MA: Blackwell.

Brown, B. (1995) *Closed Circuit Television in Town Centres: Three Case Studies*. London: Home Office.

Burgess, E. (1925) The growth of the city, in R. Park, E. Burgess and R. McKenzie (eds) *The City*. Chicago: University of Chicago Press.

Carlen, P. (1995) Virginia, criminology and the anti-social control of women, in T. Blomberg and S. Cohen (eds) *Punishment and Social Control*. New York: Aldine de Gruyter.

Carlen, P. and Worrall A. (eds) (1987) *Gender, Crime and Justice*. Buckingham: Open University Press.

Castel, R. (1991) From dangerousness to risk, in G. Burchell, C. Gordon and P. Miller (eds) *The Foucault Effect: Studies in Governmentality*. London: Harvester Wheatsheaf.

Castells, M. (1996) *The Network Society*. Oxford: Blackwell.

Castells, M. (1997) *The Power of Identity*. Oxford: Blackwell.

Castells, M. (2000) Materials for an exploratory theory of the network society, *British Journal of Sociology*, 51(1): 5–24.

Chan, J. (1997) *Changing Police Culture*. Cambridge: Cambridge University Press.

Chibnall, S. (1977) *Law and Order News*. London: Tavistock.

Choong, S. (1998) *Policing as Social Discipline*. Oxford: Clarendon Press.

Clarke, R. (1995) Situational crime prevention, in M. Tonry and D. Farrington (eds) *Building a Safer Society: Strategic Approaches to Crime Prevention*.

Clarke, R. and Cornish, D. (eds) (1986) *The Reasoning Criminal: Rational Choice Perspectives on Offending*. New York: Springer-Verlag.

Clarke, R. and Mayhew, P. (1980) *Designing Out Crime*. London: HMSO.

Cohen, S. (2002) *Folk Devils and Moral Panics*, 3rd edn. [1st pub. 1972]. London: Palladin.

Cohen, S. (1985) *Visions of Social Control*. Cambridge: Polity Press.

Cohen, S. (1987) in J. Lowman, R. Menzies and T. Palys (eds) *Transcarceration: Essays in the Sociology of Social Control*. Aldershot: Gower.

Cohen, S. (1994) Social control and the politics of reconstruction, in D. Nelken (ed.) *The Futures of Criminology*. London: Sage.

Cohen, S. (2001) *States of Denial: Knowing About Atrocities and Suffering*. Cambridge: Polity.

Cole, S. (2001) *Suspect Identities: A History of Fingerprinting and Criminal Identification*. Cambridge, MA: Harvard University Press.

Coleman, R. and Sim, J. (2000) You'll never walk alone: CCTV surveillance, order and neo-liberal rule in Liverpool City centre, *British Journal of Sociology*, 51(4): 623–40.

Collins, R. (1980) Erving Goffman and the development of modern sociology, in J. Ditton (ed.) *The View from Goffman*. London: Macmillan.

Conrad, P. (1992) Medicalization and social control, *Annual Review of Sociology*, 18: 209–32.

Cook, D. (1993) Racism, citizenship and exclusion, in D. Cook and B. Hudson (eds) *Racism and Criminology*. London: Sage.

Cooley, C. (1902) *Human Nature and the Social Order*. New York: Scribners.

Corrigan, P. (1979) *Schooling the Smash Street Kids*. London: Macmillan.

Crawford, A. (1997) *The Local Governance of Crime*. Oxford: Clarendon Press.

Crawford, A. (2000) Situational crime prevention, urban governance and trust relations, in A. Von Hirsch, D. Garland and A. Wakefield (eds) *Ethical and Social Perspectives on Situational Crime Prevention*. Oxford: Hart.

Cutter, S. (1993) *Living With Risk*. London: Edward Arnold.

Dahrendorf, R. (1985) *Law and Order*. London: Sweet and Maxwell.

Dandeker, C. (1990) *Surveillance, Power and Modernity*. New York: St. Martins Press.

Davis, M. (1990) *City of Quartz: Excavating the Future of L.A.* New York: Vintage.

Deleuze, G. (1995) Postscript on the societies of control, *October* 59: 3–7.

Dennis, N. (1997) Editor's introduction, in N. Dennis (ed.) *Zero Tolerance: Policing a Free Society*. London: IEA.

Di Mento, J. (1986) *Environmental Law and American Business: Dilemmas of Compliance*. New York: Plenum Press.

Ditton, J. (1979) *Controlology*. London: Macmillan.

Ditton, J. (1998) 'Public support for town centre CCTV schemes: myth or reality?' in C. Norris, J. Moran and G. Armstrong (eds) *Surveillance, Closed Circuit Television and Social Control*. Aldershot: Ashgate.

Dixon, D. (1997) *Law in Policing: Legal Regulation and Police Practices*. Oxford: Clarendon Press.

Dodd, N. (1999) *Social Theory and Modernity*. Cambridge: Polity.

Donzelot, J. (1979) *The Policing of Families*. London: Hutchison.

Douglas, M. (1966) *Purity and Danger*. London: Routledge and Kegan Paul.

Douglas, M. (1992) *Risk and Blame*. London: Routledge.

Douglas, M. and Wildavsky, A. (1983) *Risk and Culture*. Berkeley: University of California.

Downes, D. (1988) *Contrasts in Tolerance*. Oxford: Clarendon Press.

Downes, D. (2001) The macho penal economy: mass incarceration in the United States – a European perspective, in D. Garland (ed.) *Mass Imprisonment: Social Causes and Consequences*. London: Sage.

Downes, D. and Rock, P. (1988) *Understanding Deviance*, 2nd edn. Oxford: Oxford University Press.

Duster, T. (1971) *The Legislation of Morality: Law, Drugs and Moral Judgement*. New York: Free Press.

Eco, U. (1976) *A Theory of Semiotics*. Bloomington: Indiana University Press.

Eco, U. (1986) Function and sign: semiotics of architecture, in M. Gottdiener and A. Layopoulos (eds) *The City and the Sign*. New York: Columbia University Press.

Elias, N. (1994) *The Civilizing Process*. Oxford: Blackwell.

Ellin, N. (1997) Shelter from the storm or form follows fear and vice versa, in N. Ellin (ed.) *Architecture of Fear*. New York: Princeton Architectural Press.

Emerson, R.M. (1995) Holistic effects in social control decision-making, in R. Abel (ed.) *The Law and Society Reader*. New York: New York University Press.

Emsley, C. (1991) *The English Police: A Political and Social History*. Hemel Hempstead: Harvester Wheatsheaf.

Ericson, R. (1993) *Making Crime*, 2nd edn. Toronto: University of Toronto Press.

Ericson, R. and Haggerty, K. (1997) *Policing the Risk Society*. Oxford: Clarendon Press.

Erikson, K. (1966) *Wayward Puritans: A Study in the Sociology of Deviance*. New York: John Wiley.

Feeley, M. and Simon, J. (1994) Actuarial justice: the emerging new criminal law, in D. Nelken (ed.) *The Futures of Criminology*. London: Sage.

Felson, M. (1998) *Crime and Everyday Life*, 2nd edn. Thousand Oaks: Pine Forge Press.

Ferguson, N. (2001) *The Cash Nexus: Money and Power in the Modern World 1700–2000*. London: Penguin.

Fielding, N. (1995) *Community Policing*. Oxford: Clarendon Press.

Flusty, S. (1997) Building paranoia, in N. Ellin (ed.) *Architecture of Fear*. New York: Princeton Architectural Press.

Foucault, M. (1977) *Discipline and Punish*. London: Penguin.

Foucault, M. (1980) *The History of Sexuality*, Vol. 1. New York: Vintage.

Foucault, M. (1988) Technologies of the self, in L. Martin, H. Gutman and P. Hutton (eds) *Technologies of the Self: A Seminar With Michel Foucault*. Amherst: University of Massachusetts Press.

Foucualt, M. (1991) Governmentality, in G. Burchell, C. Gordon and P. Miller (eds) *The Foucault Effect: Studies in Governmentality*. Chicago: Chicago University Press.

Galanter, M. (1974) Why the 'haves' come out ahead: speculations on the limits of legal change, *Law and Society Review* 9.

Gandy, O. (1993) *The Panoptic Sort: A Political Economy of Personal Information*. Boulder, CO: Westview Press.

Gandy, O. (1996) Coming to terms with the panoptic sort, in D. Lyon and E. Zureik (eds) *Surveillance, Computers and Privacy*. Minneapolis: University of Minnesota Press.

Gans, H. (1979) *Deciding What's News*. London: Constable.

Garfinkel, H. (1967) *Studies in Ethnomethodology*. Cambridge: Polity.

Garland, D. (1985) *Punishment and Welfare*. Aldershot: Gower.

Garland, D. (1990) *Punishment and Modern Society*. Oxford: Clarendon.

Garland, D. (1995) Penal modernism and postmodernism, in T. Blomberg and S. Cohen (eds) *Punishment and Social Control*. New York: Aldine de Gruyter.

Garland, D. (1996) The limits of the sovereign state: strategies of crime control in contemporary society, *British Journal of Criminology*, 36(4): 445–71.

Garland, D. (2000) Ideas, institutions and situational crime prevention, in A. Von Hirsch, D. Garland and A. Wakefield (eds) *Ethical and Social Perspectives on Situational Crime Prevention*. Oxford: Hart.

Garland, D. (2001a) *The Culture of Control*. Oxford: Oxford University Press.

Garland, D. (2001b) Introduction: The Meaning of Mass Imprisonment, in D. Garland (ed.) *Mass Imprisonment: Social Causes and Consequences*. London: Sage.

Gelsthorpe, L. (2002) Feminism and criminology, in M. Maguire, R. Morgan and R. Reiner (eds) *The Oxford Handbook of Criminology*, 3rd edn. Oxford: Oxford University Press.

Giddens, A. (1971) *Capitalism and Modern Social Theory*. Cambridge: Cambridge University Press.

Giddens, A. (1987) *The Nation State and Violence*. Cambridge: Polity.

Giddens, A. (1990) *The Consequences of Modernity*. Cambridge: Polity.

Giddens, A. (1991) *Modernity and Self-Identity*. Cambridge: Polity.

Gill, P. (2000) *Rounding Up the Usual Suspects*. Aldershot: Ashgate.

Ginsburg, N. (1979) *Class, Capital and Social Policy*. London: Macmillan.

Girling, E., Loader, I. and Sparks, R. (2000) *Crime and Social Change in Middle England*. London: Routledge.

Goffman, E. (1959) *The Presentation of Self in Everyday Life*. London: Penguin.

Goffman, E. (1961) *Asylums: Essays on the Social Situation of Mental Patients*. Doubleday & Co.

Goffman, E. (1963a) *Stigma: Notes on the Management of Spoiled Identity*. London: Penguin.

Goffman, E. (1963b) *Behaviour in Public Places: Notes on the Social Organization of Gatherings*. New York: Free Press.

Goffman, E. (1971) *Relations in Public*. New York: Basic Books.

Goffman, E. (1979) *Gender Advertisements*. Cambridge, MA: Harvard University Press.

Goffman, E. (1983) The interaction order, *American Sociological Review*, 48: 1–17.

Gordon, C. (1991) Governmental Rationality: An Introduction, in G. Burchell, C. Gordon and P. Miller (eds) *The Foucault Effect: Studies in Governmentality*. Chicago: Chicago University Press.

Gough, I. (1979) *The Political Economy of the Welfare State*. London: Macmillan.

Gramsci, A. (1971) *Selections from 'The Prison Writings'*. London: Lawrence and Wishart.

Greene, J. and Mastrofski, S. (1988) *Community Policy: Rhetoric or Reality?* Praeger.

Greenwood, P., Chaiken, J. and Petersilia, J. (1977) *The Criminal Investigation Process*. Lexington, MA: D.C. Heath.

Griffiths, W. (1998) Zero tolerance: a view from London, in N. Dennis (ed.) *Zero Tolerance Policing a Free Society*, 2nd edn. London: IEA.

Gunningham, N. (1974) *Pollution, Social Interest and the Law*. London: Martin Robertson.

Gunningham, N. and Grabosky, P. (1998) *Smart Regulations: Designing Environmental Policy*. Oxford: Oxford University Press.

Gusfield, J. (1981) *The Culture of Public Problems*. Chicago: University of Chicago Press.

Habermas, J. (1989) *A Theory of Communicative Action*, Vol. 2. Cambridge: Polity.

Hacking, I. (1990) *The Taming of Chance*, 2nd edn. Cambridge: Cambridge University Press.

Hacking, I. (2000) *The Social Construction of What?* Cambridge, MA: Harvard University Press.

Hacking, I. (2002) *Historical Ontology*. Cambridge, MA: Harvard University Press.

Haggerty, K. and Ericson, R. (2000) The surveillant assemblage, *British Journal of Sociology* 51(4): 605–22.

Halbwachs, M. (1992) *On Collective Memory* [1st pub. 1941]. Chicago: University of Chicago Press.

Hall, S., Critchley, C., Jefferson, T., Clarke, J. and Roberts, B. (1978) *Policing the Crisis*. London: Macmillan.

Harcourt, B. (2001) *Illusion of Order*. Cambridge, MA: Harvard University Press.

Harvey, D. (1990) *The Urban Experience*. Baltimore: Johns Hopkins University Press.

Harvey, D. (1995) *The Condition of Postmodernity*. Oxford: Blackwell.

Hawkins, K. (1984) *Environment and Enforcement*. Oxford: Oxford University Press.

Hawkins, K. (2002) *Law as a Last Resort: Prosecution Decision Making in a Regulatory Agency*. Oxford: Oxford University Press.

Heidensohn, F. (1985) *Women and Crime*. London: Macmillan.

Hertz, N. (2001) *The Silent Takeover: Global Capitalism and the Death of Democracy*. London: William Heinemann.

Hill, S. (1981) *Competition and Control at Work*. London: Heinemann.

Hirschi, T. (1969) *The Causes of Delinquency*. Berkeley: University of California Press.

Hobsbawm, E. (1994) *Age of Extremes: The Short Twentieth Century*. London: Abacus.

Hodge, R. and Kress, G. (1988) *Social Semiotics*. New York: Cornell University Press.

Hope, T. and Sparks, R. (2000) For a sociological theory of situations (or how useful is pragmatic criminology?), in A. Von Hirsch, D. Garland and A. Wakefield (eds) *Ethical and Social Perspectives on Situational Crime Prevention*. Oxford: Hart.

Horwitz, A. (1982) *The Social Control of Mental Illness*. New York: Academic Press.

Horwitz, A. (1990) *The Logic of Social Control*. New York: Plenum Press.

Hoyle, C. (1998) *Negotiating Domestic Violence*. Oxford: Oxford University Press.

Hudson, B. (1996) *Understanding Social Justice*. Milton Keynes: Open University Press.

Hudson, B. (2002) Punishment and social control, in M. Maguire, R. Morgan and R. Reiner (eds) *The Oxford Handbook of Criminology*, 3rd edn. Oxford: Oxford University Press.

Hughes, G. (1998) *Understanding Crime Prevention*. Milton Keynes: Open University Press.

Hutter, B. (1988) *The Reasonable Arm of the Law?* Oxford: Clarendon Press.

Hutter, B. (1997) *Compliance, Regulation and Environment*. Oxford: Clarendon Press.

Hutter, B. (1999) Socio-legal perspectives on environmental law: an overview, in B. Hutter (ed.) *A Reader on Environmental Law*. Oxford: Oxford University Press.

Hutter, B. (2001) *Risk and Regulation*. Oxford: Oxford University Press.

Hutter, B. and Williams, G. (eds) (1981) *Controlling Women: The Normal and the Deviant*. London: Croom Helm.

Ignatieff, M. (1978) *A Just Measure of Pain: the Penitentiary in the Industrial Revolution, 1750–1850*. London: Macmillan.

Innes, M. (1999a) The media as an investigative resource in police murder investigations, *British Journal of Criminology*, 39(2): 268–85.

Innes, M. (1999b) 'An iron fist in an iron glove? The zero-tolerance policing debate', *Howard Journal of Criminal Justice*, 38(4): 397–410.

Innes, M. (2000) Professionalising the police informant: the British experience, *Policing and Society*, 9: 357–83.

Innes, M. (2001) 'Control creep', Sociological Research Online (6/3) http://www.socresonline.org.uk/6/3

Innes, M. (2003) *Investigating Murder: Detective Work and the Police Response to Criminal Homicide*. Oxford: Clarendon Press.

Innes, M. (in press) Signal crimes; detective work, mass media and collective memories, in P. Mason (ed.) *Criminal Visions*. Cullompton: Willan.

Janowitz, M. (1975) Sociological theory and social control, *American Journal of Sociology*, 81: 100.

Joas, H. (1993) *Pragmatism and Social Theory*. Chicago: University of Chicago Press.

John, T. and Maguire, M. (2003) *Second Round Targeted Initiative: Rollout of National Intelligence Model*. Unpublished report to the Home Office.

Johnston, L. (1992) *The Rebirth of Private Policing*. London: Routledge.

Johnston, L. (2000) *Policing Britain: Risk, Security and Governance*. London: Longman.

Johnston, L. and Shearing, C. (2003) *Governing Security: Explorations in Policing and Justice*. London: Routledge.

Jones, D. and Hood, C. (1996) Introduction, in C. Hood and D. Jones (eds) *Accident and Design: Contemporary Debates in Risk Management*. London: UCL Press.

Jones, T. and Newburn, T. (1998) *Private Security and Public Policing*. Oxford: Clarendon Press.

Kagan, R. (1978) *Regulatory Justice*. New York: Russell Sage Foundation.

Kagan, R. (2001a) *Adversarial Legalism: The American Way of Law*. Cambridge, MA: Harvard University Press.

Kagan, R. (2001b) Introduction to the Transaction Edition, in P. Nonet and P. Selznick (eds) *Law and Society in Transition: Toward Responsive Law*. New York: Transaction.

Kelling, G., Pate, A., Dieckman, D., et al. (1974) *The Kansas City Preventative Patrol Experiment*. Washington DC: Police Foundation.

Krimsky, S. and Golding, D. (eds) (1992) *Social Theories of Risk*. Westport, CT: Praeger.

Lacey, N. and Zedner, L. (1995) Discourses of community in criminal justice, *Journal of Law and Society*, 23(3): 301–25.

Lash, S. and Urry, J. (1997) *The End of Organized Capitalism*. Cambridge: Polity.

Lemert, E. (1967) *Human Deviance, Social Problems and Social Control*. New York: Prentice Hall.

Loader, I. (1997) Policing and the social: questions of symbolic power, *British Journal of Sociology*, 48(1): 1–18.

Loader, I. (2000) Plural policing and democratic governance, *Social and Legal Studies* 9(3): 323–45.

Lofland, L. (1973) *A World of Strangers: Order and Action in Urban Public Space*. Prospect Heights: Waveland Press.

Logan, J. and Molotch, H. (1988) *Urban Fortunes: The Political Economy of Space*. Berkeley: University of California Press.

Lowman, J., Menzies, R. and Palys, T. (1987) Introduction: transcarceration and the modern state of penality, in J. Lowman, R. Menzies and T. Palys (eds) *Transcarceration: Essays in the Sociology of Social Control*. Aldershot: Gower.

Luhmann, N. (1993) *Risk: A Sociological Theory*. New York: Aldine de Gruyter.

Lyman, S. and Vidich, A. (eds) (2000) *Selected Works of Herbert Blumer: A Public Philosophy for Mass Society*. Urbana: University of Illinois Press.

Lynch, M. and Bogen, D. (1996) *The Spectacle of History: Speech, Text and Memory at the Iran-Contra Hearings*. Durham: Duke University Press.

Lyon, D. (1994) *The Electronic Eye*. Cambridge: Polity.

Lyon, D. (2001) *Surveillance Society*. Buckingham: Open University Press.

McEvoy, K. (2001) *Paramilitary Imprisonment in Northern Ireland*. Oxford: Clarendon Press.

McEvoy, K. and Mika, H. (2002) Restorative justice and the critique of informalism in Northern Ireland, *British Journal of Criminology*, 42(3): 534–62.

Maguire, M. (2000) Policing by risks and targets: some dimensions and implications of intelligence-led social control, *Policing and Society*, 9(4): 315–37.

Maguire, M. (2003) Criminal investigation and crime control: thief-taking, crime-making and the CID, in T. Newburn (ed.) *A Handbook of Policing*. Cullompton: Willan.

Maguire, M. and John, T. (1995) *Intelligence, Surveillance and Informants*. London: Home Office.

Mannheim, K. (1935) *Man and Society in an Age of Reconstruction*. London: Routledge and Kegan Paul.

Manning, P. (1996) *Semiotics and Field Work*. London: Sage.

Manning, P. (1997) *Police Work*, 2nd edn. Prospect Heights: Waveland Press.

Manning, P. (2001) Theorizing policing: the drama and myth of crime control in the NYPD, *Theoretical Criminology*, 5(3): 315–44.

Marx, G. (1988) *Undercover: Police Surveillance in America*. Berkeley: University of California Press.

Marx, G. (1995) The engineering of social control: the search for the silver bullet, in J. Hagan and R. Peterson (eds) *Crime and Inequality*. Stanford: Stanford University Press.

Mathieson, T. (1997) The viewer society: Michel Foucault's panopticon revisited, *Theoretical Criminology*, 1(2): 215–34.

Mauer, M. (1997) *Intended and Unintended Consequences: State Racial Disparities in Imprisonment*. Washington: The Sentencing Project.

Mead, G.H. (1925) The genesis of the self and social control, *International Journal of Ethics*, 35(3): 251–89.

Mead, G.H. (1932) *The Philosophy of the Present*. Chicago: University of Chicago Press.

Mead, L. (1992) *The New Politics of Poverty: The Nonworking Poor in America*. New York: Basic Books.

Meier, R. (1982) Perspectives on the concept of social control, *Annual Review of Sociology*, 8: 35–55.

Melossi, D. (1990) *The State of Social Control*. Cambridge: Polity.

Melossi, D. (2001) The cultural embeddedness of social control: reflections on the comparison of Italian and North American cultures concerning punishment, *Theoretical Criminology*, 5(4): 403–24.

Merry, S. (1984) Re-thinking gossip and scandal, in D. Black (ed.) *Toward a General Theory of Social Control: Fundamentals*, Vol. 1. New York: Academic Press.

Meyrowitz, J. (1985) *No Sense of Place: The Impact of Electronic Media on Social Behaviour*. New York: Oxford University Press.

Minton, A. (2002) *Building Balanced Communities: The US and UK Compared*. London: Royal Institute of Chartered Surveyors.

Mooney, J. (1998) Moral panics and the new right: single mothers and feckless fathers – is this really the key to the crime problem?, in P. Walton and J. Young (eds) *The New Criminology Revisited*. London: Macmillan.

Moore, M. (1992) Problem solving and community policing, in M. Tonry and N. Morris (eds) *Modern Policing*. Chicago: University of Chicago Press.

Morris, N. (1995) The contemporary prison 1965–present, in N. Morris and D. Rothman (eds) *The Oxford History of the Prison*. New York: Oxford University Press.

Morris, N. and Tonry, M. (1990) *Between Prison and Probation: Intermediate Punishments in a Rational Sentencing System*. New York: Oxford University Press.

Morris, T. (1957) *The Criminal Area: A Study in Social Ecology*. London: Routledge and Kegan Paul.

Murray, C. (1994) *Underclass: The Crisis Deepens*. London: IEA.

Needham, R. (1979) *Symbolic Classification*. Santa Monica: Goodyear Publishing.

Neocleous, M. (2000) *The Fabrication of Social Order: A Critical Theory of Police Power*. London: Pluto Press.

Newburn, T. (1992) *Permission and Regulation*. London: Routledge.

Newburn, T. and Jones, T. (2002) The transformation of policing? Understanding current trends in policing systems, *British Journal of Criminology*, 42(1): 129–46.

Newman, O. (1972) *Defensible Space: People and Design in the Violent City*. London: Architectural Press.

Nonet and Selznick, P. (2001) *Law and Society in Transition*. New Brunswick: Transaction.

Norris, C. and Armstrong, G. (1999) *The Maximum Surveillance Society*. Oxford: Berg.

Offe, C. (1982) Some contradictions of the modern welfare state, *Critical Social Policy*, 2(2): 7–14.

Offe, C. (1984) *Contradictions of the Welfare State*. London: Hutchison.

O'Malley, P. (1992) Risk, power and crime prevention, *Economy and Society*, 21(3): 252–75.

Osborne, T. and Gaebler, T. (1992) *Reinventing Government: How the Entrepreneurial Spirit is Transforming the Public Sector*. Reading, MA: Addison-Wesley.

Parenti, C. (1999) *Lockdown America: Police and Prisons in the Age of Crisis*. London: Verso.

Park, R. (1925) The city: suggestions for the investigation of human behaviour in the urban environment, in R. Park and E. Burgess (eds) *The City*. Chicago: University of Chicago Press.

Park, R. (1967) *On Social Control and Collective Behaviour*. Chicago: University of Chicago Press.

Park, R. and Burgess, E. (1924) *Introduction to the Science of Sociology*. Chicago: University of Chicago Press.

Parsons, T. (1949) *The Structure of Social Action*, Vol. II [1937]. New York: Free Press.

Pasquino, P. (1991) Criminology: the birth of a special knowledge, in G. Burchell, C. Gordon and P. Miller (eds) *The Foucault Effect: Studies in Governmentality*. Chicago: Chicago University Press.

Pearson, G. (1983) *Hooligan: A History of Respectable Fears*. London: Macmillan.

Pecora, V. (2002) The culture of surveillance, *Qualitative Sociology*, 25(3): 345–58.

Perinbanayagam, R. (1990) How to do self with things, in S. Riggins (ed.) *Beyond Goffman*. Berlin: Mouton del Gruyter.

Performance and Innovation Unit (2002) *Social Capital: a discussion paper*. URL: www.cabinet-office.gov.uk/innovation/2001/futures/attachments/socialcapital.pdf.

Polk, K. (1994) *When Men Kill*. Cambridge: Cambridge University Press.

Poster, M. (1991) *The Mode of Information*. London: Sage.

Pound, R. (1968) *Social Control Through Law* [1st published 1942]. Hounden: Archon Books.

Power, M. (1997) *Audit Society: Rituals of Verification*. Oxford: Oxford University Press.

Putnam, R. (2000) *Bowling Alone: the Collapse and Revival of American Community*. New York: Simon and Schuster.

Reiner, R. (1992) *The Politics of the Police*, 2nd edn. Hemel Hempstead: Harvester Wheatsheaf.

Reiner, R. (1997) Policing and the police, in M. Maguire, R. Morgan and R. Reiner (eds) *The Oxford Handbook of Criminology*, 2nd edn. Oxford: Oxford University Press.

Reiss, A. (1984) Selecting strategies of social control over organizational life, in K. Hawkins and J. Thomas (eds) *Enforcing Regulation*. Boston: Kluwer-Nijhoff.

Renn, O. (1992) Concepts of risk: a classification, in S. Krimsky and D. Golding (eds) *Social Theories of Risk*. Westport Conn: Praeger.

Rhodes, R. (1997) *Understanding Governance: Policy Networks, Governance, Reflexivity and Accountability*. Buckingham: Open University Press.

Roche, D. (2002) Restorative justice and the regulatory state in South African townships, *British Journal of Criminology*, 42(3): 514–33.

Rock, P. (1973) News as eternal recurrence, in S. Cohen and J. Young (eds) *The Manufacture of News*. London: Constable.

Rock, P. (1979) *The Making of Symbolic Interactionism*. London: Macmillan

Rock, P. (1983) Law, order and power in late seventeenth- and early eighteenth-century England, in S. Cohen and A. Scull (eds) *Social Control and the State*. Oxford: Blackwell.

Rock, P. (1993) *The Social World of an English Crown Court*. Oxford: Oxford University Press.

Rose, N. (1990) *Governing the Soul: The Shaping of the Private Self*. London: Routledge.

Rose, N. (1996) The death of the social? Refiguring the territory of government, *Economy and Society*, 25(3): 327–56.

Rose, N. (1998) *Inventing Our Selves: Psychology, Power and Personhood*. Cambridge: Cambridge University Press.

Rose, N. (1999) *Powers of Freedom: Reframing Political Thought*. Cambridge: Cambridge University Press.

Rose, N. (2000) Government and control, in D. Garland and R. Sparks (eds) *Criminology and Social Theory*. Oxford: Oxford University Press.

Ross, C. (1901) *Social Control: a Survey of the Foundations of Order*. London: Macmillan.

Rothman, D. (1980) *Conscience and Convenience: The Asylum and its Alternatives in Progressive America*. Boston: Little Brown.

Roucek, J. (1970) *Social Control* [1947]. Westport, CT: Greenwood Press.

Rule, J. (1996) Hi-tech workplace surveillance: what's really new, in D. Lyon and E. Zureik (eds) *Surveillance, Computers and Privacy*. Minneapolis: University of Minnesota Press.

Rusche, G. and Kircheimer, O. (1939) *Punishment and Social Structure*. New York: Columbia University Press.

Sampson, R. and Raudenbusch, J. (1999) Systematic social observation of public spaces: a new look at disorder in urban neighbourhoods, *American Journal of Sociology*, 105(3): 603–51.

Schlesinger, P. and Tumber, H. (1994) *Reporting Crime*. Oxford: Oxford University Press.

Schuerman, L. and Kobrin, S. (1986) Community careers in crime, in A. Reiss and M. Tonry (eds) *Communities and Crime*. Chicago: Chicago University Press.

Scull, A. (1977) *Decarceration: Community Treatment and the Deviant – A Radical View*. Englewood Cliffs, NJ: Prentice Hall.

Scull, A. (1987) Decarceration Reconsidered, in J. Lowman, R. Menzies and T. Palys (eds) *Transcarceration: Essays in the Sociology of Social Control*. Aldershot: Gower.

Sennett, R. (1970) *The Uses of Disorder*. London: Faber.

Sennett, R. (1990) *The Conscience of the Eye: The Design and Social Life of Cities*. New York: W.W. Norton.

Shearing, C. and Stenning, P. (1987) *Private Policing*. London: Sage.

Sheptycki, J. (1998) The global cops cometh: reflections on transnationalization, knowledge work and policing subculture, *British Journal of Sociology*, 49(1): 57–74.

Sheptycki, J. (2003) *Review of the Influence of Strategic Intelligence on Organised Crime Policy and Practice*. Unpublished Report to the Home Office.

Sigler, J. and Murphy, J. (1988) *Interactive Corporate Compliance: An Alternative to Regulatory Compulsion*. New York: Quorum Books.

Silverman, E. (1999) *NYPD Battles Crime: Innovative Strategies in Policing*. Boston, MA: Northeastern University Press.

Simmel, G. (1911) The metropolis and mental life, in D. Levine (ed.) (1971) *On Individuality and Social Forms*. Chicago: University of Chicago Press.

Simon, J. (1993) *Poor Discipline: Parole and the Social Control of the Underclass*. Chicago: University of Chicago Press.

Simon, J. (2001) Fear and loathing in late-modernity: reflections on the cultural sources of mass imprisonment in the United States, in D. Garland (ed.) *Mass Imprisonment: Social Causes and Consequences*. London: Sage.

Skelton, A. (2002) Restorative justice as a framework for juvenile justice reform: a South African perspective, *British Journal of Criminology*.

Skogan, W. (1990) *Disorder and Decline: Crime and the Spiral of Decay in American Neighbourhoods*. New York: Free Press.

Slapper, G. and Tombs, S. (1999) *Corporate Crime*. London: Longman.

Slovic, P. (1992) Perceptions of risk: reflections on the psychometric paradigm, in S. Krimsky and D. Goulding (eds) *Social Theories of Risk*. Westport: Praeger.

Smart, C. (1981) Law and the control of women's sexuality: the case of the 1950s, in B. Hutter and G. Williams (eds) *Controlling Women: The Normal and the Deviant*. London: Croom Helm.

Sparks, R. (2001) Degrees of estrangement: the cultural theory of risk and comparative penology, *Theoretical Criminology*, 5(2): 159–76.

Sparks, R., Bottoms, A. and Hay, W. (1996) *Prisons and the Problem of Order*. Oxford: Clarendon Press.

Spitzer, S. (1987) Security and control in capitalist societies: the fetishism of security and the secret thereof, in J. Lowman, R. Menzies and T. Palys (eds) *Transcarceration: Essays in the Sociology of Social Control*. Aldershot: Gower.

Stanko, B. (1990) *Everyday Violence*. London: Pandora.

Stenson, K. (2000) Some day our prince will come: zero-tolerance policing and liberal government, in T. Hope and R. Sparks (eds) *Crime, Risk and Insecurity*. London: Routledge.

Sudnow, D. (1965) Normal crimes: sociological features of the penal code in a public defender's office, *Social Problems*, 12: 203–19.

Sykes, G. (1958) *The Society of Captives*. Princeton: Princeton University Press.

Sykes, G. (1995) The structural-functional perspective on imprisonment, in T. Blomberg and S. Cohen (eds) *Punishment and Social Control*. New York: Aldine de Gruyter.

Tanase, T. (1995) The management of disputes: automobile accident compensation in Japan, in R. Abel (ed.) *The Law and Society Reader*. New York: New York University Press.

Taub, R., Taylor, D. and Dunham, J. (1984) *Paths of Neighbourhood Change*. Chicago: University of Chicago Press.

Thompson, J. (1995) *The Media and Modernity: A Social Theory of the Media*. Cambridge: Polity.

Thompson, J. (2000) *Political Scandal: Power and Visibility in the Media Age*. Cambridge: Polity.

Tilley, N. (1998) Evaluating the effectiveness of CCTV schemes, in C. Norris, J. Moran and G. Armstrong (eds) *Surveillance, Closed Circuit Television and Social Control*. Aldershot: Ashgate.

Tonry, M. (1995) *Malign Neglect: Race, Crime and Punishment*. New York: Oxford University Press.

Turk, A. (1982) Social control and social conflict, in J. Gibbs (ed.) *Social Control*. Beverly Hills: Sage.

Unger, R. (1975) *Knowledge and Politics*. New York: Free Press.

Valier, C. (2001) Criminal detection and the weight of the past: critical notes on Foucault, subjectivity and preventative control, *Theoretical Criminology*, 5(4): 425–43.

Vass, A. (1990) *Alternatives to Prison*. London: Sage.

Vaughan, D. (1996) *The Challenger Launch Decision*. Chicago: University of Chicago Press.

Wacquant, L. (2001) Deadly symbiosis: when ghetto and prison meet and mesh, in D. Garland (ed.) *Mass Imprisonment: Social Causes and Consequences*. London: Sage.

Wakefield, A. (2000) Situational crime prevention in mass private property, in A. Von Hirsch, D. Garland and A. Wakefield (eds) *Ethical and Social Perspectives on Situational Crime Prevention*. Oxford: Hart.

Wardak, A. (2000) *Social Control and Deviance: a South Asian Community in Scotland*. Aldershot: Ashgate.

Websdale, N. (1999) *Understanding Domestic Homicide*. Boston, MA: Northeastern University Press.

Welsh, B. and Farrington, D. (2002) *Crime Prevention Effects of Closed Circuit Television: A Systematic Review*. London: Home Office.

Whittaker, R. (1999) *The End of Privacy: How Total Surveillance is Becoming A Reality*. New York: The New Press.

Wilensky, H. (1967) *Organizational Intelligence: Knowledge and Policy and Government and Industry*. New York: Basic Books.

Wilkins, L. (1964) *Social Deviance*. London: Tavistock.

Williams, F. (1989) *Social Policy: A Critical Introduction*. Cambridge: Polity.

Williams, R. (2000) *Making Identity Matter: Identity, Society and Social Interaction*. Durham: Sociology Press.

Willis, P. (1977) *Learning to Labour: How Working Class Kids get Working Class Jobs*. Farnborough: Saxon House.

Wilson, J.Q. (1975) *Thinking About Crime*. New York: Vintage.

Wilson, J.Q. (1980) *The Politics of Regulation*. New York: Basic Books.

Wilson, J.Q. and Boland, B. (1978) The effects of the police on crime, *Law and Society Review*, 12(3).

Wilson, J.Q. and Kelling, G. (1982) Broken windows, *The Atlantic Monthly*.

Wilson, W.J. (1996) *When Work Disappears: The World of the New Urban Poor.* New York: Alfred Knopf.

Yeager, P. (1987) Structural bias in regulatory law enforcement: The case of the Environmental Protection Agency, *Social Problems*, 34(4): 330–44.

Young, J. (1971) The role of the police as amplifiers of deviancy, in S. Cohen (ed.) *Images of Deviance*. London: Penguin.

Young, J. (1994) Incessant chatter: recent paradigms in criminology, in M. Maguire, R. Morgan and R. Reiner (eds) *Oxford Handbook of Criminology*. Oxford: Oxford University Press.

Young, J. (1999) *The Exclusive Society: Social Exclusion, Crime and Difference in Late Modernity*. London: Sage.

Zerubavel, E. (1997) *Social Mindscapes: An Invitation to Cognitive Sociology*. Cambridge, MA: Harvard University Press.

Zuboff, S. (1988) *In the Age of the Smart Machine: The Future of Work and Power*. New York: Basic Books.

Notes

Chapter 1

1 See also Meier (1982).
2 See also Horwitz (1990).
3 Support for this focus upon crime is to be found in Cohen (1985). He notes that whilst the decarceration movement described by Scull (1977) had an important impact in relation to the control of mental illness, it had little influence in respect of political responses to crime control. In response to the latter problem, there has been an almost continuous trend for more control.

Chapter 2

1 I have selected Zerubavel's formulation for particular mention as it is a potentially important and innovative recent contribution. Stated briefly, his argument is that processes of perception, mental classification and memory are subject to subtle forms of control, which pervade an individual's mental life.
2 I do not have space here to detail all of the work conducted on social control in the intervening years between Ross's and Mannheim's publications, but have focused the discussion around the key issues.
3 See also Roscoe Pound's (1942) work for a similar approach.
4 They admit that Rose's notion that 'the social' is 'dead' is something of an overstatement and is intended to be deliberately provocative, but still use it as an anchoring point in building their approach. As an alternative, I would prefer to argue that 'the social' is being re-worked to take account of the conditions associated with life in late-modernity.
5 Garland (1995) also makes this point, although Sparks (2001) notes that Feeley and Simon have both subsequently recognized this to be the case. Johnston and Shearing (2003) are explicit in recognizing that this is so.
6 See for example, the work of Donald Black (discussed in Chapter 1) who has clearly stated a belief that much of the literature on social control is overly focused upon and overemphasizes the role of the state.

Chapter 3

1 Applying this principle to a more contemporary setting Bauman (1998) argues that in the classic order-building and order obsessed constitution of modern states the archetypal fear was political revolution. But now as we develop a society based upon the principles of consumerism, it is the notion of the 'flawed consumer' that is most troubling us.
2 Ferguson (2001: 95) originally cited in Brewer, J. (1989) *The Sinews of Power*.
3 Indeed, many key theorists of social control acted as advisors to governments in this respect. It is known that both Janowitz and Blumer provided information to the American government about the manipulation of public opinion.
4 Black (1976) argues that there is a finite amount of social control in society and that a rise in the amount of formal social control will be matched by a correlated decline in the amount of informal social control.
5 A similar point is made by Horwitz (1990).
6 It is a finding that is further supported by the extensive literature on police culture (compare Chan 1997).
7 This phrase is Hacking's (1983).

Chapter 4

1 Seven year old Maria Colwell was returned to her mother and father after spending several years in foster care, and died shortly afterwards of extreme neglect and beatings. When the circumstances of the case were revealed it caused a national outcry.
2 What became known as the *Cleveland* case concerns a situation where an unexpectedly large number of children were taken into care by the local authority, mostly on the basis of a controversial diagnostic technique. The resulting Department of Health inquiry was highly critical of a number of the professionals who had taken the children into care.

Chapter 5

1 These categories are not mutually exclusive and in practice overlap. Further to which the notion that they are management functions is worth commenting upon – the police only rarely solve or eradicate these issues, more often they process and look after them.
2 Spitzer's account is particularly important here because he draws attention to the way that Karl Marx saw the provision of security as being at the very epicentre of policing. He approvingly cites Marx's 1843 comments on the French Constitution of 1793 where he remarks that 'Security is the supreme concept of civil society, the concept of the *police*, the concept that the whole society exists only to guarantee to each of its members, the preservation of his person, his rights, and his property' (Spitzer 1987: 43).
3 This acronym is used to refer to a particular management system using computer analysis of police data to assist in the identification of problems and targeting resources to them.

Chapter 6

1 This notion is described in more detail in Garland (1990). My focus on penality obviously means that more informal methods of punishing are not discussed in as much detail as more formal punishments. This imbalance reflects the wider debates concerning the definition of social control considered in the opening chapter.
2 A more extensive discussion of all of these themes can be found in Barbara Hudson's (2003) book in this series *Understanding Justice*.
3 As noted in relation to the jurisprudential perspectives, there is only sufficient space to provide the briefest outlines of the different sociological perspectives, a far more developed account is provided by Garland (1990).
4 I am grateful to Adam Reed for pointing out this disjunction.

Chapter 7

1 For a more detailed account see Ellin (1997).
2 The social semiotic perspective is described in Hodge and Kress (1988). On semiotics more generally see Eco (1976) and Manning (1996).

Chapter 8

1 The notion of a 'new surveillance' is suggested by Marx (1988), the modern/postmodern distinction is Lyon's (2001).

Chapter 9

1 Melossi (1990) reminds us that the social control of economic life has been a perennial concern stretching back to John Dewey's 'The Public and Its Problems' and Merill's 'The Stock Exchange and Social Control'.
2 These various positions are reviewed in Krimsky and Golding (1992).
3 An overview of these various instruments and approaches is provided in Hutter (1999).
4 Although as the earlier discussion of intelligence in police work identified, this is changing.

Chapter 10

1 *Guardian*, 12 June 2002, 'No 10 defends wider electronic surveillance'.

Index

Crime and Justice
Series Editor: Mike Maguire

UNDERSTANDING YOUTH AND CRIME
Sheila Brown

1998 160 pp 0 335 19505 9 Paperback c. £17.99
0 335 20004 4 Hardback c. £50.00

UNDERSTANDING CRIME DATA
Clive Coleman and Jenny Moynihan

September 1996 0 335 19518 0 Paperback c. £17.99

UNDERSTANDING WHITE COLLAR CRIME
Hazel Croall

2001 192 pp 0 335 20427 9 Paperback c. £17.99
0 335 20428 7 Hardback £52.99

UNDERSTANDING JUSTICE Second Edition
Barbara A. Hudson

August 2003 c. 224 pp 0 335 21036 8 Paperback c. £16.99
0 335 21037 6 Hardback c. £50.00

UNDERSTANDING CRIME PREVENTION
Gordon Hughes

1998 192 pp 0 335 19940 2 Paperback c. £17.99

UNDERSTANDING VIOLENT CRIME
Stephen Jones

2001 240 pp 0 335 20417 1 Paperback c. £17.99

UNDERSTANDING RISK IN CRIMINAL JUSTICE   COMING SOON!
Hazel Kemshall

August 2003 c. 176 pp 0 335 20653 0 Paperback c. £16.99
0 335 20654 9 Hardback c. £50.00

UNDERSTANDING PSYCHOLOGY AND CRIME   COMING SOON!
James McGuire

February 2004 c. 192 pp 0 335 21119 4 Paperback c. £16.99
0 335 21120 8 Hardback c. £50.00

UNDERSTANDING COMMUNITY PENALTIES
Raynor and Vanstone

2002 160 pp 0 335 20625 5 Paperback c. £17.99

UNDERSTANDING CRIMINOLOGY Second Edition
Sandra Walklate

February 2003 192 pp 0 335 20951 3 Paperback c. £16.99
0 335 20952 1 Hardback c. £50.00

Issues in Society

Series Editor: Tim May

ORGANIZATION AND INNOVATION   COMING SOON!
Guru Schemes and American Dreams
David Knights and Darren McCabe

October 2003 c. 160 pp 0 335 20684 0 Paperback c. £19.99
0 335 20685 9 Hardback c. £59.99

GOVERNING SOCIETIES   COMING SOON!
Dilemmas, Diagnoses, Departures
Mitchell Dean

December 2003 c. 160 pp 0 335 20897 5 Paperback c. £16.99
0 335 20898 3 Hardback c. £50.00

RISK, ENVIRONMENT AND SOCIETY
Ongoing Debates, Current Issues and Future Prospects
Piet Strydom

2002 208 pp 0 335 20783 9 Paperback £16.99
0 335 20784 7 Hardback £50.00

SURVEILLANCE SOCIETY
Monitoring Everyday Life
David Lyon

2001 208 pp 0 335 20546 1 Paperback £17.99
0 335 20547 X Hardback £52.99

SOCIAL EXCLUSION
David Byrne

1999 176 pp 0 335 19974 7 Paperback £16.99
0 335 19975 5 Hardback £45.00

SOCIAL SOLIDARITIES
Theories, Identities and Social Change
Graham Crow

2001 176 pp 0 335 20230 6 Paperback £17.99
0 335 20231 4 Hardback £52.99

CHILDHOOD AND SOCIETY
Growing up in an Age of Uncertainty
Nick Lee

2001 176 pp 0 335 20608 5 Paperback £17.99
0 335 20609 3 Hardback £52.99

CITIZENSHIP IN A GLOBAL AGE
Society, Culture, Politics
Gerard Delanty

2001 192 pp 0 335 20489 9 Paperback £17.99
0 335 20490 2 Hardback £52.99

WORK, CONSUMERISM AND THE NEW POOR
Zygmunt Bauman

1998 128 pp 0 335 20155 5 Paperback £17.99

HEALTH AND SOCIAL SCIENCE
A Critical Theory
Graham Scambler

2002 208 pp 0 335 20479 1 Paperback £17.99
0 335 20480 5 Hardback £52.99

Theorizing Society
Series Editor: Larry Ray

THEORIES OF SOCIAL REMEMBERING   **NEW!**
Barbara A. Misztal

August 2003 c. 192 pp 0 335 20831 2 Paperback c. £16.99
0 335 20832 0 Hardback c. £50.00

ECONOMY, CULTURE AND SOCIETY   **NEW!**
A Sociological Critique of Neo-liberalism
Barry Smart

February 2003 208 pp 0 335 20910 6 Paperback £16.99

GENDER AND SOCIAL THEORY   **NEW!**
Mary Evans

January 2003 c. 160 pp 0 335 20864 9 Paperback c. £16.99
0 335 20865 7 Hardback c. £50.00

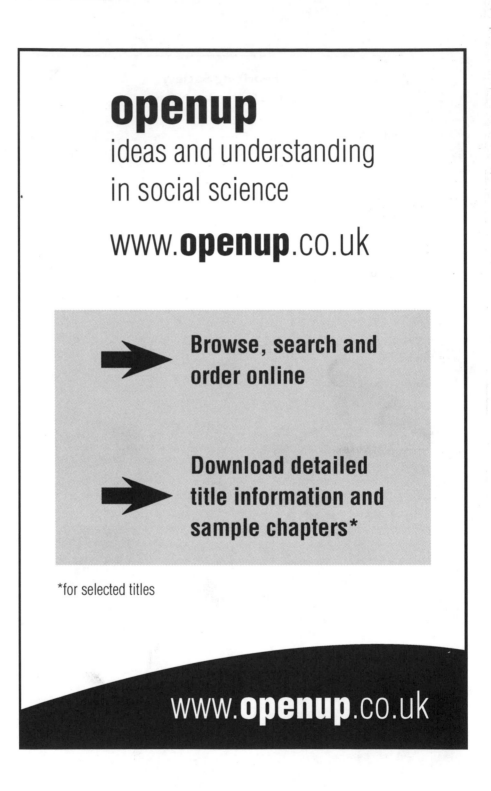